How to Enter & Win Non-Fiction & Journalism Contests

By
ALAN GADNEY

Managing Editor
CAROLYN PORTER

Facts On File Publications
New York, New York

EDITORIAL STAFF

CONTENTS

ALPHABETICAL EVENT, SPONSOR, AWARD INDEX

SUBJECT-CATEGORY INDEX

INTRODUCTION

WELCOME ... to How to Enter and Win NONFICTION WRITING & JOUR-
NALISM CONTESTS, an all new, completely up-to-date sourcebook for the
contest competitor and grant seeker in the nonfiction and journalism writing
fields (books, articles, essays, monographs, papers, and print journalism) ... one
of an ongoing series of contest-grant books covering writing and other related arts
fields.

Each book in the series focuses in detail on an individual art or medium
(Nonfiction Writing & Journalism, Fiction Writing, Film, Video-Audio-TV/Ra-
dio Broadcasting, Photography, Art, Crafts, and so on).

And each book in the series lists complete entrance information for anyone
wanting to:

- Enter their work in national and international contests, festivals, competitions, salons, shows, exhibitions, markets, tradefairs, and other award events
  and sales outlets.

- Apply for grants, loans, scholarships, fellowships, residencies, apprenticeships, internships, training and benefit programs, and free aids and services.

The books also have: ALPHABETICAL INDEXES listing each event, sponsor,
and award by its various names. SUBJECT/CATEGORY INDEXES to the entrants' specific areas of interest. Extensive CROSS-REFERENCES and DEFINI-
TIONS throughout. And introductory HELPFUL HINTS on how to analyze and
enter the events, and possibly come up a winner!

HOW THE BOOKS BEGAN

This series of contest-grant guides actually began several years ago with the
first release print of *West Texas* (a one-hour featurette I made while completing
my graduate work at the USC Cinema Department). One week after our first
showing, I sent our premiere print off to the first film festival, and the contest
entry process started to grow from there ... with one major problem, however:
The festival contact information was almost impossible to find.

After extensive research, all I could come up with were names and addresses
(and an occasional brief blurb) of intriguingly titled film events in far-off places,
but with no hard facts as to their entry requirements, eligibility restrictions,
awards, deadlines, fees, statistics, judging procedures, etc. That sort of vital information was practically nonexistent, unless you took the time and postage to write
away to every contest you discovered an address for ... which I did.

Through several years of continuous address researching, blindly writing off
for contest entry information and periodically submitting the film, *West Texas*
won 48 international film awards, and a large file of information had been col-
lected on about 180 international festivals—quite a few of which were not even
open to *West Texas* for a variety of reasons (wrong gauge, length, category, the
event turned out not to be a film festival, etc.).

The need was evident for an accurate, up-to-date, and detailed entry information source to the world's Contests, Festivals and Grants . . . Thus evolved the two editions of my previous book (GADNEY'S GUIDE TO INTERNATIONAL CONTESTS, FESTIVALS & GRANTS). Their first-of-a-kind success ultimately lead to this all new series of contest-grant guides.

ABOUT THE NONFICTION & JOURNALISM BOOK

This book (devoted solely to the fields of NONFICTION WRITING & JOUR-NALISM) is a single-source reference guide, providing you with vital entry information and statistics about a contest/grant before you even have to send away for the entry forms and shipping regulations (which you must always eventually do, as most require their own entry forms, and some have rather intricate shipping and customs requirements).

The 398 separate events listed in this volume were compiled through 3 years of active research on my earlier book, an additional year of research on this book, and thousands of questionnaires sent to worldwide writing and journalism events (many requiring repeated mailings to obtain complete and up-to-date entry information). During this process, we have totally updated, revised, and expanded the scope of the original nonfiction/journalism listings, added new competitions, and deleted a few which were too restricted or no longer in existence. (Fiction Writing sections of writing events have been included in a companion volume covering Fiction contests and grants.)

The individual events have been further grouped into 41 special-interest sub-categories (an increase in the number of subject categories over the earlier book, particularly in the areas of writing scholarships, fellowships, and grants). These subcategories are further divided and cross-referenced in the SUBJECT/CATE-GORY INDEX at the back of the book.

We have included two general types of events:

- Those AWARD EVENTS and SALES OUTLETS to which entrants may submit their works in order to receive SOMETHING OF VALUE in return, such as contests, festivals, competitions, salons, shows, exhibitions, markets, tradefairs, and various other award and sales programs primarily for new and unknown works.

- And BENEFIT PROGRAMS to which individuals or organizations may apply for some type of AID or SERVICE, such as grants, money and equipment loans, scholarships, fellowships, residencies, apprenticeships, internships, training programs, and so on.

Due to page length restrictions we have given condensed listings to those events that (1) are restricted to members of a specific organization, or limited to residents of a small city or geographical area (usually of less than state size), or (2) are not open to general entry but whose participants are nominated or invited by the sponsors or national selecting organizations. Workshops, seminars, conferences, schools, service programs, and the like, have only been listed if they are free, have free benefits attached, or encompass a contest, festival, grant, scholarship, fellowship, residency, etc.

We have listed as much detailed information about each separate event as possible (that is, as much as could be culled from the materials provided us by the event—usually including current addresses, dates, deadlines, complete entry requirements, eligibility and fee information, awards available, judging aspects, catch clauses, purpose, theme, sponsors, average statistics, where held, and various historical aspects). All information was transcribed from the questionnaires and entry materials provided us and edited to fit the format of the book. (See HOW TO USE THE BOOK for description of format.)

The information listed is the most current we could obtain, and will normally be revised and updated every two or three years in this continuing reference series.

We have also included older events when there was no direct confirmation that the events had gone out of existence. Many events come and go in an on-again, off-again manner, depending on their finances, administration changes, and other factors . . . again, good reason to ALWAYS WRITE TO AN EVENT BEFORE ENTERING YOUR WORK. Most events require entry forms, which they provide. Many have special shipping regulations. And, as we have condensed and edited their rules and regulations, it is best to write for the complete versions (especially important in interpreting the meanings of occasional tricky "catch clauses" about the use and ownership of winning entries). Also remember to send along a self-addressed, stamped return envelope (SASE), particularly to smaller events operating on tight postage budgets.

It would be almost impossible to give an exact figure for the total amount of money offered through this book. Some events give cash, others give equipment (of varying value depending on how badly you need the equipment or how much you can sell it for), and others give trophies, cups, plaques, medals, certificates, etc. (all of great value to the winner, but of little real monetary worth). Grant sources, on the other hand, may offer millions of dollars in direct financial aid. Probably the safest thing to say about the total amount of money offered through this book is that it is well into the millions.

HOW TO USE THIS BOOK

In the TABLE OF CONTENTS you will find that this volume has been divided into a series of "special-interest" SUBCATEGORIES. Each contains all those events whose primary emphasis is within that particular subcategory. The listing is usually alphabetical—first those in the United States, followed by other countries in alphabetical order.

At the start of each subcategory is an italicized INTRODUCTORY SECTION giving (1) specific contents of that subcategory, (2) definitions, and (3) "also see" CROSS-REFERENCES to similar events in other subcategories in the book.

To find additional events accepting entries in your specific interest area (but which may be listed in other subcategories because their primary emphasis is stronger in those areas), use the SUBJECT/CATEGORY INDEX at the back of the book. This lists subjects of special interest by an identifying code number for each event. The code number is located in the box above each event.

To find a specific event, sponsor, or award by name, use the ALPHABETICAL EVENT/SPONSOR/AWARD INDEX at the back of the book (again listing entries by identifying code number). In this index, sponsors and events are usually listed by full names, abbreviations, and unique titles.

EACH EVENT consists of (1) a current address and telephone number; (2) month/season held; (3) introductory paragraph, including entry restrictions, date of establishment, former names, purpose, theme, motto, sponsors, average statistics, historical information, facilities and other aspects; (4) technical entry regulations and categories; (5) eligibility requirements; (6) awards; (7) judging aspects and catch clauses; (8) sales terms; (9) entry fees; (10) deadlines. All have a similar format designed for easy use, with the five most important aspects of each event noted in bold type:

1. Identifying Code Number (in box)
2. Name of event
3. Month/Season of event
4. Entrant restrictions
5. Type of event and subject-category

With these five main points in mind, a potential entrant can quickly skim through a series of events to find those of particular interest.

HOW TO ANALYZE AN EVENT

We have usually provided enough information about each event to help you in making various determinations before you send away for entry forms, shipping regulations, and additional instructions. These are some of the points you should consider in your analysis.

• **When is the event held?** The month/season held is designated by bold type immediately following the address.

• **When is the entry deadline?** Months of entry are found in the DEADLINES section at the end of each event listing, and are usually well in advance of the month held. The event should be contacted about the specific entry date for the year you are applying.

• **Do I qualify?** Entrant restrictions are listed in bold type in the first sentence, and may be further clarified in the ELIGIBILITY section.

• **Does my work qualify?** The type of event and specific subject categories are listed in bold type at the beginning of the second and subsequent paragraphs. Various technical entry requirements follow each.

• **How much does it cost?** Costs and hidden costs are found in the ENTRY FEE section.

• **What are the prizes?** Found in the AWARDS section are prizes varying from trophies, cups, plaques, and medallions (of personal value), to cash, trips, equipment, and services (of a more material value—meaning you may be able to resell them at a later date if you already have better equipment, cannot take the trip, or do not want the services). Exhibition, distribution, broadcast, sale, and publication may also be offered, but should always be analyzed in terms of their financial and legal implications (what you get for what you have to give in return, and how valuable your entry may become in the future).

• **What are the catch clauses?** A few events have tricky qualifying clauses, condensed in the JUDGING section. These may involve claims to use and ownership (sometimes of all entries, and on an extensive basis), or responsibility in the event of loss, damage, nonreturn, etc.

Occasionally the actual entry forms and regulations may be rather vague as to whether the sponsors just keep a copy of your winning entry or whether they receive full ownership of the work (and for what use). Possibly, in these instances, you should write to the sponsors for further clarification.

• **How is my work judged?** The number of judges, judging procedures, and criteria are listed in the JUDGING section. It is important to understand that during preliminary judging (sometimes performed by the event's staff and aides), many entries may be immediately disqualified because of failure to adhere to the various contest regulations, or eliminated because of technical flaws or oversights (good reason always to send away for, and to read carefully, the latest rules). This is especially true of large contests that thousands enter. Sponsors have to narrow the competition as rapidly and efficiently as possible, and the first to go are the rule breakers and sloppy entries.

A program of the event or listing of past winners may give you an overall feel for the event (if it is conservative or liberal, oriented in certain directions, etc.). There is the possibility of talking to past entrants and winners in order to get an idea of specific likes and dislikes of the event and its judges. Or if you know who the judges will be, you may be able to make an educated guess as to what they will choose. However, I have found that it is almost impossible to predict how judges will act on anything other than the widest of generalities. Judges change from year to year, the philosophy of the event may alter, and single-judge contests put you at the mercy of that particular year's judge. So, you can never really outguess the judges.

• **How old is the event?** Usually included in the first sentence is the founding date, the inference being that the older the event, the more stable and reputable it is.

• **How large is the event?** Average attendance, distribution, and sales figures can often be found in the first paragraph, indicating the potential promotional and sales values of participating in the event.

• **What is the duration of an event, and how long will it tie up my entry materials?** The number of days the event is usually held is found in the first paragraph; the entry and return-of-material dates are in the DEADLINES section.

• **What is the competition?** Average statistics on number of entries, entrants, countries competing, acceptances into final competition, and winners can be found in the first paragraph, giving some idea of possible competition in future events.

• **How legitimate is the event?** This can be determined to some extent by the names of familiar sponsors, cosponsors, financial supporters, and those organizations that officially recognize the event—again, all found in the opening paragraph, and giving some idea of reputability. Also important may be the purpose, theme, and motto.

These are just a few of the aspects to examine before writing away for further information, entry forms, the most current regulations . . . and before sending away your work.

YEARLY PLANNING GUIDE

This book can also serve as a planning guide for your contest entries throughout the year. By using the SUBJECT/CATEGORY INDEX, you can get an overall picture of the various world events accepting entries in your areas of interest. We would then suggest setting up a calendar, listing those events you wish to enter by (1) the date you should write away for entry forms and current rules (several months before the actual entry month), (2) the entry dates, and (3) the dates the event is held, which will give you some indication of when the sponsor will be announcing the winners and returning your materials.

HELPFUL HINTS ON HOW TO WIN

Here are a few recommendations to enhance your chances of winning:

• ANALYZE THE STATISTICS—Look at the average statistics (found in the first paragraph of an event listing) to determine the size of your competition. Remember, you should always calculate the number of awards/honors given against the number of entrants, and not just analyze on total entrants alone. Larger events with a greater number of entrants and more awards may in reality have a higher winner-ratio than smaller events with only one award. You may also stand a better chance of winning in newer events which have not yet built up their patronage.

• ANALYZE THE TYPE OF EVENT—Based on past winner/award listings, is the event consistently conservative or liberal in its selections (or does it change moods from one year to the next)? If a contest says it leans toward contemporary or experimental works, you should take this into account before entering. You may also wish to try and analyze how the judges will vote, again based on past records and who the current judges are. (See HOW TO ANALYZE AN EVENT for additional information.)

• PATRONIZE THE SPECIALIZED EVENTS—If you have a specialized entry, while it will normally qualify for more generalized contests, you might begin by concentrating on those events which have a special interest in, or specific subject categories for your particular entry. Because of their highly specialized nature, these contests may get fewer entries, and if your work fits their interests, you should stand a better chance of winning. You might also consider patronizing those events that have changing annual themes by designing your entry to fit that particular year's needs.

• FOLLOW THE RULES—The contest rules (obtained directly from the event) should be studied carefully, first to find hidden clauses, and second to ensure you will not be inadvertently excluded because you entered the wrong category, sent an incorrect entry fee or no return postage, entered with improper technical aspects, or not enough supplementary information, etc. So read the rules and follow them, and fill out the entry forms completely. Rule breakers usually are disqualified, sometimes even before the preliminary judging. Then, to further cut down the number of competitors, most judges go strictly by the regulations, automatically discarding those entries that in any way deviate from the rules.

• KEEP IT CLEAN—Keep it technically perfect. Again, judges will usually reject sloppy entries (sometimes these don't even reach the judges, but are weeded out by the contest staff). So send only clean entries in good condition. No dirty covers, messy type, ultra-thin paper, smudges, spots, or ripped pages. All of these reflect badly on your entry's artistic content. And if the sponsors tell you they want an entry mounted in a special cover or written in a specific format, you had better follow their instructions. Also, it is best to send a duplicate rather than your original work (unless they request the original, in which case you should study their rules carefully to see if you will ever get your original back).

• SEND IT AHEAD OF TIME—Send your materials well in advance of the entry deadlines. Last-minute entries may get abbreviated handling by judges who have already looked over the earlier entries and have made up their minds. They may not get listed in the contest programs, which have already gone to the printers—and if they are shown, they may be scheduled during the least desirable exhibition times. And of course, *late* entries are usually sent back unopened.

• SEND PUBLICITY AND INFORMATION MATERIALS—Send supporting materials unless positively prohibited. (Definitely send them when they are requested.) Every little bit helps: biographical, technical, and project background information; publicity and press materials; still photos, production philosophy, synopsis, translation, transcription (and advertising materials if appropriate). The judges may occasionally use some of these in making their final decisions, and the events may use the publicity in their programs, flyers, and press rooms. Remember to send along any special technical instructions or return shipping requests you feel are needed.

• USE PROPER SHIPPING—First a word about the U.S. and international mail systems (as opposed to international Air Freight; some foreign contests even prohibit the use of air freight, as the entries may become held up in customs). Provided your entries are properly packaged, sealed, marked, stamped, and insured, and have correctly filled-out customs stickers (information about all of this is available through the U.S. Post Office), they should be able to travel almost anywhere in the world with relative safety. (This is based on personal experience. *West Texas* was mailed to a large number of film festivals all over the world, and I never lost a print or received one back damaged in transit.)

Remember always to ship by air to overseas competitions (as boat mail may take as long as three months from the U.S. to Australia, for example). On domestic U.S. shipments, you can mail at various rates lower than First Class, if you take into account the time for possible delays. (Again, contact the post office for information about mailing costs and times.)

Of course, if you have a heavy international shipment (a large box of books for example), you may be over the postal weight limitations, and have to ship by Air Freight. In this case, it may be best to contact a customs house broker/international freight forwarder about services and charges.

Short overseas messages will travel very rapidly by international telegram. And always remember to enclose sufficient return postage and a correctly sized self-addressed stamped return envelope (SASE) when requested. Finally, if your entry arrives with "Postage Due," it could be a negative factor in the contest staff preselection process.

A WORD ABOUT GRANTS

It would take an entire volume to discuss all the "ins" and "outs" of grant solicitation. However, we can touch on a few of the more important aspects.

• FIND OUT AS MUCH AS POSSIBLE about a potential grant source before investing the time in sending a proposal. Write to the granting organization for more information—and once you have this information, analyze it and focus your energies on the most likely prospects.

• WRITE AN INQUIRY LETTER—a brief letter of introduction, to see if they are interested in your project. Include a short description of the project and its unique aspects, background information about yourself and your sponsoring organization, the proposal budget, and ask them if they would be interested in further information. Keep your introductory letter brief, to the point, well written, easy to understand, and not exaggerated. If the foundation is interested, it will request what it needs, which may run anywhere from an expanded summary to a full-scale proposal and budget.

• GET AN ORGANIZATION TO SPONSOR YOU—Many foundations restrict their granting to only nonprofit, tax-exempt organizations, institutions, etc. However, this does not necessarily prohibit you from securing a grant from them. Simply get a nonprofit organization to sponsor you and your project, and have the organization apply for the grant in their name. Many organizations offer grant solicitations as one of their services, and this can have benefits for the sponsoring organizations: You give them credit and publicity through your finished project. They have a track-record as a successful fund raiser, which may help them in obtaining future grants. And they can even be paid through your budget for handling certain administrative and bookkeeping duties.

• GET SOME NAMES ON YOUR SIDE—well-known persons in the roles of advisors, technical consultants, etc. can help greatly toward building an impressive project package.

• TRY SPECIAL INTEREST GROUPS—If you have designed a project involving a special interest (a Medical Book, for example), rather than only approaching sources that grant your medium (Books), you might consider going to those grant sources that fund the special interest instead (i.e., Medical Grants). Or you may find similar money sources through special-interest organizations, associations, institutions, and businesses. The public library is a good place to start your search.

WHY ENTER CONTESTS

Finally, a word about the positive benefits of entering your work in contests, festivals, and competitions.

To start with, it is an extremely good way to test (and prove) the artistic and commercial value of your work before professional judges, critics, and the public. There is also the challenge of the competition—the excitement and glamour of knowing that your work is being seen in contests, festivals, salons, exhibitions, and publications around the world. Your entry competes with those of your peers —and if it reaches the finals and wins, there is the great personal satisfaction and certification of acceptance.

If you do win, you can win substantial cash prizes, trips, art items, equipment, services, exhibition, distribution, broadcast, publication, sales, trophies, and other awards. There can be useful free publicity for both you and your work, through (1) press information and literature released by the event, (2) the writings and reviews of others about your work, and (3) your own promotional materials designed around your winnings.

All of this can bring valuable international exposure through the print and broadcast media, and the resulting recognition and prestige can certainly help to sell both your award-winning work and yourself as an award-winning writer. The end benefits can be sales, valuable contacts, jobs, contracts, increased fees, and the financing of other projects.

How does this translate into real terms . . . The 48 international film awards won by *West Texas* resulted directly in: (1) a large number of valuable art objects, trophies, and awards; (2) enough cash winnings to cover all the film festival entry fees, shipping, promotion, and other costs; (3) an enormous amount of free personal publicity; (4) the eventual sale and distribution of the film; (5) the writing and directing of a subsequent feature-length theatrical, *Moonchild;* (6) several paid speaking engagements; (7) a TV script assignment; (8) a stint as a film magazine contributing editor; and (9) eventually to writing this series of books on contests and grants . . . So, the entering of contests and the winning of awards in many ways can be quite profitable.

THE CHANGING NATURE OF NONFICTION WRITING CONTESTS

In the three years since my previous book was published, several changes have taken place in the number and types of nonfiction writing contests and grants offered throughout the world. Two interesting aspects should be noted:

First, there has been a distinct increase in the overall number of article and essay contests currently available (many of which have definite commercial ramifications—the acquiring of high-quality material for special "awards" issues of literary magazines and book anthologies). All of this can be of great benefit to the article writer or essayist; they not only win a cash prize, but may also have their work published as well.

The second and possibly more important increase has come in the number of nonfiction writing grants, scholarships, fellowships, residence and emergency assistance grants currently available (aided in part by the leadership in government grant funding over the past few years). Let us hope that these grant outlets can continue through aid from private sources.

A FEW CLOSING THOUGHTS — While I have found the vast majority of events to be highly reputable and continually striving to improve their quality, there are still a few bad exceptions (lost entries, withheld awards, judging problems, etc.).

However, the interesting thing is that just as numbers and types of events change from year to year, so do most of these questionable conditions. Just when you hear someone complain about an unfair judging process, the next year the judges change, and that same person may come out a winner. Or the rules and administration change, and what was once a suspect practice disappears.

With this in mind, there has been no attempt on our part to editorialize about the occasional bad occurrences we hear of. This is strictly a reference guide (not a critical work). We list all those events which qualify, from the largest to the smallest, the oldest to the youngest, the well-known and the not so well-known. And we have tried to print enough information about each event to give you a firm basis upon which to decide whether or not to write for further information. (See HOW TO ANALYZE AN EVENT.)

It should also be stated that we do not endorse (or accept any responsibility for the conduct of) the events listed in this book.

Finally, no book of this type can ever be all-inclusive. That would be virtually impossible. Each year hundreds of new events start up, old ones lapse or go out of business, only to be replaced by similar events in a new form. As I have mentioned, there is constant growth and progression based on general changes in the art and media fields. However, considering the many individual events we have listed, each as thoroughly as possible within the edited format, and each updated and verified to the best of our knowledge based on entry materials and questionnaires provided us, we feel that we have brought you quite a comprehensive reference guide.

A special thank you to the American Library Association (the Reference and Adult Services Division, Reference Committee) for awarding the previous contest book an "OUTSTANDING REFERENCE SOURCE OF THE YEAR" . . . and to the many readers and reviewers of that book for their favorable response. These honors have been extremely gratifying.

And an additional thanks and grateful appreciation to the many events, sponsors, contributors, and correspondents who have so graciously provided us with the information included in this directory.

As a final reminder, please remember that to ensure you have the latest information, complete regulations, and proper entry forms, ALWAYS WRITE TO AN EVENT BEFORE ENTERING YOUR WORK

And please advise us of any new Contests and Grants you may know of, so that we may include them in our future editions.

Alan Gadney
Festival Publications
P.O. Box 10180
Glendale, California 91209 U.S.A.

NON-FICTION & JOURNALISM

ARTICLE, ESSAY (General Nonfiction Writing)

General Nonfiction Writing, Article, Essay, including Biography-Autobiography, Criticism-Review, and HIGH SCHOOL, JUVENILE, YOUTH. (Also see other ARTICLE, ESSAY.)

1

Arkansas Writers' Conference (AWC) Literary Awards
Anna Nash Yarbrough, Director
510 East Street
Benton, Arkansas 72015 U.S.A.
Tel: (501) 778-2833

June

International; entry open to all; annual; established 1944. Purpose: to help writers become better. Sponsored by AWC; Arkansas Pioneer Branch, NLAPW. Average statistics: 200 attendance. Held at annual 2-day AWC Conference in Arkansas. Tickets: $1.50 per day. Have lectures, workshops. Also sponsor Short Story and Poetry Contests; awards for Conference participants.

ESSAY CONTEST: Various Subjects, unpublished; typed. Categories: Assigned Subject in 1200 words; Assigned Subject in 1000 words.

ARTICLE CONTEST: Various Categories, unpublished; typed. Categories: Any Subject (1500 words, entrant must attend; 2500 words); Assigned Subject (1000 words); Historical about Arkansas by Arkansas Resident (2000 words).

AWARDS: $100 Alice Leigh Gift; $75, $50, $25 Gifts.

JUDGING: Include SASE for prose. Not responsible for loss or damage. All materials without SASE destroyed.

ENTRY FEE: $3 registration fee (nonreturnable).

DEADLINES: Entry, May. Awards, June.

2

Hospitalized Veterans Writing Project (HVWP)
Veterans Voices Magazine
5920 Nall, Room 117
Mission, Kansas 66202 U.S.A.

March, June, October

National; **entry restricted to U.S. hospitalized-outpatient veterans;** triannual; established 1946. Purpose: to encourage creative writing, art, photography, recreation-rehabilitation to hospitalized-outpatient veterans. Sponsored and supported by HVWP, nonprofit volunteer service organization. Average statistics: 47 entries, 20 entrants. Publish *Veterans'*

Voices, triannual magazine established 1951 for creative writing, art (Margaret Sally Keach, founder-publisher; Margaret Clark, editor). Also sponsor $50 Joseph Posik Award (By nomination only), $15 Logan Art Award, poster contest, HVWP Scholarship for English or Journalism graduate work at Veterans Administration hospital. Second contact: Hospitalized Veterans Writing Project, 4801 Linwood Blvd., Kansas City, Missouri 64128.

ARTICLE CONTEST: Various Categories, unpublished, original; 1-4 pages typed double-spaced; 3 entries maximum. Require 1 original, 3 copies, service serial number; entries mailed by hospital staff member. Categories: Courage-Determination, Disability, Humor, Marine, My Country, Patriotic, Other.

AWARDS: $125 First, $75 Second Prize, Charlotte Dilling Memorial Patriotic Award for patriotic articles. $85 First, $65 Second Prize, Disabled American Veterans Writing Award for article on disability. $30 Major Katherine Stull Valor Prose Award for article detailing special courage-determination experience. $25 Gordon Thompson Humor Award. $25 Margaret H. Tyler Humor-Prose Award. $15 Beginners' Prose Award. $15 Juanita Harvey Prose Award. Prizes for John Abercrombie Humor Award; Ruth Cheney Streeter Prose Award; Ned Edwards Award for Best Story by or about Marine.

JUDGING: No entries returned.

ENTRY FEE: None.

DEADLINES: Entry, awards, March, June, October.

3

Illinois Wesleyan University (IWU) Writers' Conference Awards
Kate Romani, Coordinator
IWU Writers' Conference
Illinois Wesleyan University
Bloomington, Illinois 61701 U.S.A.
Tel: (309) 556-3065

August

International; **entry restricted to Conference participants;** annual; established 1977. Cash awards to **Conference Article Writing, Biography-Autobiography-Research, Personal Essay, Juvenile,** unpublished, 20-page maximum. Purpose: to offer writers opportunity to work with professionals have manuscripts critiqued. Sponsored and supported by IWU, United Methodist Church; Central Illinois Branch, National League of American Pen Women. Average statistics: 40 entries, 60 attendance, 5 awards. Held at Illinois Wesleyan University for 1 week in August. Have workshops, seminars, critiques, conferences. Second contact: Bettie Wilson Story, Conference Director, IWU, Bloomington, Illinois 61701. Entry, June. Conference, August.

4

John H. McGinnis Award
Southwest Review
Margaret L. Hartley, Editor
Southern Methodist University
Dallas, Texas 75275 U.S.A.
Tel: (214) 692-2263

February

International; **entry restricted (published in Southwest Review);** biennial; established 1960. $500 **Award to Essay** published in *Southwest Review* during 2 years previous. Judging by staff. Awards, February.

5

Kay Snow Writing Contest
Willamette Writers, Inc.
Mrs. Philip C. Herzog,
Treasurer-Agent
3622 S.E. Lambert Street
Portland, Oregon 97202 U.S.A.
Tel: (503) 777-1236

August

International; **entry open to U.S. and Canada;** annual; established 1969. Purpose: to honor founder of Willamette Writers Club, nonprofit educational organization established 1965 to encourage, provide meeting place for writers. Sponsored and supported by Willamette Writers. Held during annual Willamette Writers Conference in Portland, Oregon for 2 days; 150-200 attendance. Have workshops, speakers. Tickets: approximately $65. Publish monthly bulletin. Also sponsor Poetry and Fiction Writing Contests. Second contact: Jim White, P.O. Box 808, Portland, Oregon 97207.

WRITING CONTEST: Nonfiction, original, unpublished; 1500 words maximum, 1 entry per category, double-spaced (photocopies OK). No photos, illustrations. Categories: General, Juvenile.

AWARDS: $100 First, $50 Second, $25 Third Prize, each category. 1 prize per entrant.

JUDGING: Based on originality, significance, effectiveness of style, artistry. May withhold awards; print winners in monthly bulletins. Entrants retain all rights. No entries returned.

ENTRY FEE: Free (members), $5 each (nonmembers).

DEADLINES: Entry, June. Awards, August.

6

McKendree Writers' Conference Writing Contests
Evelyn Best, Director
105 Florence Street
Lebanon, Illinois 62254 U.S.A.
Tel: (618) 537-2568

May

International; entry open to all; annual; established 1954. Purpose: to promote writing inspiration, encouragement, fellowship. Sponsored by McKendree Writers' Conference, Illinois Arts Council. Held at McKendree College, Lebanon, Illinois, for 1 day. Publish quarterly newsletter. Also sponsor Fiction Writing, Play, Poetry Contests. Second contact: Helen Church, President, St. Louis Street, Lebanon, Illinois 62254.

ARTICLE CONTEST: Nonfiction, any type, original, unpublished, typed on one side, double-spaced, unsigned, 3000-word maximum, unlimited entries.

AWARDS: $25 First, $15 Second, $10 Third Place, each category. Winners published in MWA publication.

JUDGING: May withhold awards. No entries returned.

ENTRY FEE: $1 each category.

DEADLINES: Entry, March. Winners announced, May.

7

Mississippi Valley Writers' Conference (MVWC) Awards
Writers' Studio
David R. Collins, Director
3403 45th Street
Moline, Illinois 61265 U.S.A.
Tel: (309) 762-8985

June

International; **entry restricted to Conference participants;** annual; established 1974. 11 $25 Awards to **Conference Writing,** unpublished. Sponsored by MVWC. Average statistics: 60 entrants, 20 awards. Held at Augustana College, Rock Island, Illinois for 4 days. Judging by workshop leaders. Second contact: Bess Pierce, MVWC, Augustana College, Rock Island, Illinois 61201. Awards, June.

8

Museroom
Center for Internationalising the Study of English (CIE)
Mike Hazard, Director
628 Grand Avenue, #307
St. Paul, Minnesota 55105 U.S.A.
Tel: (612) 222-2096

Periodic

International; entry open to all; periodic; established 1974. Formerly called WALT WHITMAN INTERNATIONAL MEDIA COMPETITION to 1976. Purpose: to promote, encourage literature and media. Sponsored by CIE.

WRITING CONTEST: Various Types and Themes.

AWARDS: Not specified.

ENTRY FEE: Not specified.

DEADLINES: Not specified.

9

National Council of Teachers of English (NCTE) Achievement Awards in Writing
Leona Blum, Director
1111 Kenyon Road
Urbana, Illinois 61801 U.S.A.
Tel: (217) 328-3870

February

National; **entry restricted to U.S.**

high school juniors (nomination by school teachers-students); annual; established 1956. Achievement Awards, Commendation Certificates, College Admission and Financial Assistance Recommendations for **High School Juniors' Writing Skills.** Purpose: to encourage writing in schools, honor outstanding English students. Sponsored and supported by NCTE, nonprofit educational association; Maurice R. Robinson Fund. Average statistics: 6000 entrants, over 850 finalists. Entry, February.

10

PEN Writing Award for Prisoners
PEN American Center
Karen Kennerly, Executive Secretary
47 Fifth Avenue
New York, New York 10003 U.S.A.
Tel: (212) 255-1977

May

National; **entry restricted to U.S. prisoners;** annual; established 1974. Sponsored by 1800-member PEN American Center (founded 1922), division of 10,000-member, 80-country International PEN (Poets, Playwrights, Essayists, Editors, Novelists), founded 1921 as independent, nonprofit world association of writers. Supported by NEA. Average statistics: 1500 entries. Also sponsor PEN Literature Awards, PEN Translation Awards, PEN Fund for Writers; Lucille J. Mednick Memorial Award ($500, annual) for distinguished service to literary community and commitment to serve the young, unrecognized, unpopular (by nomination only).

ESSAY CONTEST: Nonfiction, unpublished; 5000 words maximum, 1 per entrant.

ELIGIBILITY: Unpublished (prison publications excepted), double-spaced typed or handwritten, on 8 1/2x11-inch paper; by U.S. prisoners incarcerated September previous to March current year.

AWARDS: $100 First, $50 Second, $25 Third Prize, each category.

JUDGING: By 5 judges.

ENTRY FEE: None.

DEADLINES: Entry, March. Winners announced, May.

11

Playboy Magazine Annual Awards
Patricia Papangelis, Administrative Editor
919 North Michigan Avenue
Chicago, Illinois 60611 U.S.A.
Tel: (312) 751-8000

Annual

International; **entry restricted to writing published by Playboy Magazine;** annual; established 1956. Cash Awards, Medallion to **Playboy Magazine Writing, Illustration, Photography, Cartoons.** Purpose: to recognize and award *Playboy's* most significant contributors during year. Sponsored and judged by *Playboy Magazine.*

12

Scholastic Writing Awards
Scholastic Inc.
50 West 44th Street
New York, New York 10036 U.S.A.

May

International; **entry restricted to U.S., Canadian students under age 20;** annual; established 1926. Considered largest student writing program in U.S. Pupose: to recognize creative writing of junior, senior high school students in U.S., U.S. territories, Canada. Sponsored by Scholastic Inc. Supported by Scholastic, Smith-Corona,

International Paper Company, National Broadcasting, Paper Mate. Recognized by National Association of Secondary School Principals. Average statistics: 200,000 entries in writing, art, and photography divisions. Also have original song category. Also sponsor art and photography awards, annual Lucky Book Club Four Leaf Clover Awards to Scholastic Book Service published authors of age 7-8 children's books (established 1971).

ESSAY CONTEST: Personal or Formal Nonfiction. Divisions: Senior Grades 10-12 (Personal Essay: 600-1500-word highly personal work that instructs, explains, entertains; Formal Essay: 600-1500-word newspaper editorial or work that conveys information or maintains, defends point of view); Junior Grades 7-12 (500-1500 words any topic, personal experience, event, problem; may be serious or humorous).

ARTICLE CONTEST: Humor, 600-1500-word satire, parody, or anecdote. Senior Division Grades 10-12 only.

REVIEW CONTEST: Critical Evaluation, 600-1500-word review or critical account of literature work or author. Senior Division Grades 10-12 only.

ELIGIBILITY: U.S., Canadian students under age 20, grades 7-12, regularly and currently enrolled in public or nonpublic schools (including U.S. territories, U.S.-sponsored schools abroad). Original work, typed double-spaced on plain 8 1/2x11-inch paper. Entries may be submitted by students (with teacher verification) or by teachers. Limit 3 entries per student. Teachers may submit 10 entries maximum in each competitive class. No plagiarism, joint authorship; no entries copyrighted, printed in copyrighted publications, entered in award competitions (NCTE Awards excepted), or currently submitted for publication (uncopyrighted school newspapers or magazines excepted).

AWARDS: National Honor Awards: 3 $100 First, 3 $50 Second, 3 $25 Third, 10 $15 Fourth Place Awards, each class in Senior and Junior-Senior Divisions. 3 $50 First, 3 $25 Second, 3 $15 Third, 10 $10 Fourth Place Awards, each class in Junior. Up to 30 Honorable Mentions, Merit Certificates, each classification. 3 Typewriters to teachers for most outstanding group of entries, any division or classification. $250 Kenneth M. Gould Memorial Award to Senior for outstanding ability in varied forms, creative writing. $500 International Paper Company Scholarship to Senior for outstanding critical review. 2 $250 National League of American Pen Women Scholarships to Seniors showing outstanding creative writing ability. Winners may be published in *Literary Cavalcade*, other Scholastic magazines.

JUDGING: By authors, educators, editors. Based on originality, quality of expression, writing skill. National winners property of sponsor for possible publication (may edit for reading level, space requirements). No entries returned.

ENTRY FEE: None.

DEADLINES: Entry, February. Awards, May.

13

Sinclair Community College Creative Writing Contest
Gary Mitchner
Department of English
444 West Third Street
Dayton, Ohio 45402 U.S.A. Tel: (513) 226-2594

March

International; entry open to all; annual; established 1967. Purpose: amateur writers meet and gather advice from professional writers. Sponsored by Sinclair Community College, Ohio Arts Council. Held at annual Writers' Workshop at the college, for 2 days; 250 attendance. Tickets: $2 (presentation) $20 (Workshop). Also sponsor Fiction Writing and Poetry Contest.

WRITING CONTEST: **Nonfiction,** unpublished; typed double-spaced on 8 1/2x11-inch paper; 5000-word limit.

AWARDS: $60 First Place, each adult category. $30 Second, $20 Third Place. Scholarship to high school First Place, each category. Merit Certificates. Winners published in Writers' Workshop booklet.

JUDGING: By Sinclair English Department. No entries returned. Not responsible for loss or damage.

ENTRY FEE: $4, adults. $2, high school students.

DEADLINES: Entry, January. Judging, February. Awards, March.

14

Spectrum Magazine Writing Contest
Associated Students: UC Santa Barbara (UCSB)
Joan L. Chappell, Managing Editor
Box 14800
University of California at Santa Barbara
Santa Barbara, California 93107 U.S.A.

Spring

International; **entry restricted to students, nonprofessionals;** annual; established 1957. Changed from quarterly to annual in 1979. Purpose: to publish student, nonprofessional work. Sponsored by UCSB English

Department, Associated Students, Alumni Association. Supported by UCSB sales of *Spectrum Magazine.* Average statistics: 700 entries, 250 entrants, 50 awards. Have readings. Publish *Spectrum Magazine* (annual). Second contact: Ellen Girardeau, 6504 Seville, Apartment 7, Goleta, California 93017.

ESSAY-LETTERS CONTEST: Any Subject, published, unpublished, reasonable length, translations acceptable, unlimited entries. No simultaneous submissions.

AWARDS: Winners published in magazine.

JUDGING: By 8-10 student judges. Copyright reverts to author after publication. Not responsible for loss or damage.

ENTRY FEE: None. Entrant pays postage (include SASE).

DEADLINES: Entry, February. Judging, February-March. Winners notified, April. Publication, May.

15

Writer's Digest Creative Writing Competition
Henry E. Dorfman, Director
9933 Alliance Road
Cincinnati, Ohio 45242 U.S.A.
Tel: (513) 984-0717

October

International; entry open to all; annual. Sponsored by *Writer's Digest,* F & W Publishing Corporation. Publish *Writer's Digest* (monthly). Also sponsor short story and poetry contests.

ARTICLE CONTEST: Any Subject, original, unpublished, not accepted for publication elsewhere; 2500-word limit; 1 entry, typed double-spaced on one side of 8 1/2x11-inch white paper. No F & W employees.

AWARDS: Grand Prize Best Overall Entry (including short story, poetry contests), $500, silver cup, and name engraved on sponsor's plaque. First Place, electric typewriter and commemorative plaque. Second-Third Places, commemorative plaques. Fourth-100th Places, Certificates of Achievement. Grand-Third Prize winners published in winners booklet.

JUDGING: Based on saleability. Sponsor retains one-time publication rights to Grand-Third Prize winners. No entries returned.

ENTRY FEE: None. Entrant pays postage.

DEADLINES: Entry, June. Winners notified, October; announced, November issue.

16

Writers' Forum Writing Contests
Pasadena City College
Jane Hallinger
1570 Colorado Blvd.
Pasadena, California 91108 U.S.A.
Tel: (213) 578-7261

May

Regional; **entry open to Southern California;** annual; established 1952. Sponsored by Writers' Forum, Pasadena City College. Held at Pasadena City College for 1 1/2 days. Tickets: $10. Also sponsor Short Story and Poetry Contests.

ESSAY CONTEST: Any Subject, not previously published in major magazine. Categories: Adults, College, High School Students.

AWARDS: Cash Prizes.

JUDGING: Entrant retains all

rights. Not responsible for loss or damage.

ENTRY FEE: None.

DEADLINES: Awards, May.

17

Youth Magazine Creative Arts Awards
132 West 31st Street
New York, New York 10001 U.S.A.

Summer

National; **entry restricted to U.S. youth age 13-19;** annual. Sponsored by *Youth Magazine.* Also have art, sculpture contests. Second contact: *Youth Magazine,* room 1203, 1505 Race Street, Philadelphia, Pennsylvania 19102; tel: (215) 568-3950

ARTICLE CONTEST: **By Youth,** including true-to-life experiences. Limit 5 entries.

ESSAY CONTEST: **By Youth,** including editorials. Limit 5 entries.

AWARDS: Winners published in special awards issue of *Youth Magazine.*

JUDGING: Only nonwinners returned.

ENTRY FEE: None.

DEADLINES: Entry, May. Awards, Summer.

18

Edmonton Journal Literary Awards
Promotion Department
Box 2421
Edmonton, Alberta T5J 2S6
CANADA

Summer

Regional; **entry restricted to Ed-** monton **Journal area novice writers;** annual; established 1962. Sponsored and supported by *Edmonton Journal.*

ARTICLE CONTEST: **Nonfiction,** original, unpublished; 2000 words maximum, limit 1 per entrant.

ELIGIBILITY: Must be year-round residents of *Edmonton Journal's* trading zone (northern Alberta, Peace River Block, Yukon and Northwest Territories; southern boundary is east-west line through and including Red Deer; western boundary is Rocky Mountains; eastern boundary is Saskatchewan border). No previous working writers; *Edmonton Journal* employees and immediate families; elementary, junior, senior high school students.

AWARDS: $500.

JUDGING: Sponsor may divide, withhold award; publish winner. Not responsible for loss or damage.

ENTRY FEE: Not specified.

DEADLINES: Entry, April. Award, Summer.

ARTICLE, ESSAY (Historical)
Article, Essay, Dissertation, Paper, including AMERICAN, NORTH AMERICAN WEST, SCOTTISH, ART, ARCHAEOLOGY, ANTIQUARIAN, FILM. (Also see other ARTICLE, ESSAY.)

19

Allan Nevins Prize
Society of American Historians
Professor Kenneth T. Jackson
610 Fayerweather Hall

Columbia University
New York, New York 10027 U.S.A.
Tel: (212) 280-2555

April

National; **entry open to U.S.**; annual; established 1960. Sponsored by Columbia University and Society of American Historians, in cooperation with Harcourt Brace Jovanovich; Harper & Row; Little, Brown and Company; W. W. Norton; Random House-Alfred A. Knopf; Harvard University Press; Oxford University Press. Also sponsor Francis Parkman Prize Competition.

DISSERTATION   CONTEST: American History, manuscripts dealing with American arts, literature, science, biographical studies. Submission by chair of department or sponsor of dissertation; limit 2 manuscripts per department. Require receipt of doctorate or successful defense of dissertation in preceding year.

AWARDS: $1000 First Prize and publication by one of sponsoring publishers.

JUDGING: Based on good writing, high-quality scholarship, contribution to historical knowledge.

ENTRY FEE: Not specified. Entrant pays postage (include SASE).

DEADLINES: Entry, December. Award, April.

20

Ohio University Film Conference Film Papers
Athens Center for Film and Video
Stephen Andrews, Coordinator
384 Lindley Hall
P.O. Box 388
Athens, Ohio 45701 U.S.A. Tel: (614) 594-6888

April

International; entry open to all; annual. Purpose: to bring together diverse but related approaches to film study. Sponsored by Athens Center for Film and Video. Supported by NEA, Ohio Arts Council, Ohio University College of Fine Arts. Held at Ohio University and Athena Cinemas (Athens, Ohio) for 4 days. Tickets: $15 general, $7.50 students. Also sponsor Athens International Film Festival, Athens Video Festival.

PAPER   PRESENTATION: Film History Study, various yearly themes, 10-15 pages (double-spaced) or 15 minutes in length. Require 2 copies plus 100-word abstract.

AWARDS: None.

ENTRY FEE: None.

DEADLINES: Registration, September. Submission of papers, January. Conference, April.

21

Ray A. Billington Award
Western History Association (WHA)
William D. Rowley, Executive Secretary
Department of History
University of Nevada
Reno, Nevada 89557 U.S.A.

October

International; **entry restricted to periodical editors;** annual. Named after Ray A. Billington, first WHA president. Purpose: to encourage authors, editors to seek excellence in western history field. Sponsored by WHA. Held at WHA annual meeting. Publish *Western Historical Quarterly.*

PERIODICAL   ARTICLE   CONTEST: North America Western History, published in regular periodical July previous to July of contest year; about North American West (including Alaska, Canada, Mexico); 1 entry per editor, 3 copies, each with nomination letter.

AWARDS: $300 to article author. $100 to publishing journal.

JUDGING: By 3-person committee. Based on contribution to knowledge, skill and imaginativeness of research, literary quality.

ENTRY FEE: None.

DEADLINES: Entry, July. Awards, October.

22

Society of Cinema Studies (SCS) Conference Film Papers
Dan Leab
121 East 78th Street
New York, New York 10021 U.S.A.
Tel: (212) 737-2715

April

International; **entry restricted to SCS members;** annual; established 1955. Presentation of **Film History Papers** by SCS members. Purpose: dissemination of scholarly knowledge about film history. Sponsored by SCS. Average statistics: 50 entrants. Publish *Cinema Journal* and *Moving Image* (newsletter). Awards, April.

23

Reginald Taylor Essay Prize
British Archaeological Association (BAA)
Paul Everson, Hon. Editor
County Planning Department
County Offices
Newland, Lincoln, ENGLAND
Tel: 0522-29931, ext. 109

May

International; entry open to all; annual. Established on legacy of E. Reginald Taylor, former secretary of BAA.

Purpose: to encourage original research on archaeological, art-historical, antiquarian subjects, particularly by young scholars. Sponsored by BAA, founded 1843. Also sponsor annual conference on British cathedrals.

ESSAY CONTEST: Archaeology, Art History, Antiquarian (Roman era to A.D. 1830), original, unpublished, 7500 words maximum.

AWARDS: 30 pounds, invitation to read essay before BAA, publication in *BAA Journal.*

JUDGING: By BAA Editorial Committee. Not responsible for loss or damage.

ENTRY FEE: None.

DEADLINES: Entry, December. Winner announced, May.

24

Royal Historical Society Essay Prizes
Secretary, Royal Historical Society
University College London
Gower Street
London, WC1E 6BT, ENGLAND
Tel: 01-367-7532

Spring

International; entry open to all; annual. Sponsored and supported by the Royal Historical Society of University College London. Sanctioned by an Order of the Chancery Division of the High Court of Justice.

ESSAY CONTEST: History *(Alexander Prize Essay),* original, unpublished; typed, text 6000 words maximum, footnotes 2000 words maximum. Require cover letter. No previous winners.

Scottish History *(David Berry Essay),* limited to reigns of James I-James VI; original, unpublished; 6000-10,-

000 words (excluding footnotes, appendices), typed. No previous winners.

AWARDS: Silver Medal and entrant reads Alexander Essay at last meeting of Society. Best Berry Essay 100 pounds.

JUDGING: By Royal Historical Society members. May require evidence of authorship. Not responsible for loss or damage.

ENTRY FEE: Not specified. Entrant pays postage (include SASE).

DEADLINES: Entry,   October. Awards, Spring.

ARTICLE, ESSAY (Medical, Scientific)

Article, Essay, Paper, including
FOREST CONSERVATION,
HANDICAPPED-DISABLED,
OPERATIONS RESEARCH,
PHOTOGRAMMETRY,
PSYCHOLOGY,
READING-LEARNING DISABILITY,
UNDERWATER. (Also see other
ARTICLE, ESSAY.)

25

AAAS Socio-Psychological Prize Competition
American Association for the
Advancement of Science (AAAS)
8th Floor
1776 Massachusetts Avenue N.W.
Washington, District of Columbia
20036 U.S.A.

January

International; entry open to all; annual; established 1952. Purpose: to encourage in social inquiry the develop-

ment, application of dependable methodology that has proved fruitful in natural sciences. Held in Washington, D.C., at AAAS annual meeting.

ESSAY CONTEST: **Human Psychological-Social-Cultural Behavior,** unpublished or published since previous January; in English; 120 pages maximum, 5 copies each entry and 5 copies 1200-word maximum abstract. Require complete analysis of problem, relevant data and interpretation. Should foster comprehension of psychological-social-cultural human behavior, deal with observation, construction of social process, group behavior, interpersonal behavior. No theoretical formulations, empirical studies.

AWARDS: $1000 AAAS Socio-Psychological Prize.

JUDGING: By AAAS officers.

ENTRY FEE: None. Entrant pays postage (include SASE)

DEADLINES: Entry, July. Award, January.

26

"Ability Counts" Research Writing Contest
President's Committee on
Employment of the Handicapped
Mrs. Juanita E. Campbell, Public
Information Specialist
Washington, District of Columbia
20210 U.S.A.

Spring

National; **entry restricted to U.S. high school students;** annual; established 1949. Sponsored and supported by President's Committee on Employment of the Handicapped, Governor's Committee on the Handicapped, Disabled American Veterans, AFL-CIO state federations and councils. Recognized by National Association of Secondary School Principals.

ESSAY CONTEST: Handicapped-Disabled, various yearly themes; original, 3 pages maximum; in English; typed double-spaced on 8 1/2x11-inch paper. Require teacher signature.

ELIGIBILITY: U.S. public-private-parochial high school students (grades 11-12) in a state, Virgin Islands, Puerto Rico, or District of Columbia.

AWARDS: $2000 First, $1500 Second, $900 Third, $600 Fourth, $500 Fifth Prize. Certificates, Plaques. Plaques to winners' high schools. Judge Robert S. Marx First Place National Award. State, Local Prizes, Scholarships. Transportation to Washington, D.C., expenses to First Place State winners.

JUDGING: State contest conducted by Governors' Committees on Employment of the Handicapped (c/o State Chairman, State Capitol). First Place State Winners go to National judging. Based on content significance, program impact, organization, expression, clarity, neatness, personal interviews and observations.

ENTRY FEE: None. Entrant pays postage (include SASE).

DEADLINES: Entry,   March. Awards, Spring.

27

Bausch & Lomb Photogrammetric Award
American Society of Photogrammetry (ASP)
105 North Virginia Avenue
Falls Church, Virginia 22046 U.S.A.
Tel: (703) 534-6617

Spring

National; **entry restricted to U.S. undergraduate and graduate college,**

university students; annual. Purpose: to stimulate U.S. college students' photogrammetric interest. Sponsored by ASP. Supported by Bausch & Lomb Inc. Also sponsor $3000 Wild Heerbrugg Photogrammetric Fellowship Award for photogrammetry graduate education; III Talbut Abrams Award for authorship-recording of current, historical, engineering, scientific developments in photogrammetry; Autometric Award for technical publication on photographic interpretation.

ESSAY CONTEST: Photogrammetry, (map-making science-art of obtaining surveys by photography), unpublished, 4000 words maximum, 5 maximum per college-university; describing new use, adaptation, improvement of photogrammetry or photogrammetry equipment.

AWARDS: $250 each to graduate and undergraduate winner; round trip to annual convention in Washington, D.C.; 3 years paid Society membership.

JUDGING: By 3-member committee. Based on originality, comprehension of principles, organization, English. May withhold awards.

ENTRY FEE: None. Entrant pays postage (include SASE).

DEADLINES: Entry,   January. Awards, Spring.

28

Forest History Society Awards
Journal of Forest History
Ronald J. Fahl, Editor
109 Coral Street
Santa Cruz, California 95060 U.S.A.

August

International; **entry restricted to magazine editors;** annual; established

1971. Sponsored by Forest History Society. Also sponsor $500 Forest History Society Book Award (biennial) for manuscript, published book on forest history or conservation; $150 Federick K. Weyerhaeuser Award for article in *Journal of Forest History*.

ARTICLE CONTEST: Forest-Conservation History, published in previous year, 4 copies or offprints. No *Journal of Forest History* articles.

MAGAZINE ARTICLE CONTEST: Forest-Conservation History. Requirements, restrictions same as for Article.

AWARDS: $150 Theodore C. Blegen Award to Best Article.

JUDGING: By 3 judges.

ENTRY FEE: None.

DEADLINES: Entry, May. Awards, August.

29

International Reading Association (IRA) Albert J. Harris Award

Drew Cassidy, Public Information Officer
800 Barksdale Road
P.O. Box 8139
Newark, Delaware 19711 U.S.A.
Tel: (302) 731-1600

Spring

International; entry open to all; annual. Purpose: to honor outstanding contribution to diagnosis and remediation of reading, learning disabilities. Sponsored by IRA, 65,000-member, nonprofit, educational association with members in over 85 countries, dedicated to reading instruction improvement, reading habit development. Supported by Institute for Reading Research. Held at IRA Convention annual awards banquet. Also sponsor IRA Children's Book Award;

Outstanding Dissertation of the Year Award; Print Media Award; Milton D. Jacobson Memorial Award (article published in *Reading Research Quarterly* in previous year). Second contact: Dr. Helen K. Smith, 5840 Red Road, Apartment 129, Miami, Florida 33143.

ARTICLE CONTEST: Reading-Learning Disability Diagnosis or Remediation, published in professional journal or monograph between June previous and June current year. Submit 7 copies of originals, photostats of publication title page.

AWARDS: $500.

JUDGING: by IRA special committee. No entries returned. Not responsible for loss or damage.

ENTRY FEE: None.

DEADLINES: Entry, October. Award, Spring.

30

Operations Research Society of America (ORSA) Research Paper Awards

Jesse L. Turner, Business Manager
428 East Preston Street
Baltimore, Maryland 21202 U.S.A.
Tel: (301) 528-4146

Annual

National; **entry restricted (selection by ORSA members);** annual; established 1954 (Lanchester), 1974 (Nicholson). Frederick W. Lanchester Prize of $2000 and Medal for **Operations Research Paper.** George E. Nicholson, Jr., Memorial Award First ($300) and Second ($150) Prizes for **Student Operations Research Paper.** Sponsored by ORSA, established 1952 to describe, understand, predict behavior of man-machine systems operating in natural environments.

31

Aqua Space Aquatic Research Competition
Aquatic Exploration and Research
Associates (AERA)
Dale Woodyard, Director
Department of Psychology
University of Windsor
Windsor, Ontario N9B 3P4 CANADA
Tel: (519) 253-4232

October-November

International; entry open to all; annual; established 1977. Purpose: to educate public about aquatic world, AERA aquatic projects. Theme: Aquatic Education. Sponsored by AERA. Average statistics: 500 entries (includes films, photos), 60 entrants, 30 finalists, 9 winners, 300 attendance. Held at University of Windsor. Tickets: $3.50. Publish *AERALOG Newsletter* (bimonthly). Also sponsor Oris Award for Marine Environmental Journalism. Second contact: Glen Adams, 10275 Shenandoah Court, Windsor, Ontario, Canada.

PAPER CONTEST: **Underwater Research,** report using format appropriate to type of research. Require photographs, diagrams, other documentation. No previous winners. Categories: Underwater Archaeology, Biology, Geology, Geography, Behavior Research.

AWARDS: Joe MacInnis Award for Best Research Paper. Trophies, prizes, each category.

JUDGING: By professional, experienced judges. May withhold awards. Sponsor may make copies for publicity. Not responsible for loss or damage.

ENTRY FEE: $5 each. Entrant pays postage.

DEADLINES: Entry, October. Event, October-November. Materials returned, January.

ARTICLE, ESSAY (Religious, Humanitarian)
Article, Essay, including FAITH, PRAYER. (Also see other ARTICLE, ESSAY.)

32

Conference on Christianity and Literature (CCL) Student Writing Contest
Editor of Christianity and Literature
Calvin College
Grand Rapids, Michigan 49506
U.S.A. Tel: (616) 949-4000, ext. 264

Spring

International; **entry restricted to U.S., Canadian undergraduates;** annual; established 1974. Purpose: to encourage student writing on relation of religion to literature-life experience. Sponsored by CCL, founded 1956 as international organization for understanding relationship between Christianity and creation, study, teaching of literature. Supported by William B. Eerdmans Publishing Co. Average statistics: 180 entries. Publish *Christianity and Literature* (quarterly journal). Also sponsor CCL Book of the Year Award. Second contact: Roy Battenhouse, English Department, Indiana University, Bloomington, Indiana 47401.

ESSAY CONTEST: **Religion and Literary Criticism.**

AWARDS: First, Second, Third Prizes. Prizes are books.

ENTRY FEE: None. Entrant pays postage.

DEADLINES: Entry, March. Judging, April. Awards, May.

| 33 |

Explorer Writing Awards
Explorer Magazine
Raymond Flory, Editor-Publisher
538 West Grove Street
Mishawaka, Indiana 46544 U.S.A.

Spring, Fall

International; entry open to all; semiannual; established 1960. Sponsored and supported by *Explorer Magazine.*

ARTICLE CONTEST: Travel, Personal Experience (describing answered prayer), original, unpublished; 300 words maximum.

AWARDS: First Prize, $10 and plaque; $5 Second, $4 Third, $3 Fourth Prizes.

JUDGING: By subscribers.

ENTRY FEE: Not specified. Entrant pays postage (include SASE).

DEADLINES: Entry, not specified. Awards, Spring, Fall.

| 34 |

Guideposts Youth Writing Contest
Guideposts Magazine
747 Third Avenue
New York, New York 10017 U.S.A.
Tel: (212) 754-2200

Winter

International; **entry restricted to high school juniors, seniors or foreign equivalent grades;** annual. Sponsored by *Guideposts Magazine*

(monthly).

ARTICLE CONTEST: **Personal Experience in Faith Nonfiction,** unpublished, first-person, original, 1200 words maximum, in English, typed, double-spaced. About writer's memorable, moving, true personal experience, making reader sense writer's faith in God. No *Guideposts* employees or children.

AWARDS: Accredited-college scholarships to be used within 5 years after graduation ($4000 First, $3500 Second, $3000 Third, $2500 Fourth, $2000 Fifth, $1000 Sixth-Tenth Place); manual portable typewriters (11th-30th Prizes). Sponsor owns winning manuscripts.

ENTRY FEE: None. Entrant pays postage (include SASE).

DEADLINES: Entry, November. Awards, Winter.

| 35 |

International Humanist Essay Contest
Nelson Joe Raglione, Public Relations
P.O. Box 36
Lachine, Quebec H8S 4A5 CANADA
Tel: (514) 631-6796

June-July

International; entry open to all; monthly (from 1982); established 1981. Purpose: to develop ecological and humanistic understanding among all people. Theme: My Ideal World. Motto: "To help just one desperate person, to feed just one starving child, we unite." Sponsored by International Humanist Foundation, nonprofit organization without religious, political, commercial ties, set up for world peace and brotherhood. Recognized by U.N. Publish information on international humanism. Second contact:

Mr. Derek Rafuse, (514) 627-5474.

ESSAY CONTEST: Humanitarian, 1-page essay entitled "My Ideal World."

AWARDS: $200 First Prize. All contestants receive membership card.

JUDGING: Based on humanistic content, not on style or neatness. All entries read and returned. Not responsible for loss or damage.

ENTRY FEE: $1 each. Sponsor pays return postage.

DEADLINES: Entry, Award, June-July; possible monthly from 1982.

ARTICLE, ESSAY (Sociology, Culture)

Article, Essay, Paper, including ANTHROPOLOGY, POPULAR AMERICAN CULTURE, ITALIAN-AMERICAN, SOCIAL PROTEST-PHILOSOPHY. (Also see other ARTICLE, ESSAY.)

36

Bryant Spann-Eugene V. Debs Memorial Prize
Bryant Spann Memorial Prize Committee
Department of History
Indiana State University
Terre Haute, Indiana 47809 U.S.A.

Fall

International; entry open to all; annual; established 1979. Purpose: to encourage writings against social injustice, in tradition of Eugene V. Debs. Sponsored and supported by Eugene V. Debs Foundation, founded 1974. Also have annual award to person best

serving mankind.

ARTICLE-ESSAY CONTEST: Social Protest-Justice, published or unpublished; any length; in English; 100-line limit, typed, double-spaced on 8 1/2x11-inch paper, limit 2 per entrant. Submit 5 copies each entry with 5 copies summary of each entry's relevance to Debs social protest tradition.

AWARDS: $600 Spann-Debs Memorial Prize.

ENTRY FEE: None. Entrant pays postage (include SASE).

DEADLINES: Entry, April. Judging, May-August. Award, October-November. Materials returned, September.

37

Conference on Culture and Communication (CCC) Call for Papers
Temple University
Dr. Richard Chalfen, Director
Department of Anthropology
Philadelphia, Pennsylvania 19122
U.S.A. Tel: (215) 787-7775, 787-7616

March

International; entry open to all; biennial (even years); established 1974. Alternates with Conference on Visual Anthropology (COVA) Film and Video Exhibitions. Purpose: to explore interrelations between culture and communication. Sponsored by Temple University Anthropology and Radio-Television-Film Departments. Held in Walk Auditorium, Ritter Hall, Temple Unviersity. Have discussions, symposia, audiovisual equipment. Also sponsor photo essay exhibit.

PAPER READING: Culture and Communication. Submit abstract, under 175 words (typed, single-spaced) and-or session proposal, plus 2 copies. Categories: various sub-themes.

AWARDS: Small stipends to some invited participants.

ENTRY FEE: None.

DEADLINES: Entry, November. Conference, March.

38

Design for Living Contest
The March Society
Charles A. Mills, Awards Chairman
14531 Stephen Street
Nokesville, Virginia 22123 U.S.A.

Summer

International; entry open to all; annual; established 1974. Sponsored by The March Society. Publish *Journal of The March Society*.

ESSAY CONTEST: Social-Philosophical Theme, regarding program for dealing with social-philosophical problems. Various yearly themes. Other requirements, restrictions not specified.

AWARDS: $100 First, $25 Second Prize. 5 Honorable Mentions. All entries eligible for first publication in *Journal*.

JUDGING: Based on writing quality, originality, cogency of thinking, presentation and viability of alternative solutions. Entrant retains all rights.

ENTRY FEE: None.

DEADLINES: Entry, June. Awards, Summer.

39

Leonardo Covello Award in Italian-American Studies
American-Italian Historical Association (AIHA)
209 Flagg Place
New York, New York 10304 U.S.A.

October

International; **entry restricted to graduate students, doctorates;** annual. Purpose: to promote understanding of Italian experience in America. Sponsored by AIHA, nonprofit educational organization founded 1966 to create true understanding of American-Italian experience, encourage American-Italian studies. Held at annual AIHA meeting for 1 day. Publish regional, national newsletters. Also sponsor annual national conference, group programs, resource depositories, information network.

ESSAY CONTEST: Italian-American Experience, article-length manuscript, 2 copies. Require vita. Encourage original research, synthesis, new interpretations by graduate students or doctorate recipients in past 3 years.

AWARDS: $200 Leonard Covello Award.

JUDGING: By 5 judges. May withhold award.

ENTRY FEE: None.

DEADLINES: Entry, July. Event, October.

40

Popular Culture Association (PCA) Meeting Papers
Pat Browne
Popular Culture Center
Bowling Green State University
Bowling Green, Ohio 43403 U.S.A.
Tel: (419) 372-2981

Spring

International; **entry restricted to U.S., Canadian PCA members;** annual; established 1970. Presentation of **Popular American Culture Papers.** Purpose: to study artistic and commercial products designed for mass consumption. Sponsored by PCA. Held at various U.S. locations for 5 days in Spring. Average statistics: 1000 attendance. Tickets: $15-$20.

41

Curl Essay Prize
Royal Anthropological Institute of
Great Britain and Ireland
56 Queen Anne Street
London W1M 9LA, ENGLAND Tel: 01
486 6832

Winter

International; entry open to all; annual; established 1951. Sponsored by Royal Anthropological Institute of Great Britain and Ireland. Also sponsor anthropological scholarships to British nationals.

ESSAY CONTEST: **Anthropological Results-Analysis,** 10,000 words maximum; relating to results, analysis of anthropological work; 3 copies.

AWARDS: 250 pound Curl Bequest Prize. Possible publication of essays.

ENTRY FEE: None.

DEADLINES: Entry, September.

ARTICLE, ESSAY (Other)
Article, Essay, Dissertation, Monograph, Paper, Writing, including AMERICAN INDUSTRY, COPYRIGHT LAW, FAMILY ORIENTED, FANTASY, PACIFIC TRAVEL, READING, SENIOR CITIZEN, STAMPS, IN FRENCH and LATIN.

42

Alliance Francaise National French Contest
Federation of French Alliances in the United States
Jean-Jacques Sicard, Coordinator
22 East 60th Street
New York, New York 10022 U.S.A.
Tel: (212) 644-1820

Spring

National; **entry restricted to U.S. students sponsored by members;** annual; established 1975. $75-$300 (to high school students); Paris-study scholarship, $100-$300 (college-university students) under age 25 for **Theme Essay in French.** Alliance Francaise, French Club, or contest sponsor must sponsor students. Sponsored by Federation of French Alliances in the United States. Also sponsor $1000 Summer Scholarships for study in France. Awards, Spring.

43

International Conference on the Fantastic in the Arts
Thomas Burnett Swann Fund
Dr. Robert A. Collins, Coordinator
College of Humanities
Florida Atlantic University
Boca Raton, Florida 33431 U.S.A.
Tel: (305) 395-5100, ext. 5238

March

International; entry open to all; annual; established 1979. Purpose: to recognize, emphasize, explore tradition of the fantastic in Western literature; promote writers in the field. Sponsored by Thomas Burnett Swann

Fund. Recognized by Modern Language Association. Average statistics: 7 countries, 500 attendance. Held at Florida Atlantic University for 4 days. Have shows, exhibits, readings, lectures. Publish *Sentient Cosmos* (newsletter), *The Scope of the Fantastic* (annual essay collection). Also sponsor Annual Workshop on Teaching Science Fiction.

WRITING PRESENTATION: Fantasy, 30-minute maximum readings. Require query, 100-word abstract, biographical information.

MONOGRAPH-PAPER PRESENTATION: Fantasy. Requirements, restrictions same as for writing.

AWARDS: Noncompetitive. Sponsor claims first serial rights to academic articles, monographs; insures solicited material only.

ENTRY FEE: $30 registration.

DEADLINES: Materials, December. Acceptance, January. Event, March.

44

International Reading Association (IRA) Dissertation of the Year Award
Drew Cassidy, Public Information Officer
800 Barksdale Road
P.O. Box 8139
Newark, Delaware 19711 U.S.A.
Tel: (302) 731-1600

Spring

International; entry open to all; annual. Purpose: to honor outstanding dissertation in reading fields. Sponsored by IRA, 65,000-member, nonprofit, educational association with members in over 85 countries, dedicated to reading instruction improvement, reading habit development. Supported by Institute for Reading

Research. Held at IRA Convention annual awards banquet. Also sponsor IRA Children's Book Award; Albert J. Harris Award; Print Media Award. Second contact: Dr. Robert J. Tierney, Center for the Study of Reading, University of Illinois, 51 Gerty Drive, Champaign, Illinois 61820.

DISSERTATION CONTEST: Reading, Related Field, completed between June previous and August current year; any research approach (historical, survey, experimental), submit 10 copies.

AWARDS: Not specified.

JUDGING: By IRA committee. Based on approach, scholarly qualifications, significance. No entries returned. Not responsible for loss or damage.

ENTRY FEE: None.

DEADLINES: Entry, September. Award, Spring.

45

Nathan Burkan Memorial Competition
American Society of Composers, Authors and Publishers (ASCAP)
ASCAP Building
One Lincoln Plaza
New York, New York 10023 U.S.A.
Tel: (212) 595-3050

Fall

International; **entry restricted to law students;** annual; established 1938. Named for Nathan Burkan, copyright authority and ASCAP's first General Counsel. Purpose: to increase interest in copyright law, improve legal writing. Sponsored by ASCAP, founded 1914 as public nondramatic performance, music licensing, and collection organization of composers, lyricists, music publishers. Also sponsor grants to writer members for concert-public music, grants to young U.S. citizen-resident composers, ASCAP-Deems Taylor Awards for Writing on Music.

ESSAY CONTEST: Copyright Law, 50 pages maximum, by second- or third-year law students in accredited law schools. Submit 2 copies, typed double-spaced on 8 1/2x11-inch paper, covered. No collaborations.

AWARDS: $250 First, $100 Second Prize at local law schools. $3000, $2000, $1500 National Awards and publication in *ASCAP Copyright Law Symposium.* Honorable Mentions.

JUDGING: Local winners at local law schools. National by panel of U.S. justices.

ENTRY FEE: None.

DEADLINES: Entry,   August. Awards, Fall.

46

Ozark Writers and Artists Guild Writing Contest
Maggie Smith, Director
Box 411
Siloam Springs, Arkansas 72761
U.S.A. Tel: (501) 524-3591

July

International; entry open to all; annual; established 1935. Purpose: to provide workshop of writers and artists for idea-exchange in friendly atmosphere. Sponsored by Siloam Springs Writers and Northwest Arkansas Branch of American Pen Women. Supported by Siloam Springs banks, savings and loans, individuals. Recognized by Poets' Roundtable of Arkansas. Held at John Brown University for 1 day. Tickets: $6 (luncheon). Have seminar, speakers, poetry for popular-vote award.

ILLUSTRATED ARTICLE CONTEST: Family-Oriented, unpublished; on 8 1/2x11 paper, 800 words maximum, with black and white photo or drawing, 1 per entrant. Must not have won over $10.

AWARDS: $25 First, $15 Second, $10 Third Prize. 2 Honorable Mentions. Touring exhibition of winners.

JUDGING: All entries read in entirety by judge in appropriate field. No entries returned. Not responsible for loss or damage.

ENTRY FEE: $4 1-4 entries. $1 each additional.

DEADLINES: Entry, June. Awards, July.

47

Pacific Travel Story Contest
Pacific Area Travel Association (PATA)
Graham Hornel, Director, Public Relations
228 Grant Avenue
San Francisco, California 94108
U.S.A. Tel: (415) 986-4646

February

International; entry open to all; annual; established 1958. Sponsored by PATA, nonprofit association founded 1951 to stimulate travel to, among Pacific Basin countries-island groups. Held at PATA annual conference. Also sponsor Pacific Film Contest, Publicity Photo Contest, Travel Poster Contest, Promotional Travel Brochure Contest (all open to PATA members only).

ARTICLE CONTEST: Pacific Travel Newspaper, Magazine, published December of previous to November of contest year; 1 per category,

2 unmounted copies, tearsheets or clippings showing publication date and name. Require English translation of foreign language entries (except French, Germn). Categories: Best Story Any Language, In French, In German, In English, Self-Illustrated Story (any language), Newspaper Story (any language), Magazine Story (any language). No travel trade publications.

AWARDS: Excellence Certificates, inclusion on PATA Media Familiarization programs lists, hosted trips to PATA destinations, Best Each Category. Grand Prize winner presented on stage at conference.

JUDGING: Based on motivational impact, "friendly Pacific" image, informational value, writing skill.

ENTRY FEE: None.

DEADLINES: Entry, November. Awards, February.

48

Philip H. Ward Memorial Award Competition
American First Day Cover Society (AFDCS)
Sol Koved, Editor
14 Samoset Road
P.O. Box 23
Cranford, New Jersey 07016 U.S.A.

October

International; **entry restricted to philatelic publications;** annual; established 1964. Named after Philip H. Ward, Jr., pioneer first day cover (FDC) collector, journalist. Purpose: to encourage publication of FDC literature. Sponsored by AFDCS. Held at AFDCS annual convention-exhibition. Have information, translation services; meetings, exhibits. Publish *First Days* (bimonthly journal). Also sponsor First Day Cover Stamp Com-

petition (open to major exhibitions with separate FDC category). Second contacts: Barry Newton, Award Committee Chairman, P.O. Box 5152, Akron, Ohio 44313; Mrs. Marge Finger, Executive Secretary, P.O. Box 23, Elberon, New Jersey 07740; John Jezek, President, P.O. Box 1031, No. Riverside, Illinois 60546.

ARTICLE CONTEST: First Day Cover Stamps, published in philatelic press during previous calendar year, 3 copies (photocopies OK). Material published in *First Days* automatically considered.

AWARDS: Silver Plaque for excellence in FDC story or research. Honorable Mentions.

JUDGING: By 3 philatelist-writers. Based on style, depth of research, scholarship, readability, impact.

ENTRY FEE: None.

DEADLINES: Entry, January. Awards, October.

49

United States Industrial Council (USIC) Educational Foundation Essay Contest
John G. Hutchens, President
P.O. Box 2686
Third Floor, Realtors Building
Nashville, Tennessee 37219 U.S.A.
Tel: (615) 256-5961

September

National; **entry open to U.S.;** annual; established 1980. Purpose: to promote awareness of need to support measures for revitalizing American industry. Sponsored and supported by USIC, nonprofit educational institution founded 1933, concerned with promoting interest in free enterprise system.

ESSAY CONTEST: American Industry, 1000 words minimum, typed, double-spaced. Require author biography, statement of originality, permission to USIC to publish.

AWARDS: $1000. Publication in Foundation Special Report.

ENTRY FEE: None. Entrant pays postage (include SASE).

DEADLINES: Entry, June. Winner announced, September.

50

Writing in the Autumn Competition
Rocky Mountain Writers Guild, Inc.
James D. Hutchinson, President
2969 Baseline Road
Boulder, Colorado 80303 U.S.A.
Tel: (303) 444-4100

June

National; **entry restricted to U.S. seniors age 62 or older;** annual. Purpose: to encourage senior citizens to write and compete. Sponsored by Rocky Mountain Writers Guild, Inc. Average statistics: 49 awards. Publish newsletter. Also sponsor creative writing workshops, technical writing seminars, marketing conferences, literary services.

ESSAY CONTEST: Senior Citizen Theme, unpublished, original, true; 1200-word limit.

AWARDS: $100 First, $50 Second Prize. Subscriptions, mementos, plaques, publication.

JUDGING: Sponsor claims first North American rights. Not responsible for loss or damage.

ENTRY FEE: $2 each. Entrant pays postage (include SASE).

DEADLINES: Entry, April. Awards, June.

51

International Contest for Latin Prose
Institute of Roman Study
Latin Office
Piazza dei Cavalieri di Malta 2
00153 Rome, ITALY Tel: 573-442

Spring

International; entry open to all; annual; established 1949. Sponsored by Ministry for Cultural Environment of Italy and City of Rome, Rome Institute of Study. Held during Birth of Rome (Natale di Roma) Celebration.

ESSAY CONTEST: In Latin Prose, unpublished, any genre, theme; scholastic or traditional; 1 entry, typed or printed; 5 copies. No previous winners. Categories: Teacher-Latin Scholar (1500 words minimum), Student (1000 words minimum). Require student verification of enrollment.

AWARDS: 500,000 Lire and "Praemium Vrbis" (sculptured silver She-wolf) to teachers-scholars. 250,000 Lire and Silver Medallion, 100,000 Lire and Diploma, to students. Honorable Mentions.

JUDGING: By 5 judges. Institute may publish winners.

ENTRY FEE: None.

DEADLINES: Entry, January. Awards, Spring.

BOOK (the Arts, Media)
Book, Article, including ARCHITECTURE HISTORY, DANCE, ILLUSTRATED ART, MOTION

PICTURES, MUSIC, PHOTOGRAPHIC HISTORY, POET-POETRY, RADIO, TELEVISION, THEATER. (Also see other BOOK.)

| 52 |

Alice Davis Hitchcock Book Award

Society of Architectural Historians (SAH)
Suite 716
1700 Walnut Street
Philadelphia, Pennsylvania 19103
U.S.A. Tel: (215) 735-0246, 735-0224

April

International; **entry restricted to North American authors;** established 1949. Purpose: to recognize distinguished scholarship in architecture history. Sponsored and supported by SAH.

BOOK CONTEST: Architecture History, published November, 2 years previous, to October current year. May include urban development, garden, stage design, books dealing in part with architecture. Submit 4 copies with publication date.

AWARDS: Alice Davis Hitchcock Book Award Plaque, citation in SAH Journal.

JUDGING: By 3 professors of architecture.

ENTRY FEE: None.

DEADLINES: Entry, November. Award, April.

| 53 |

ASCAP-Deems Taylor Awards for Writing on Music

American Society of Composers, Authors and Publishers (ASCAP)
ASCAP Building
One Lincoln Plaza
New York, New York 10023 U.S.A.
Tel: (212) 595-3050

Fall

National; **entry open to U.S.;** annual; established 1967. Named after Deems Taylor, composer, critic, commentator, former ASCAP President. Sponsored by ASCAP, founded 1914 as public nondramatic performance music licensing-collection organization of composers, lyricists, music publishers. Also sponsor ASCAP Foundation Grants to Young Composers ($1000 and $1500 to young U.S. citizen, resident composers); ASCAP-Raymond Hubbell Musical Scholarships ($1000 to institutions to assist young composers, performers, teachers); Nathan Burkan Memorial Competition.

BOOK CONTEST: Music Nonfiction, published in U.S., in English, during previous calendar year; unlimited entries. Submit 4 copies. No instructional texts or fiction.

ARTICLE CONTEST: Music Nonfiction Newspaper, Magazine. Requirements same as for Book. Submit 4 copies, 1-10 articles per entry, collated in folder.

AWARDS: Books: $500 to authors, Plaques to publishers. Articles: $250 to authors, Plaques to publishers.

JUDGING: By 6 professionals, academicians. No entries returned.

ENTRY FEE: None.

DEADLINES: Entry, February. Awards, Fall.

54

Broadcast Industry Conference
Broadcast Preceptor Award
San Francisco State University
(SFSU)
Janet Lee Miller, Darryl R. Compton,
Co-chairs
1600 Holloway Avenue
San Francisco, California 94132
U.S.A.

April

International; entry open to all; annual; established 1950. Purpose: to honor writers with accomplishments, contributions of highest importance to broadcast industry standards and achievements. Sponsored and supported by SFSU Broadcast Industry. Held during Broadcast Industry Conference at SFSU (annually). Also sponsor Broadcast Media Awards for Film, Video, Audio; Records at Random, Victoria St. Clair, Albert Johnson Awards for SFSU students.

BOOK CONTEST: **Media Literature,** published during previous calendar year, 2 copies. Require biography, achievement outline, 8x10-inch photo, supporting materials. Categories: Production, Performance, Industry Leadership, Academic Leadership.

AWARDS: 12 Preceptor Awards.

JUDGING: By SFSU Faculty. Based on outstanding achievement. Sponsor keeps copies of nominees for Broadcast Archives.

ENTRY FEE: None.

DEADLINES: Entry, February. Awards, April.

55

De La Torre Bueno Prize
Dance Perspective Foundation
Selma Jean Cohen, President
29 East Ninth Street
New York, New York 10003 U.S.A.
Tel: (212) 777-1594

April

International; entry open to all; annual; established 1973. Named after Jose Rollin de la Torre Bueno, late senior editor, Wesleyan University Press. Purpose: to honor best book-length manuscript on dance. Sponsored and supported by Dance Perspectives Foundation, Wesleyan University Press. Second contact: Wesleyan University Press, 55 High Street, Middletown, Connecticut 06457.

BOOK CONTEST: **Dance,** unpublished; any area, subject, approach. Request list of intended illustrations. No technical manuals, textbooks.

AWARDS: $100, Honor Certificate, and publication by Wesleyan University Press (unless other publisher already contracted).

JUDGING: By 3 judges. Based on research quality, depth of synthesis, literary style, originality, significance.

ENTRY FEE: None. Entrant pays postage.

DEADLINES: Entry, December. Awards, April.

56

Photographic History Prize
Photographic Historical Society of New York
Harvey V. Fondiller, Chairman, Awards Committee
P.O. Box 1839
Radio City Station
New York, New York 10019 U.S.A.
Tel: (212) 662-7589

Summer

International; entry open to all; annual; established 1975. Sponsored by Photographic Historical Society of New York.

BOOK CONTEST: Photographic History, published in English during previous year.

AWARDS: $250 for Distinguished Achievement in Photographic History. $100 Special Citation.

ENTRY FEE: None.

DEADLINES: Entry, April. Awards, Summer.

57

Poetry Society of America Awards

Charles A. Wagner, Executive Secretary
15 Gramercy Park
New York, New York 10003 U.S.A.
Tel: (212) 254-9628

Spring

National; entry open to U.S.; biennial (odd years). Instrumental in establishing Pulitzer Prize for poetry. Purpose: to foster wide interest in poetry (Cane Award established by Harcourt Brace Jovanovich to honor famous poet-lawyer). Sponsored by Poetry Society of America (PSA), nonprofit cultural organization founded 1910. Supported by publishers, editors, foundations, corporations, patrons. Have seminars, workshops, educational programs, library, advisory service. Publish *PSA Bulletin* (quarterly), major anthologies, 5 centennial memorial editions. Also sponsor membership and nonmembership awards, grants.

BOOK-PROSE CONTEST: About Poet or Poetry *(Cane Award)*. Given

in odd years and published in even years. Submit 4 copies (by publisher).

AWARDS: $500 Melville Cane Award.

JUDGING: Require reprint rights for one-time use of sample poems. Rights revert to winning authors upon publication in bulletin.

ENTRY FEE: None.

DEADLINES: Entry, December.

58

Theatre Library Association (TLA) Awards

Louis A. Rachow
Booth-Hampden Library, The Players
16 Gramercy Park
New York, New York 10002 U.S.A.

Spring

National; entry restricted to U.S. publishers; annual; established 1968 (Freedley Award), 1973 (TLA Award). George Freedley Award named for late theatre historian, critic, author, first curator of New York Public Library Theatre Collection. Sponsored by TLA, national organization founded 1937 to further gathering, preserving, availability of theater resources through libraries, museums, private collections. Also sponsor workshops on preservation of library materials. Awards made at cocktail reception. Tickets: $15 individuals, $25 institutions. Second contact: Richard M. Buck, Secretary-Treasurer, TLA, 111 Amsterdam Avenue, New York, New York 10023

BOOK CONTEST: Live Theater Performance *(Freedley Award)*, published in U.S. in previous calendar year; 4 copies (includes vaudeville, puppetry, pantomime, circus).

Recorded   Performance-Motion Pictures-Television   *(TLA Award)*, published in previous calendar year, 4 copies.

ELIGIBILITY: No galley sheets, proofs, or textbooks, bibliographies, dictionaries, anthologies, published collections of articles-essays, reprints, dance-ballet, opera.

AWARDS: George Freedley Award Scroll, TLA Awards Scroll main awards. Honorable Mentions may be awarded.

JUDGING: By 3 judges, each award. Based on scholarship, readability, general contribution to knowledge. Not responsible for loss or damage.

ENTRY FEE: None.

DEADLINES: Entry, January. Awards, Spring.

59

Jerusalem International Book Fair Art Book Competition
Gershon Polak, Executive Director
22 Jaffa Road
Jerusalem 91000, ISRAEL
Tel: 02-232251

April

International; **entry restricted to publishers;** biennial (odd years); established 1969. Sponsored by Israel Museum. Average statistics: 190 entries, 15 countries (Art Book Competition); 40,000 books, 1018 publishers, 45 countries, 108,000 attendance (Book Fair). Held during Jerusalem International Book Fair (founded 1963) for 6 days. Also sponsor not open to entry $3000 Jerusalem Prize (founded 1963, sponsored by Municipality of Jerusalem) to author whose work expresses "Freedom of the Individual in Society."

BOOK CONTEST: **Illustrated Art** (archaeology, fine arts, architecture, applied arts, photography), published

during previous 2 years; 3 titles maximum.

AWARDS: International Art Book Prize, original publisher and designer invited to Jerusalem, awarded Original Art Work and Gold Medal. 4 Honorable Mention Silver Medals. Winners exhibited at Fair and Israel Museum.

JUDGING: By 4-member international designer-art historian jury. Based on design, production, content. Sponsor keeps 2 copies for exhibition.

ENTRY FEE: None.

DEADLINES: Entry, January. Book Fair, April.

60

Ondas Awards
Radio Barcelona
Joaquin Pelaez, Executive Secretary
Calle de Caspe, No. 6
Barcelona 10, SPAIN
Tel: 343-302-22-66

October-November

International; entry open to all; annual; established 1954. Purpose: to exalt artistic, cultural values of radio, television; reward outstanding international works, professionals. Sponsored by Radio Barcelona (Manuel G. Teran, President). Supported by Sociedad Espanola de Radiofusion (SER). Average statistics: 160 entries, 40 entrants, 24 countries. Held in Barcelona. Also sponsor Premio Holanda European Philips Contest for Young Scientists, Inventors. Second contact: Jean Michel Bamberger, General Executive Secretary, Gran Via, No. 32 (9), Madrid 13, Spain; tel: 341-232-80-00.

BOOK CONTEST: **Television, Radio Communications Media,** published, 2 copies. Limit 2 per entrant. Require 5 photos of entrant, biographical note.

AWARDS: Ondas Award, Silver Winged Horse Trophies for outstanding work in artistic, news, cultural fields; or increased solidarity between peoples through communication.

JUDGING: All entries reviewed by minimum 5 international radio, TV professionals. Sponsor retains copy for archival use.

ENTRY FEE: None.

DEADLINES: Entry, July. Judging, October. Event, November.

BOOK (Biography, Essay Collection)

Book, including AUTOBIOGRAPHY, CHILDREN'S. (Also see other BOOK.)

61

English-Speaking Union Book Award
English-Speaking Union of the United States
John I. B. McCulloch, President
16 East 69th Street
New York, New York 10021 U.S.A.
Tel: (212) TR9-6800

Annual

International; **entry restricted to African, Asian, Third World nonnative-speakers of English (selection by Union);** annual; established 1974. $2000 (and travel expenses to award presentation) English-Speaking Union Book Award to **Best Biography in English by Writer from Asia, Africa, Third World.** Purpose: to foster among English-speaking peoples understanding, mutual trust, friend-

ship. Sponsored by 32,000-member English-Speaking Union of the United States. Also sponsor Fiction-Poetry-Drama Book Award; Books-Across-the-Sea (international book exchange-aid to foreign American studies programs); loan program of Commonwealth books to U.S. libraries; Traveling Librarian Program; grants for British study-travel; scholarships; fellowships.

62

Pan-American International Literary Awards
Pan-American Publishing Company
Rose Calles, Editor
P.O. Box 1505
Las Vegas, New Mexico 87701
U.S.A. Tel: (505) 454-0132

March

International; entry open to all; annual; established 1978. Purpose: to enable unpublished writers to have their works published and awarded. Sponsored and supported by Pan-American Publishing Company. Average statistics: 100 entries, 3 awards. Also sponsor Novel, Short Story Collection, and Experimental Book Contests.

BOOK CONTEST: Essay Collection, original, unpublished, in English; typed double-spaced, 1 copy (carbon or photocopy acceptable).

AWARDS: $250 First, $100 Second, $50 Third Prize (including Fiction entries). First Prize winner offered standard publishing contract, minimum 10% royalties, publication by sponsor. All entries considered for publication.

JUDGING: By panel of judges. All entries read in entirety. Not responsible for loss or damage.

ENTRY FEE: $25. Entrant pays postage (include SASE).

DEADLINES: Entry, December. Awards, March. Materials returned, April.

63

Whitbread Literary Awards
Booksellers Association of Great Britain & Ireland
Andrea Livingstone, Administrator
154 Buckingham Palace Road
London SW1W 9TZ, ENGLAND
Tel: (01) 730-8214(5)(6)

November-December

National; **entry restricted to United Kingdom and Ireland publishers of U.K.-Irish authors;** annual; established 1971. Purpose: to acknowledge literary merits, readability qualities of books. Sponsored and supported by Whitbread Brewery; administered by The Booksellers Association of Great Britain & Ireland. Average statistics: 200 entries (including Fiction), 3 awards. Held during 1-day awards luncheon in London. Have Conference and Trade Exhibition in Spring. Also sponsor Children's Fiction and Novel contests.

BOOK CONTEST: Biography-Autobiography, published, 4 book or proof copies.
Children's, published, 4 book or proof copies. Should be primarily literary rather than pictorial.

ELIGIBILITY: First published in U.K.-Ireland October previous year to November current year; by authors domiciled in U.K.-Ireland for preceding 5 years. Submission only by publishers who have books in stock. Page proofs acceptable with prior permission. No galley proofs.

AWARDS: 2500 pounds each to Best Biography or Autobiography, Best Children's Book (including Fiction), Whitbread Book of the Year (chosen from all entries). Award bands supplied to winners' publishers. Sponsor may provide liaison between publishers and Booksellers Association.

JUDGING: By panel of 3 judges appointed by Whitbread in consultation with Booksellers Association. May vary, withdraw categories or conditions, consider unsubmitted books. No entries returned.

ENTRY FEE: None.

DEADLINES: Entry, July (published before July), September (published July-November). Awards, November-December.

64

James Tait Black Memorial Prizes
University of Edinburgh
Department of English Literature
David Hume Tower, George Square
Edinburgh EH8 9JX, SCOTLAND
Tel: 031-667-1011, ext. 6259

January

International; **entry restricted to British publications;** annual; established 1918. Named for James Tait Black of A & C Black Ltd., book publishers. Sponsored by University of Edinburgh. Supported by estate of James Tait Black, Scottish Arts Council.

BOOK CONTEST: Biography, published by British publisher in award year, in English. May be published simultaneously or slightly earlier in another country. Submit 2 copies.

AWARDS: 1000 pounds.

JUDGING: By Regius Professor of Rhetoric, English Literature at University of Edinburgh and assistants. Judging not limited to entries. Not responsible for loss or damage.

ENTRY FEE: None.

DEADLINES: Entry, open. Judging, continuous. Winners announced, February.

BOOK (Business, Legal, Political)

Book, Article, including PREVENTIVE LAW, PUBLIC ADMINISTRATION, RISK INSURANCE, EUROPEAN UNITY, LEGAL BIBLIOGRAPHY. (Also see other BOOK.)

65

American Risk and Insurance Association (ARIA) Awards

Dr. Richard E. Johnson, Executive Director
Department of Risk Management and Insurance
Brooks Hall University of Georgia
Athens, Georgia 30602 U.S.A.
Tel: (404) 542-4290

August

International; entry open to all; annual; established 1970. Purpose: to encourage research advancing knowledge of risk and insurance. Sponsored by ARIA (over 2000 members). Supported by Massachusetts Mutual Life Insurance Co. (Wright Award), Woodman Accident and Life Co. and Insurance Co. of North America Foundation (Kulp Award). Average statistics: 40 entries, 10 semifinalists. Held at ARIA annual meeting. Also sponsor Journal of Risk and Insurance Awards for outstanding articles published in journal (quarterly).

BOOK CONTEST: Risk and Insurance, published 2 years prior to award; 1 copy (further copies may be requested).

AWARDS: $1000 Clarence A. Kulp Memorial Award, $1000 Elizur Wright Award.

JUDGING: By Awards Committee Chair.

ENTRY FEE: Not specified.

DEADLINES: Awards, August.

66

Emil Brown Fund Preventive Law Prize Awards

Louis M. Brown
Sanders, Barnet and Goldsmith
1901 Avenue of the Stars, Suite 850
Los Angeles, California 90067 U.S.A.

Open

International; entry open to all; annual. Sponsored by Emil Brown Fund.

BOOK CONTEST: Preventive Law, published.

ARTICLE CONTEST: Preventive Law, published in law review, bar journal, or other professional publication.

AWARDS: $1000 Emil Brown Fund Preventive Law Prize Award. $500 Student Award (for published student work). Special Awards.

JUDGING: By 5 judges. May withhold awards, consider unsubmitted material.

ENTRY FEE: None.

DEADLINES: Open.

67

**Joseph L. Andrews
Bibliographical Award**
American Association of Law
Libraries (AALB)
Executive Secretary
53 West Jackson Boulevard
Chicago, Illinois 60604 U.S.A.
Tel: (312) 939-4764

June

International; **entry restricted
(nomination by AALB committee);**
annual; established 1967. Certificates
to **Legal Bibliographical Literature.**
Sponsored by AALB. Held at AALB
annual meeting. Award, June.

68

Louis Brownlow Book Award
National Academy of Public
Administration (NAPA)
Dr. Erasmus H. Kloman, Senior
Research Associate
1225 Connecticut Avenue N.W.
Washington, District of Columbia
20036 U.S.A. Tel: (202) 828-6519

November

National; **entry restricted to U.S.
professionals;** annual; established
1967. Purpose: to recognize outstanding
contributions on contemporary
topics of interest to field of public administration.
Sponsored by NAPA,
private, nonprofit organization
founded 1967 to establish source of
advice, counsel to governments, public
officials on problems of public administration.
Average statistics: 50 entries,
1 winner. Presented during
Academy's fall meeting. Have symposia,
workshops, educational programs,
conferences.

BOOK CONTEST: **Public Administration,**
published during previous 2
years; 3 copies; about constructive
treatment of important problem, significant
development, or performance
of government institution. No textbooks,
essay collections by different
authors.

AWARDS: $500 cash award and
Plaque.

JUDGING: By 3 NAPA members.
Based on factual accuracy, new insight,
fresh analysis, readable style,
original ideas contributing to understanding
of governmental institutions
and how they can effectively serve
public.

ENTRY FEE: None.

DEADLINES: Entry, May. Judging,
Summer. Award, November.

69

**Thomas Newcomen Award in
Business History**
Business History Review, Harvard
Business School
Albro Martin, Editor
215 Baker Library
Soldiers Field
Boston, Massachusetts 02163 U.S.A.
Tel: (617) 495-6364

Triennial

National; **entry restricted to U.S.
published books;** triennial; established
1964. Named after Thomas
Newcomen, inventor of atmospheric
steam engine (1712). Purpose: to stimulate
scholarly research-publication in
history of business enterprise. Sponsored
and supported by 17,000-member
Newcomen Society in North
America (founded 1923) and *Business
History Review,* international quarterly
journal of Harvard University
Graduate School of Business Administration.
Recognized by Business History
Conference and AHA. Average
statistics: 150 entries, 10 semifinalists,
5 finalists, 1 award. Also sponsor

$300, $150 Newcomen Awards in Business History and scrolls to articles published in *Business History Review;* $200 Newcomen Awards in Material History for thesis in material-industrial history; residence grant for business history study-research at Harvard University. Second contact: Newcomen Society in North America, P.O. Box 113, Downington, Pennsylvania 19335.

BOOK CONTEST: Business History, published in U.S., tracing interactions of businesspersons; studying adjustment of business-businesspersons to their economic, political, and social environments; examining history of firms, industries. Submit 3 copies. No books on non-U.S. business.

AWARDS: $1000 Prize. Honorable Mentions. Scrolls.

JUDGING: By 3-member panel.

ENTRY FEE: Not specified.

DEADLINES: Not specified.

69 70

Adolph Bentinck Prize
Robert Lange, General Secretary
33 Rue Poissonniere
Paris 75002, FRANCE

December

International; entry open to all; annual; established 1973. Purpose: to commemorate, continue Adolph Bentinck's lifelong fight for European cause, liberty, closer understanding among nations. Held in various European capitals.

BOOK CONTEST: European Unity, published during previous 2 years; with summary in English or French if in another language.

AWARDS: Adolph Bentinck Prize,

15,000 French francs for service to European idea, peace, struggle against intolerance-fanaticism.

ENTRY FEE: None.

DEADLINES: Entry, April. Awards, December.

BOOK (for Children, Youth)

Book, including BIOGRAPHY, GRAPHICS, ILLUSTRATED, PICTURE STORY BOOK, PEACE-SOCIAL JUSTICE-WORLD COMMUNITY. (Also see other BOOK CATEGORIES.)

71

American Library Association (ALA) Awards and Citations Program (Children's)
Children's Services Division
50 East Huron Street
Chicago, Illinois 60611 U.S.A.
Tel: (312) 944-6780

Winter

National; **entry restricted to U.S. (nomination by ALA);** annual. Mildred L. Batchelder Citation to publisher for **Foreign Children's Book** published in U.S. Randolph Caldecott Medal to U.S. citizen-resident illustrator for **Children's American Picture Book.** John Newberry Medal to U.S. citizen-resident for **American Children's Literature.** Laura Ingalls Wilder Medal to author-illustrator for **U.S. Children's Literature** contribution over period of time (triennial). Sponsored by Children's Services Division of American Library Association (ALA). Also sponsor Awards and Citations for Librarianship, Reference

Works. Awards, Winter.

72

Boston Globe-Horn Book Awards
The Boston Globe
Stephanie Loer, Children's Book Editor
Boston, Massachusetts 02170 U.S.A.
Tel: (617) 359-8542

September

National; **entry restricted to U.S. publishers;** annual; established 1967. Purpose: to honor children's books of excellence. Sponsored by *The Boston Globe,* Horn Book, Inc. Held at fall conference of New England Library Association.

BOOK CONTEST: Children's, published in U.S. in year prior to award; 3 maximum per publisher, each category. Submit 5 copies each book. No textbooks, new or revised editions. Categories: Nonfiction, Illustration.

AWARDS: $200 and Pewter Bowl, each category. Pewter Plate to Runners-Up, each category. 3 Honor Books, each category. Winners featured at Boston Globe Book Festival, John B. Hynes Auditorium, Boston.

JUDGING: By 3 judges appointed by editor of *Horn Book Magazine.*

ENTRY FEE: None.

DEADLINES: Entry, March. Awards, Fall.

73

Charlie May Simon Children's Book Award
James A. Hester, Chair
10213 Sylvan Hills Road
North Little Rock, Arkansas 72116 U.S.A.

September

National; **entry restricted to U.S.(selection by members);** annual; established 1971. Medallion to **Author of Children's Literature** published in previous 2 years. Named after Charlie May Simon, Arkansas author of more than 25 books. Purpose: to promote children's reading of literature. Sponsored by Arkansas Department of Education, state colleges, universities, civic organizations. Average statistics: 18-24 entries, 1 award. Held at annual banquet. Sponsoring agencies select 18-24 books for Arkansas school children Master Reading List. Children grades 4-6 vote in March. Second contact: Elementary School Council, Arkansas Department of Education, Little Rock, Arkansas 72201. Award, September.

74

Children's Reading Round Table (CRRT) Award
Children's Reading Round Table of Chicago
Caroline Rubin, Bulletin Editor
1321 East 56th Street
Chicago, Illinois 60637 U.S.A.

May

regional; **entry restricted (nomination by CRRT members);** annual; established 1953. $100 and Plaque to individual for **Continuing Contribution to Children's Books** (usually in Chicago-Midwest area). Formerly called MIDWEST AWARD. Purpose: to honor authors, illustrators, editors, librarians, teachers working in children's books field. Sponsored and supported by 600-member CRRT, established 1931. Also sponsor CRRT literature conference (even years), summer seminars for children's book writers and illustrators (odd years). Second contact: Ellen Schweri, President, 5735 North Washtenaw, Chicago, Illinois 60659. Event, May.

75

Dorothy Canfield Fisher Children's Book Award

Vermont Department of Libraries
Carol Chatfield, Chair
138 Main Street
Montpelier, Vermont 05602 U.S.A.

June

National; **entry restricted to U.S. publishers;** annual; established 1956. Purpose: to encourage Vermont school children to read more and better books; honor memory of Dorothy Canfield Fisher, Vermont literary figure. Sponsored by Vermont Congress of Parents and Teachers, Vermont Department of Libraries. Also sponsor Fiction Book Contest.

BOOK CONTEST: **Children's Nonfiction-Biography,** published during preceding copyright year for grades 4-8, by living American authors.

AWARDS: Illuminated Scroll to author.

JUDGING: 30-book Master List chosen by 8-member committee; Vermont school children (grades 4-8) vote for favorite.

ENTRY FEE: None.

DEADLINES: Entry, February. Master List selection, March. Children vote, April. Award, June.

76

George G. Stone Recognition of Merit

George G. Stone Center for
Children's Books
Harper Hall
Claremont University Center
Claremont, California 91711 U.S.A.

February

Regional; **entry restricted (nomination by Southern California school children, teachers);** annual; established 1965. Scroll to **Children's Book or Author** for increasing awareness of world. Sponsored by George G. Stone Center for Children's Books. Held at annual Claremont Reading Conference for Young People. Final selection by school librarians. Awards, February.

77

Golden Archer and Little Archer Award Program

University of Wisconsin-Oshkosh
Dr. Shirley Wilbert, Dr. Norma Jones
Department of Library Science
Oshkosh, Wisconsin 54901 U.S.A.
Tel: (414) 424-2313

Fall

National; **entry restricted to U.S. (nomination by school students);** annual; established 1974 (Golden Archer), 1976 (Little Archer). Golden Archer Award Medal and Certificate to **Children's Book** (grades 4-8), Little Archer Award Medal, Certificate to **Children's Picture Story Book** (grades K-3); published in previous 5 years by living American author. Named after Marion Fuller Archer. Purpose: to honor juvenile books by living American authors. Sponsored by Department of Library Science, University of Wisconsin-Oshkosh. Held during Fall Conference at UW-Oshkosh. Judging: preliminary by Wisconsin elementary and middle school students; final by 6-member committee. Event, Fall.

78

Golden Kite Award

Society of Children's Book Writers
(SCBW)
Stephen Mooser, President
P.O. Box 296, Mar Vista Station

Los Angeles, California 90066 U.S.A.
Tel: (213) 347-2849

March

National; **entry restricted to SCBW members;** annual; established 1973. Golden Kite Statuette, Honor Book Certificate to **Children's Book Writers.** Sponsored by 400-member Society of Children's Book Writers. Have annual national children's book writers' conference. Publish *Bulletin* (bimonthly). Also sponsor $750 **Work-in-Progress Grant to Children's Book Writer** (SCBW Member). Second contact: Sue Alexander, SCBW, 6846 McLaren, Canoga Park, California 91307. Awards, March.

79

Hans Christian Andersen Awards for Books for Children
International Board on Books for Young People (IBBY), United States National Section
John Donovan, Executive Director
Children's Book Council
67 Irving Place
New York, New York 10003 U.S.A.

April

International; **entry restricted (nomination by IBBY National Sections);** biennial; established 1956. Medals and Diplomas (2) to living **Children's Book Author and Illustrator.** Sponsored by IBBY, founded 1951 for international understanding through children's literature. Publish international honor list of children's books. Second contact: Leena Maissen, Secretary, IBBY, Leonhardsgraben 38A, CH-4051 Basel, Switzerland. Awards, April.

80

International Reading Association (IRA) Children's Book Award
Drew Cassidy, Public Information Officer
800 Barksdale Road
P.O. Box 8139
Newark, Delaware 19711 U.S.A.
Tel: (302) 731-1600

Spring

International; **entry restricted to publishers;** annual; established 1975. Purpose: to recognize promising, unestablished authors in children's book field. Sponsored by IRA, 65,000-member nonprofit educational association with members in over 85 countries, dedicated to reading instruction improvement, reading habit development. Supported by Institute for Reading Research. Held at IRA Convention awards banquet. Also sponsor Print Media Awards (outstanding reporting in newspapers, magazines, wire services); Broadcast Media Awards for Radio and Television (dealing with reading, literacy); Outstanding Dissertation of the Year Award. Second contact: Zena Sutherland, 1418 East 57th Street, Chicago, Illinois 60637.

BOOK CONTEST: Children's, published, copyrighted in calendar year prior to award, any language. Publisher submits 7 copies. Must be first or second book by author.

AWARDS: $1000 stipend, Medal. Honor Book awards to other outstanding entries.

JUDGING: By IRA committee. No entries returned. Not responsible for loss or damage.

ENTRY FEE: None.

DEADLINES: Entry, November. Awards, Spring.

81

Irma Simonton Black Award
Bank Street College of Education
Publications-Communications
Division
610 West 112th Street
New York, New York 10025 U.S.A.

Spring

International; entry open to all; annual; established 1973. Named for Irma Simonton Black, educator-author-editor. Sponsored by Bank Street College of Education.

BOOK CONTEST: Young Children, published during previous year.

AWARDS: Irma Simonton Black Award Scrolls, to author and illustrator of outstanding book for young children. Award Seal for cover.

JUDGING: By Publications-Communications Division of Bank Street College (children participate in judging). Based on storyline, language, illustration.

ENTRY FEE: None.

DEADLINES: Entry, January. Awards, Spring.

82

Jane Addams Children's Book Award
Women's International League for Peace and Freedom
1213 Race Street
Philadelphia, Pennsylvania 19107
U.S.A.

September

International; **entry restricted to publishers;** annual; established 1953. Purpose: to award book promoting peace, social justice, world community; combining literary merit with world community-social justice

themes. Theme: Children's Books That Build for Peace. Sponsored by Jane Addams Peace Association, founded 1948 to foster understanding between world peoples; Women's International League for Peace and Freedom, founded 1915 with Jane Addams as first president. Second contact: Annette C. Blank, 5477 Cedonia Avenue, Baltimore, Maryland 21206.

BOOK CONTEST: Peace-Social Justice-World Community for Children, published previous year, in English or English translation; for preschool to high school age.

AWARDS: Jane Addams Scroll and Silver Seals for book jacket. Honor Scrolls.

JUDGING: By national librarian committee.

ENTRY FEE: None.

DEADLINES: Awards, September 6 (Jane Addams's birthdate).

83

Kerlan Collection Award
Children's Literature Research
Collections (CLRC)
Dr. Karen N. Hoyle, Curator
109 Walter Library
University of Minnesota
Minneapolis, Minnesota 55455
U.S.A. Tel: (612) 373-9731

Spring

International; **entry restricted (nomination by member-staff);** annual; established 1975. Kerlan Collection Award (Plaque) to **Creator of Children's Literature.** Purpose: to recognize creation of children's literature; donation to Kerlan Collection for study of children's literature. Sponsored and supported by CLRC, University of Minnesota Libraries. Held at University of Minnesota for 1 day.

Also sponsor exhibitions, conferences. Event, Spring.

84

Mark Twain Award
Missouri Library Association (MLA)
Marilyn Lake, Executive Secretary
402 South Fifth Street
Columbia, Missouri 65201 U.S.A.

May

National; **entry restricted to U.S. (nomination by members)**; annual; established 1972. Mark Twain Award, Bronze Bust, travel expenses to conference to U.S. author for **Children's Book** (published 2 years previous). Sponsored by MLA and Missouri Association of School Librarians (MASL). Held at MASL Conference. Have workshops. Also sponsor Literary Awards to Missouri author who has written a **Book on Missouri Life;** Meritorious Achievement Award for Contribution to Missouri library cause. Judging by Missouri school children (grades 3-8). Second contact: Jane Benson, Frank Hughes Memorial Library, 210 East Franklin, Liberty, Missouri 64068. Entry, May.

85

Regina Medal Award
Catholic Library Association (CLA)
Matthew R. Wilt, Executive Director
461 West Lancaster Avenue
Haverford, Pennsylvania 19041
U.S.A. Tel: (215) 649-5250

April

International; **entry restricted (nomination by CLA);** annual; established 1959. Silver Medal to individual for **Children's Literature.** Purpose: to recognize continued distinguished contribution to children's literature. Sponsored by CLA, professional association promoting Catholic principles through library resources, services, publications, education. Held at annual CLA Convention. Also sponsor $1500 Reverend Andrew L. Bouwhuis (graduate) Scholarship in library science (open to college seniors, graduates); $1000 member-only World Book-Childcraft Award Scholarships in school, children's librarianship. Award, April.

86

Southern California Council on Literature for Children and Young People Book Awards
Fullerton Public Library
Carolyn Johnson
353 West Commonwealth Avenue
Fullerton, California 92632 U.S.A.
Tel: (714) 738-6339

Annual

Regional; **entry restricted to Southern California residents (selection by members);** annual; established 1961. Plaques to **Southern California Authors, Illustrators of Children's Books.** Purpose: to promote interest in literature; establish excellence standards. Sponsored by 450-member Southern California Council on Literature for Children and Young People. Publish *The Sampler* (quarterly newsletter). Also sponsor annual Spring workshop. Second contact: Joan Blumenstein, Orange Public Library, 101 North Center Street, Orange, California 92666; tel: (714) 532-0379.

87

University of Southern Mississippi Medallion
Jeannine Laughlin, Director
Children's Book Festival
School of Library Service
Southern Station, Box 5146
Hattiesburg, Mississippi 39401
U.S.A. Tel: (601) 266-7167

March

International; entry open to all (nomination by general public); annual; established 1969. Purpose: to recognize outstanding achievement in children's literature. Sponsored by School of Library Service, University of Southern Mississippi. Held during annual Children's Book Festival at University of Southern Mississippi for 2 days.

BOOK CONTEST: Children's Literature.

AWARDS: Silver Medallion to Best author-illustrator.

JUDGING: Nomination by general public; winners by national committee.

ENTRY FEE: None.

DEADLINES: Awards, March.

88

William Allen White Children's Book Award
Emporia State University
George V. Hodowanec, Executive Director
William Allen White Library
1200 Commercial
Emporia, Kansas 66801 U.S.A.
Tel: (316) 343-1200, ext. 205

April

International; **entry open to authors residing in U.S., Canada, Mexico (by nomination);** annual; established 1952. Award program expanded to include Braille, large print, recorded books for handicapped children, 1974. Purpose: to encourage Kansas children to read and enjoy good books. Sponsored by Emporia State University, William Allen White Library. Supported by William Allen White Library Endowment Fund, es-

tablished 1969. Also sponsor May Massee Workshop.

BOOK CONTEST: Children's Nonfiction, published in previous calendar year. No translations, anthologies, textbooks. No nominations by publishers, authors.

AWARDS: William Allen White Medal, invitation to speak at Library Colloquium.

JUDGING: Master List selected by Book Selection Committee and Kansas citizens. Kansas school children (grades 4-8) vote for favorite. Final by Book Selection Executive Committee. Based on originality, vitality, clarity, factual accuracy (where applicable), sincerity, respect for reader.

ENTRY FEE: None.

DEADLINES: Selection, January-October. Children's vote, March. Winner announced, April. Award, Fall.

89

Children's Book of the Year Award
Children's Book Council of Australia (CBCA), Queensland Branch
Robyn Collins, Judges' Secretary
G.P.O. Box 1319
Brisbane, Queensland 4000,
AUSTRALIA Tel: 07-2218400, ext. 227

July

National; **entry restricted to Australia;** annual; established 1946. $2500 (Aust.) and Medal to **Australian Children's Book, Children's Picture Story Book.** Purpose: to promote, encourage writing of children's books in Australia. Sponsored by CBCA (formerly called Sydney International Children's Book Week Committee to 1958). Supported by CBCA, state government. Average statistics: 80 entries. Publish *Reading Time* (reviewing journal). Also sponsor seminars, workshops. Awards, July.

90

Alvine-Belisle Prize
Association for the Advancement of the Sciences and Documentation Techniques (ASTED)
Marthe Laforest, Librarian
360, Rue le Moyne
Montreal, Quebec H2Y 1Y3
CANADA Tel: (514) 844-8023

October

National; **entry open to Canada;** annual; established 1974. Purpose: to encourage editors, authors of French literature for young readers. Sponsored by Comite de Litterature de Jeunesse, ASTED. Supported by ASTED. Average statistics: 50-60 entries. Held during ASTED Congress.

BOOK CONTEST: For Youth in French, first published in Canada during previous year, in French. Publishers submit 2 copies per entry.

AWARDS: $500   Alvine-Belisle Prize.

JUDGING: By 5 ASTED-member librarians. No entries returned. Not responsible for loss or damage.

ENTRY FEE: None.

DEADLINES: Judging, September. Award, October.

91

Marie-Claire Daveluy Prize
Association for the Advancement of the Sciences and Documentation Techniques (ASTED)
360 Rue le Moyne
Montreal, Quebec H2Y 1Y3
CANADA

Open

National; **entry restricted to French-Canadian residents aged 15-21;** annual; established 1969 (formerly Maxine Prize). Purpose: to encourage youth to write Canadian works for youth. Sponsored by ASTED.

BOOK CONTEST: For Youth in French, original, interesting to youth age 12-15 (prose, narrative). Submit manuscript in French, 75 pages minimum, typed.

AWARDS: $700   Marie-Claire Daveluy Prize. $300 Second Prize. Possible publication of winners.

ENTRY FEE: None.

DEADLINES: Open.

92

Vicky Metcalf Award
Canadian Authors Association (CAA)
24 Ryerson Avenue
Toronto, Ontario M5T 2P3 CANADA
Tel: (416) 868-6916

Spring

National; **entry open to Canada;** annual; established 1963. Purpose: to stimulate writing for children. Sponsored by CAA, Mrs. Vicky Metcalf. Held at CAA Awards Dinner. Also sponsor CAA Poetry, Play-Script, Fiction book Contests.

BOOK   CONTEST: Children's nonfiction or picture books of interest to young people. Submit nominating letter in triplicate listing nominee's published works.

AWARDS: $1000 Vicky Metcalf Award.

JUDGING: By 3 judges.

ENTRY FEE: None.

DEADLINES: Entry, March.
Awards, Spring.

93
Children's Book Circle (CBC)
Eleanor Farjeon Award
The Bodley Head
Rona Selby, Secretary
9 Bow Street
Covent Garden, London WC2E 7AL,
ENGLAND Tel: 01-836-9081, ext.
222

May

International; **entry restricted (nomination by members);** annual; established 1965. Eleanor Farjeon Award of 500 pounds for **Distinguished Service to Children's Books.** Sponsored by CBC (founded 1962). Held in London; 200-300 attendance. Award, May.

94
Library Association Medals
Miss A.E.L. Hobart, Development
Secretary
7 Ridgmount Street
London WC1E 7AE, ENGLAND
Tel: 01-636-7543

National; **entry restricted (nomination by members);** annual; established 1936 (Carnegie), 1955 (Greenaway), 1962 (Wheatley), 1970 (Besterman, McColvin). Carnegie Medal to **Children's Book** (fiction-nonfiction). Kate Greenaway Medal for **Children's Book Illustrations** (fiction-nonfiction) to artist. Wheatley Medal to **Index.** Besterman Medal to **Bibliography or Literature Guide.** McColvin Medal to **Reference Book.** For books in English, first published in United Kingdom during preceding year (Wheatley, during preceding 3 years). Sponsored by The Library Association, established 1877. Judged by Library Association and Youth Librar-

ies Group.

95
Other Award
Children's Book Bulletin
4 Aldebert Terrace
London SW8 1BH, ENGLAND

July

National; **entry restricted to Great Britain;** annual; established 1975. Commendations to **British Published Children's Books.** Purpose: to show new writing, illustration for children; widen literary experience for young people. Sponsored by *Children's Book Bulletin.* Event, July.

96
Times Educational Supplement
Information Book Awards
Times Newspapers Limited
Michael Church, Literary Editor
P.O. Box 7 New Printing House
Square
Gray's Inn Road
London WC1X 8EZ, ENGLAND
Tel: 01 837 1234

October

International; **entry restricted to Great Britain-Commonwealth book publishers;** annual; established 1972. Purpose: to induce improvement in quality of children's books. Sponsored by *Times Educational Supplement,* Times Newspapers.

BOOK CONTEST: Children's, originated in Great Britain-Commonwealth September previous to August current year. Submit 3 copies. Categories: Junior (to age 9), Senior (10-16).

AWARDS: Junior Award, Senior Award, to authors, 150 pounds each. 150 pounds to winners' illustrators at judges' discretion.

JUDGING: By 3 judges each category, together with Editor. Entrants retain all rights. Not responsible for loss or damage.

ENTRY FEE: None.

DEADLINES: Entry, August. Awards, October.

| 97 |

Bologna Children's Book Fair Prizes
Ente Autonomo per le Fiere di Bologna
Dr. G. C. Alberghini, Secretary General
Piazza Costituzione 6
40128 Bologna, ITALY Tel: (051) 503050

April

International; **entry restricted to Book Fair exhibitor publishers;** annual; established 1964. Purpose: to recognize remarkable illustration-graphic value from international high-quality children's books. Sponsored by and held at Bologna Children's Book Fair. Average statistics: (Graphic Prize) 134 entrants, 500 entries, 20 countries; (Erba Prize) 142 entrants, 500 entries, 20 countries. Have Illustrators' Exhibition. Tickets: free.

BOOK CONTEST: Children-Youth Graphics *(Graphic Prize),* published, 1 or more entries, 5 copies. Categories: For Children, For Youth. **Children's Illustrated** *(Erba Prize),* published, 1 or more entries, 3 copies.

ELIGIBILITY: Published for first time January of second year previous to January of current year. Publishers must confirm participation by December of previous year. Also open to fiction entries.

AWARDS: Critici in Erba Prize, Gold Plate to publisher of Best Illus-

trated Book. Graphic Prize for Children, Graphic Prize for Youth, Gold Plates. Winners displayed at Fair.

JUDGING: Erba Prize by 9-child committee (ages 6-9) from 50 Bologna schools. Graphic Prizes by committee from Study Centre "G. B. Bodoni" in Parma, based on graphic, artistic, technical criteria. Not responsible for loss, delay, or damage. No entries returned.

ENTRY FEE: None. Entrant pays postage, delivery charges, customs duties.

DEADLINES: Entry, January. Judging, February. Awards, April.

BOOK (Criticism)
Book, Script, Newspaper, Magazine, including DRAMATIC CRITICISM, EXPLICATION, and HUMAN CONDITION, SCIENCE. (Also see other BOOK.)

| 98 |

Explicator Literary Foundation Prize
J. Edwin Whitesell
3241 Archdale Road
Richmond, Virginia 23235 U.S.A.

Fall

International; entry open to all; annual. Sponsored by Explicator Literary Foundation, dedicated to encouragement of explication de texte as method of literary study, analysis.

BOOK CONTEST: English-American Literature Explication, published during previous year.

AWARDS: $300 and Bronze Plaque

for Best Book of Explication in English-American literature.

JUDGING: By 4 judges.

ENTRY FEE: None.

DEADLINES: Entry, February. Awards, Fall.

| 99 |

George Jean Nathan Award for Dramatic Criticism
Dorothy E. Hinz, Corporate Communications
350 Park Avenue
New York, New York 10022 U.S.A.
Tel: (212) 350-4469

December

National; **entry open to U.S.;** annual; established 1958. Purpose: to encourage, assist in developing drama criticism; stimulate intelligent playgoing. Considered one of richest, most distinguished awards in American theater. Sponsored and supported by George Jean Nathan Trust. Administered by Manufacturers Honover Trust, 600 5th Avenue, New York, New York 10020; tel: (212) 957-1620.

BOOK CONTEST: U.S. **Dramatic Criticism,** published in U.S.

NEWSPAPER-MAGAZINE CONTEST: U.S. Dramatic Criticism, published in U.S.

SCRIPT CONTEST: U.S. **Television, Radio Dramatic Criticism,** broadcast in U.S.

ELIGIBILITY: Published, broadcast in U.S. during theatrical year (July-June), dealing with current productions or with drama of the past.

AWARDS: $5000, Silver Medallion, Certificate for Best Drama Criticism.

JUDGING: Preliminary by committee, final by Cornell, Princeton, Yale University English Department heads. Based on critical, perceptive theater criticism.

ENTRY FEE: None. Require citizenship proof.

DEADLINES: Entry, September. Judging, October. Awards, December.

| 100 |

Phi Beta Kappa Book Awards
Phi Beta Kappa
1811 Q Street N.W.
Washington, District of Columbia
20009 U.S.A.

December

International; **entry restricted to U.S. published books;** annual; established 1950 (Gauss), 1959 (Science), 1960 (Emerson). Purpose: (Emerson Award) to recognize interpretive syntheses carrying forward humane learning, deeper understanding of man; (Science Award) to stress literate-scholarly interpretations of physical-biological sciences, mathematics; encourage books symbolizing importance of science in humanistic studies. Sponsored by Phi Beta Kappa. Also sponsor $7000 Mary Isabel Sibley Fellowship for 1-year advanced study, research, writing in Greek language-history-archaeology (1981), French language-literature (1982) by unmarried women, age 25-35, with doctorate or doctoral dissertation pending (entry, January).

BOOK CONTEST: Literary Scholarship-Criticism *(Gauss Award),* published, containing critical-historical introduction; 7 copies.
Human Condition *(Emerson Award),* published, studies of intellectual-cultural condition of man; should contribute to historical, philosophical, religious interpretations of human

condition; 7 copies. No limited, purely technical studies.

Science   Literature   *(Science Award)*, published; 7 copies.

ELIGIBILITY: Originally published in U.S. June of previous to May of current year by single writer or closely collaborating scholars. If foreign publication prior to U.S., must be by arrangement with U.S. publisher (or U.S. publication must follow within 60 days). Submission by presses; each entry submitted for 1 award only. Single volumes of multivolume works must stand independently. No translations, research reports, highly specialized or technical, previously published as a whole (except published as magazine, newspaper, learned journal articles).

AWARDS: $2500 each Christian Gauss Award, Ralph Waldo Emerson Award, Phi Beta Kappa Award in Science.

ENTRY FEE: None.

DEADLINES: Entry, June. Awards, December.

101

Grand Prize for Literary Criticism
Syndicat des Critiques Litteraires
Robert Andre, General Secretary
Hotel de Massa
38 rue du Faubourg-Saint-Jacques
75014 Paris, FRANCE Tel: 3220647

Fall

National; **entry restricted to France and Belgium;** annual; established 1945. 3000 French francs to **Best French Language Literary Criticism Book** (including biography, essay, research), published in previous year. Sponsored by Syndicat des Critiques Litteraires. Supported by Centre National des Lettres, Academie Francaise. Judging by 15-member commit-

tee. Award, Fall.

BOOK (Culture, Sociology, Anthropology)
Book, Article, Monograph, Essay, including AFRICAN, AMERICAN, FOLKLORE, FRENCH MINORITY, JEWISH, NAZI HOLOCAUST, QUEBEC, WOMEN. (Also see other BOOK.)

102

American Sociological Association (ASA) Awards
Russell R. Dynes, Executive Officer
1722 N Street N.W.
Washington, District of Columbia
20036 U.S.A. Tel: (202) 833-3410

August

International; entry open to all; annual (Scholarship and Teaching Awards), biennial (Bernard Award); established 1980 (Scholarship Award), 1977 (Bernard Award). Sponsored by ASA. Held at ASA annual meeting. Also sponsor ASA Career Award and DuBois-Johnson-Frazier Award for distinguished scholarship in field of sociology; Minority Fellowship Program for Ph.D. studies in applied sociology.

BOOK   CONTEST: Sociology *(Contribution to Scholarship Award)*, published within 3 preceding calendar years, in English.
Sociology   Teaching-Learning *(Contributions to Teaching Award)*, for outstanding contributions to undergraduate-graduate teaching and learning of sociology.
Women   in   Society   *(Bernard*

Award), single, series, or cumulative work; detailed nomination statement required.

MONOGRAPH CONTEST: Sociology *(Contribution to Scholarship Award)*. Requirements same as for Sociology Book.

ARTICLE CONTEST: Sociology *(Contribution to Scholarship Award)*. Requirements same as for Sociology Book.

Women in Society *(Bernard Award)*. Requirements same as for Women in Society Book.

AWARDS: Certificate of Recognition for Distinguished Contribution to Scholarship Award, Distinguished Contributions to Teaching Award, Jessie Bernard Award. Sorokin Lectureship to Contribution to Scholarship Award Winner.

JUDGING: By members of ASA Selection Committee.

ENTRY FEE: Not specified.

DEADLINES: Entry, March (Scholarship and Bernard Award), May (Teaching Award). Awards, August.

| 103 |

Association of Jewish Libraries (AJL) Book Awards
Hazel B. Karp, Chair, Book Award Committee
880 Somerset Drive N.W.
Atlanta, Georgia 30327 U.S.A.
Tel: (404) 237-5882, 634-7388

June

National; **entry open to U.S.;** annual; established 1968. Purpose: to honor, encourage books with Jewish themes or backgrounds for young readers. Sponsored by AJL. Average statistics: 50 entries, 100-200 attendance. Held at AJL National Convention for 3 days. Have workshops, convention, exhibits. Also sponsor Library Science Scholarship to student in Judaic field. Second contact: Barbara Leff, AJL National President, Stephen S. Wise Temple, 15500 Stephen S. Wise Drive, Los Angeles, California 90025.

BOOK CONTEST: Jewish Interest Juvenile, original, published previous calendar year, in English.

AWARDS: AJL Book Award, Plaque or Scroll to author, award and publicity-promotion for winning book. Sydney Taylor Body of Work Award.

JUDGING: By 5 Judaic librarians. May withhold awards. All entries read, reviewed in writing.

ENTRY FEE: None.

DEADLINES: Entry, open. Judging, continuous. Winners announced, Spring. Award, June.

| 104 |

Chicago Folklore Prize
University of Chicago
Chair, Department of Germanic Languages & Literatures
1050 East 59th Street
Chicago, Illinois 60637 U.S.A.
Tel: (312) 753-3883

Spring

International; entry open to all; annual; established 1928. Purpose: to encourage study of folklore in its many forms. Sponsored by University of Chicago. Supported by International Folklore Association. Also sponsor $1000 Harriet Monroe Poetry Award (by committee nomination only).

MONOGRAPH CONTEST: Folklore, published, in major Western language, 3 copies. Request publishers submit entries. No articles, dissertations, former major award winners.

AWARDS: $100 (maximum) First Prize for important contribution to study of folklore. Honorable Mentions, other prizes, at judges' discretion and fund availability.

JUDGING: By 3 judges. May withhold awards. No entries returned.

ENTRY FEE: None.

DEADLINES: Entry, April. Awards, Spring.

| 105 |

Herskovits Award
African Studies Association
Maxine Driggers
255 Kinsey Hall
University of California, Los Angeles (UCLA)
Los Angeles, California 90024 U.S.A.
Tel: (213) 206-8011

October-November

National; **entry restricted (selection by members);** annual. Award to **Scholarly Publication about Africa** (published-distributed in U.S.). Sponsored by UCLA African Studies Association, founded 1957. Also have Film Festival. Award, October-November.

| 106 |

James Mooney Award
Southern Anthropological Society
Harriet J. Kupferer
Department of Anthropology
University of North Carolina
Greensboro, North Carolina 27405
U.S.A. Tel: (919) 379-5132

Spring

International; entry open to all; annual; established 1976. Purpose: to encourage distinguished writing in anthropology. Sponsored by Southern Anthropological Society.

BOOK CONTEST: New World Anthropology, unpublished manuscript, in English, approximately 100,-000 words, typed double-spaced; may be prehistoric, historic, contemporary. Require description letter. No previous, current publication or awards pending.

AWARDS: James Mooney Award for Studies of New World Societies and Cultures, $1000 and publication by University of Tennessee Press (293 Communications Building, Knoxville, Tennessee 37916). Based on best description, interpretation of people-culture of distinctive New World population.

JUDGING: Preliminary and final. May withhold award.

ENTRY FEE: None.

DEADLINES: Entry, December. Award, Spring.

| 107 |

National Jewish Book Awards
Jewish Welfare Board (JWB) Jewish Book Council
15 East 26th Street
New York, New York 10010 U.S.A.
Tel: (212) 523-4949

Spring

International; **entry restricted to U.S., Canadian authors-translators (nomination by Council members);** annual. Gerrard and Ella Berman Award ($500) for **Jewish History Book** (no books on Holocaust). Frank and Ethel S. Cohen Award ($500) for **Jewish Thought Book.** Leon Jolson Award ($500) for **Nazi Holocaust Period Nonfiction Book** in English, Yiddish, Hebrew, published during previous 3 calendar years. Morris J. Kaplun Memorial Award ($500) for **Nonfiction Book on Israel.** William Frank Memorial Award ($500) for **Jewish**

Children's Book. Workmen's Circle Award ($500) for **Yiddish Literature Book in Yiddish** (may be essays or memoirs). Leon R. Gildesgame Award ($500) for book on the Visual Arts for **Book of Jewish Interest in Art** published during previous 2 calendar years. Citations to publishers of winning books. All books in English, published during previous calendar year unless otherwise specified. No anthologies, reprints, new editions. Purpose: to promote greater awareness of American-Canadian-Jewish literary creativity. Sponsored by JWB Jewish Book Council. Awards, Spring.

108

Ralph Henry Gabriel Prize in American Studies

American Studies Association (ASA)
Roberta K. Gladowski, Executive Director
307 College Hall/CO
University of Pennsylvania
Philadelphia, Pennsylvania 19104
U.S.A. Tel: (215) 243-5408

December

International; **entry restricted to ASA members;** annual; established 1975. Ralph Henry Gabriel Prize in American Studies, $1000 advance royalties, publication by Greenwood Press (honorable mentions may also be nominated for publication), to **American Civilization Book,** unpublished, in English. Named after Ralph Henry Gabriel, an ASA founder. Purpose: to encourage publication of American Studies scholarship by younger members of profession. Sponsored by ASA and Greenwood Press. Publish *American Quarterly* (ASA newsletter). Entry, December.

109

Champlain Prize

Le Conseil de la Vie Francaise en Amerique (CVFA)
Pauline Dumais, Chef du Secretariat
59 rue d'Auteuil
Quebec G1R 4C3, CANADA
Tel: (418) 692-1150

July

International; **entry restricted to French-speaking minorities in Canada, U.S.;** biennial (alternates yearly between fiction, nonfiction); established 1957. Named after founder of Quebec. Purpose: to encourage literary production among French-speaking minorities living outside Quebec; create in Quebec interest in these French-speaking minorities. Sponsored and supported by CVFA. Held at CVFA annual meeting.

BOOK CONTEST: French Minority Experience in French; published in previous 3 years or under contract at time of submission. Submit 4 copies of work, curriculum vitae.

ELIGIBILITY: By French-speaking authors born, raised in minority situation in U.S. or Canada, or Quebec-born authors who at time of publication have lived at least 3 years in minority situation; or residents of Quebec whose work bears on French-speaking minorities.

AWARDS: $1000 Champlain Prize and Certificate, travel and expenses to awards ceremony. Honorable Mention.

JUDGING: By 3-member jury. May withhold awards.

ENTRY FEE: None.

DEADLINES: Entry, December. Awards, July.

| 110 |

La Presse Prize for Literature
Antoine Des Roches, Public
Relations Director
7 rue Saint-Jacques
Montreal, Quebec H2Y 1K9
CANADA

November

National; **entry restricted;** annual; established 1975. $7500 to **Quebec French Culture Literature** (critical-philosophical-artistic essay) by French Canadians-legal immigrants. Award, November.

| 111 |

Amaury Talbot Prize
Barclays Bank Trust Company Ltd
Central Administration Office, Trustee
Office
Radbroke Hall
Knutsford, Cheshire WA16 9EU
ENGLAND Tel: Knutsford (0565)
3888, ext. 2639

Annual

International; entry open to all; annual; established 1955. Sponsored by Barclays Bank Trust Company Ltd. Supported by Amaury Talbot Fund.

BOOK CONTEST: **African Anthropological Research,** published during current calendar year, 2 copies.

ARTICLE CONTEST: **African Anthropological Research,** published during current calendar year, 2 copies.

ELIGIBILITY: Preference first to Nigeria, second to West Africa, third to other African regions.

AWARDS: 300 pound Amaury Talbot Fund Prize.

JUDGING: By panel nominated by Oxford Institute of Social An-

thropology and Royal Anthropological Institute. No entries returned.

ENTRY FEE: None.

DEADLINES: Entry, January. Awards, not specified.

BOOK (Education, Library, Bibliography)
Book, Article, Monograph, Paper, including BOOK-TYPOGRAPHY BIBLIOGRAPHY. (Also see other BOOK.)

| 112 |

American Library Association (ALA) Awards and Citations Program (Librarianship)
50 East Huron Street
Chicago, Illinois 60611 U.S.A.
Tel: (312) 944-6720

Winter

International; **entry restricted to U.S., Canada (nomination by ALA members);** annual. Francis Joseph Campbell Citation Medal for **Library Service to the Blind** (including writing-publication). Library History Round Table Award of $500 for **Library History Research Essay** (unpublished manuscript, maximum 25 pages). Library Research Round Table (LRRT) Research Award of $500 for **Library Research Paper** (maximum 75 pages). Joseph W. Lippincott Award of $1000, Citation for **Professional Librarianship** (including published writing). Esther J. Piercy Award for **Technical Service Librarianship** (including professional literature; to librarian with 10 years maximum experience). Herbert W. Putnam Honor Award of $500 grant-in-aid to **Ameri-**

can **Librarian** for writing, travel to improve profession. RSTD Resources Section Publication Award of Citation for college-university library acquisitions **Monograph, Article, Paper.** Ralph R. Shaw Award of $500, Citation for **Library Literature** (periodic). H. W. Wilson Library Periodical Award of $500, Certificate for **Library Periodicals** (U.S.-Canada, periodic). Sponsored by ALA. Also sponsor Awards and Citations for Reference, Children's Works; Scholarships for library education-study. Awards, Winter.

113

Educator's Award
Delta Kappa Gamma (DKG) Society International
Executive Secretary
P.O. Box 1589
Austin, Texas 78767 U.S.A.
Tel: (512) 478-5748

Spring

International; **entry restricted to women from DKG countries;** annual; established 1946. Purpose: to recognize women's contributions to education which may influence the profession. Sponsored by DKG Society International and held at its international convention (even years) or 1 of 4 regional conferences (odd years).

BOOK CONTEST: Education, published; copyrighted (first edition, English translation) during previous calendar year; by 1-2 women from DKG country; in fields of research, philosophy, other stimulating-creative areas. Submit 5 copies, nominating letter, copyright date. No methods-skill books, textbooks, unpublished manuscripts, children's books.

ELIGIBILITY: DKG countries include U.S., Canada, Costa Rica, El Salvador, Finland, Guatemala, Iceland,

Mexico, Netherlands, Norway, Sweden, U.K.

AWARDS: $1500 Educator's Award for book influencing future directions in teaching. Based on editing, format, style, international interest.

JUDGING: By 5 judges. May withhold, divide award.

ENTRY FEE: None.

DEADLINES: Entry, February. Award, Spring.

114

Gold Medal for Services to Bibliography
Bibliographical Society
Mrs. M. M. Foot, Secretary
British Library
Great Russell Street
London WC1, ENGLAND
Tel: 01-636-1544, ext. 354

Periodic

International; **entry restricted (selection by members);** periodic; established 1929. Gold Medal for **Services to Bibliography** (including writing). Purpose: to honor distinguished bibliographers. Sponsored and supported by Bibliographical Society, established 1892. Publish *The Library* (quarterly journal). Also sponsor bibliographical lectures.

115

International League of Antiquarian Booksellers (ILAB) Bibliographical Prize
Dr. Frieder Kocher-Benzing, Secretary
Rathenaustrasse 21
D-7000 Stuttgart 1, WEST GERMANY (FRG)

Summer

International; entry open to all;

triennial; established 1962. Sponsored by ILAB, international association of National Associations of Antiquarian Booksellers. Second contact: Bob de Graaf, President, Zuidelinde 40, 2421 AK Nieuwkoop, Netherlands.

BOOK CONTEST: Book-Typography Bibliography-Research, unpublished or published in 3 years preceding entry date, in universally used language, 2 copies; learned bibliography or book-typography history research of general interest. No specialized-sale or public library catalogs, periodicals.

AWARDS: $1000 Bibliographical Prize. May publish winner.

JUDGING: By President of ILAB, Secretary of Triennial Prize, 1 ILAB member, and 3 persons of bibliographical knowledge. Unpublished preferred over published. May withhold Award. Winner retains all rights. Unpublished returned, published property of ILAB.

ENTRY FEE: None.

DEADLINES: Entry, December of second year preceding award. Award, Summer.

BOOK (History)

Book, Article, Monograph, Historical Writing, including AMERICAN, NORTH AMERICAN, CANADIAN, COLONIAL, CONFEDERATE, CIVIL WAR-RECONSTRUCTION, ENGLISH, LINCOLN THEME, NEW YORK, SOUTHERN. (Also see other BOOK.)

| 116 |

Bancroft and Loubat Prizes
Columbia University
202A Low Memorial Library
New York, New York 10027 U.S.A.

Spring

International; entry open to all; annual (Bancroft, established 1948); every 5 years (Loubat, established 1893). Sponsored and supported by Columbia University, founded 1912.

BOOK CONTEST: American History, Diplomacy *(Bancroft Prize),* published during previous year or by December after entry; originally written in English or published translation in English. Submit 4 copies, published or page-proof copy. No volumes of papers, letters, speeches (unless edited by author), or books reporting recent personal experiences of Americans within limited time, geographic area. Categories: History (including biography), Diplomacy.
North American History, Geography, Ethnology, Philology or Numismatics *(Loubat Prize),* printed and published in English.

AWARDS: Bancroft, $4000 each category. Loubat, $1200 First, $600 Second Prize.

JUDGING: Bancroft, by Prize Committee; previous winners eligible.

ENTRY FEE: None. Entrant pays postage (include SASE).

DEADLINES: Entry,   October. Awards, Spring.

| 117 |

Civil War Round Table of New York Awards
George M. Craig, Chairman
83-12 St. James Street
Elmhurst, New York 11373 U.S.A.
Tel: (212) NE9-1172

February

International; entry open to all; annual; established 1960. Purpose: greater appreciation of life, works of Abraham Lincoln. Sponsored and supported by Civil War Round Table of New York. Held at Round Table dinner meeting. Also sponsor Fletcher Pratt Award (to best book dealing with Civil War); awards for Lincoln-theme musical works, paintings, radio-television programs. Second contact: Arnold Gates, 168 Weyford Terrace, Garden City, New York 11530.

BOOK   CONTEST: Lincoln Theme.

ARTICLE   CONTEST: Lincoln Theme.

AWARDS: $100, copy of Lincoln Bust, Plaque.

JUDGING: By committee. Not responsible for loss or damage.

ENTRY FEE: None.

DEADLINES: Entry, December. Awards, February.

118

Confederate Memorial Literary Society Awards for Historical Research and Writing
Museum of the Confederacy
Dr. Edward D. C. Campbell, Jr., Director
1201 East Clay Street
Richmond, Virginia 23219 U.S.A.
Tel: (804) 649-1861

June

National; entry open to U.S.; annual; established 1970. Purpose: to encourage, recognize research in Middle Period of U.S. History. Sponsored and supported by Museum of the Confederacy. Average statistics: 25 entries. Held at Museum of the Confederacy,

Richmond, Virginia. Have film, lecture series. Also sponsor Founders Award for research or editing of primary sources resulting in publication of 1 or more volumes.

BOOK   CONTEST: Confederate Narrative History, published and copyrighted in previous year, 4 copies.

ARTICLE CONTEST: Confederacy. Requirements same as for Book.

MONOGRAPH CONTEST: Confederacy. Requirements same as for Book.

AWARDS: Jefferson Davis Award for Book, Award of Merit for Article or Monograph. Each award is Citation and Impression of Great Seal of the Confederacy.

JUDGING: By researchers-writers per award. Sponsor keeps copy for library.

ENTRY FEE: None

DEADLINES: Entry, February. Winners announced, May. Awards, June.

119

Francis Parkman Prize Competition
Society of American Historians, Inc.
Prof. Kenneth T. Jackson
610 Fayerweather Hall
Columbia University
New York, New York 10027 U.S.A.
Tel: (212) 280-2555, (914) 666-5721

April

International; entry open to all; annual; established 1957. Purpose: to stimulate history writing as literature; emphasize that literary distinction should accompany solid historical scholarship. Sponsored by Society of

American Historians, Inc. Held in New York at formal dinner. Also sponsor Allan Nevins Prize.

BOOK CONTEST: U.S. Colonial, National History, published during previous calendar year; 4 copies; unlimited entry. Studies in religious, legal, technological, diplomatic history eligible.

AWARDS: $500 Francis Parkman Prize, engraved Bronze Medal and Certificate to Best Entry.

JUDGING: By 3 judges.

ENTRY FEE: None.

DEADLINES: Entry,   January. Award, April.

120

Harry S. Truman Book Award
Harry S. Truman Library Institute
Benedict K. Zobrist, Secretary
Harry S. Truman Library
Independence, Missouri 64050
U.S.A. Tel: (816) 833-1400

Spring

International; entry open to all; biennial; established 1963. Named after 33rd U.S. president. Formerly called DAVID D. LLOYD PRIZE to 1980. Sponsored and supported by Harry S. Truman Library Institute. Held in Independence, Missouri. Also sponsor Tom L. Evans Research Grant to postdoctoral scholars and Institute Grants to younger scholars, for investigating political, economic, social development of U.S. during Truman's public career.

BOOK CONTEST: Harry S. Truman Presidential Period, dealing primarily and substantially with political, economic, social development aspects of U.S. between April 12, 1945 and January 20, 1953 (Truman's public career). Require 3 copies.

AWARDS: Not specified.

ENTRY FEE: None.

DEADLINES: Entry, January. Judging, January-April. Awards, May.

121

Jamestown Prize
Institute of Early American History
and Culture
Norman Fiering, Editor of
Publications
Box 220
Williamsburg, Virginia 23185 U.S.A.

Spring

International; **entry restricted to unpublished book authors;** annual. Formerly called JAMESTOWN FOUNDATION AWARD and INSTITUTE MANUSCRIPT AWARD. Sponsored by Institute of Early American History and Culture. Supported by Jamestown Foundation, University of North Carolina Press, College of William and Mary, Colonial Williamsburg Foundation.

BOOK CONTEST: Early American Scholarly History, unpublished, on early American history, culture (America before circa 1815, or related history of British Isles, Europe, West Africa, Caribbean); typed, double-spaced; not in contention for another award.

AWARDS: $1500 Jamestown Cash Prize and publication by University of North Carolina Press.

JUDGING: Preliminary and final.

ENTRY FEE: None.

DEADLINES: Entry, open. Winner announced, Spring.

| 122 |

Jules F. Landry Award
Catherine Silvia, Promotion Manager
Louisiana State University Press
Baton Rouge, Louisiana 70803
U.S.A. Tel: (504) 388-2210

Continuous

International; entry open to all; annual. Sponsored by Louisiana State University (LSU) Press. Also sponsor Literature Contest.

BOOK CONTEST: **Southern History, Biography,** unpublished manuscript.

AWARDS: $1000 Landry Award and publication by LSU Press (includes Literature Contest).

ENTRY FEE: None.

DEADLINES: Open.

| 123 |

National Historical Society (NHS) Book Prizes
William C. Davis, President
Box 1831
Harrisburg, Pennsylvania 17105
U.S.A. Tel: (717) 255-7713

Summer, Winter

International; entry open to all; annual; established 1972 (NHS Prize); biennial, established 1980 (Wiley Prize; named after late Civil War historian Bell I. Wiley). Purpose: to encourage historians in producing sound, readable history. Sponsored by NHS. Publish *American History Illustrated* (magazine). Also sponsor Members' Award for Excellence in Writing for article in *American History Illustrated.*

BOOK CONTEST: **First American History Nonfiction** *(NHS Prize),* published in previous calendar year, 3 copies. No manuscripts, theses, dissertations.

Civil War-Reconstruction *(Wiley Prize),* published during 2 previous calendar years, 3 copies. Nominated by publisher. No manuscripts, theses, dissertations.

AWARDS: $1000 NHS Book Prize in American History for new author. $1000 Bell I. Wiley Book Prize for Civil War-Reconstruction History.

JUDGING: By 3 historians.

ENTRY FEE: None.

DEADLINES: Entry, February (Wiley), May (NHS). Winners announced, September (NHS), November (Wiley).

| 124 |

New York State Historical Association Manuscript Award
Dr. Wendell Tripp, Editorial Associate
Cooperstown, New York 13326
U.S.A. Tel: (607) 547-2508

July

International; entry open to all; annual; established 1973. Purpose: to award superior unpublished book-length monographs dealing with New York State history. Sponsored by New York State Historical Association. Average statistics: 72 entries, 18 finalists. 5 winners published or accepted for publication by major university presses to date. Held in Cooperstown, New York. Have annual seminars.

BOOK CONTEST: **New York State History** (historical biographies and manuscripts dealing with literature, the arts, accepted if methodology is historical), unpublished, book-length, typed, double-spaced. No carbon copies.

AWARDS: $1000 and publication assistance.

JUDGING: By 10-member editorial board of *New York History* (quarterly journal). All entries reviewed in entirety. May withhold award.

ENTRY FEE: None.

DEADLINES: Entry, January. Judging, June. Winner announced, July.

| 125 |

Pacific Coast Branch of American Historical Association Awards
John A. Schultz, Secretary-Treasurer
University of Southern California
Los Angeles, California 90007 U.S.A.
Tel: (213) 743-5295

August

International; **entry restricted to U.S., Canadian Pacific Coast authors;** annual; established 1932. Sponsored by Pacific Coast Branch of the American Historical Association. Held at sponsor's annual convention.

BOOK CONTEST: First Scholarly History, first full-length work by scholar-author living in 10 Mountain-Pacific Coast States, Alaska, Hawaii, or Canada's 2 western provinces. Require 3 copies.

AWARDS: $200 Prize.

JUDGING: By 3 judges.

ENTRY FEE: None.

DEADLINES: Entry, May. Award, August.

| 126 |

Phi Alpha Theta Book and Manuscript Awards
Phi Alpha Theta International
Dr. Donald B. Hoffman, Secretary
2812 West Livingston Street
Allentown, Pennsylvania 18104
U.S.A.

December

International; **entry restricted to members;** annual. $500 Awards to **Published History Books** (First Published and Subsequent Published), and **Publication of Historical Manuscript** (book-length, 50,000-150,000 words). Sponsored by Phi Alpha Theta International Honor Society in History. Awards at PAT-American Historical Association luncheon in December.

| 127 |

Simon Baruch University Award
United Daughters of the Confederacy (UDC)
Memorial Building
328 North Blvd.
Richmond, Virginia 23220 U.S.A.

November

International; entry open to all; biennial; established 1904 as essay contest in southern history; book, monograph awards established 1923. Purpose: to assist young professionals in publication of theses, dissertations, writings; encourage research in southern history. Sponsored by UDC.

BOOK CONTEST: Southern Confederate History, unpublished; 75,000 words minimum, typed, double-spaced.

MONOGRAPH CONTEST: Southern Confederate History, unpublished; 25-50,000 words, typed, double-spaced.

ELIGIBILITY: Southern history in or near period of Confederacy or bearing on causes leading to secession, War Between the States; presented in scholarly form, based (at least in part) on primary sources; within 15 years of author's U.S. college or university higher degree graduation, or by students with accepted theses, dissertations. Require registrar attendance statement, biographical data, passport photo.

AWARDS: $1500 grant-in-aid for publication (winner makes printing arrangements).

JUDGING: By 3 historians. Based on research effectiveness, originality, accuracy, excellence of style. 9 copies published book, property of UDC; 52 may be purchased for state library distribution. Nonwinners returned. May withhold award.

ENTRY FEE: Not specified.

DEADLINES: Entry, May. Award, November.

| 128 |

Society of Colonial Wars Awards
Joan Sumner, Executive Secretary
122 East 58th Street
New York, New York 10022 U.S.A.

Various

International; entry open to all; annual; established 1951. Purpose: to promote wider knowledge, encourage material on life and times of early America. Sponsored by Society of Colonial Wars. Also sponsor awards for music, art, photography.

BOOK CONTEST: Colonial Period, bound volumes or pamphlets.

WRITING CONTEST: Colonial Period.

ELIGIBILITY: At least 75% of content must be in Colonial Period (1607-1775).

AWARDS: Parchment Citations of Honor and Bronze Medallions to winners. Honorable Mention Citations. Sponsor may withhold awards.

ENTRY FEE: None.

DEADLINES: Open.

| 129 |

Southern Historical Association (SHA) Book Awards
Bennett H. Wall, Secretary
History Department
University of Georgia
Athens, Georgia 30602 U.S.A.
Tel: (404) 546-7040

Various

National; **entry open to U.S. citizens;** annual (Sydnor Award even years; Simkins Award odd years). Sponsored by SHA. Also sponsor Ramsdell Award for article on southern history published in *Journal of Southern History,* Fletcher M. Green Award for graduate student article in *Journal.*

BOOK CONTEST: Southern History, published. Categories: Book *(Sydnor Award),* First Book *(Simkins Award).*

AWARDS: Charles S. Sydnor Award for Book on Southern History, $500 and Certificate. Francis Butler Simkins Award for First Book on Southern History, $200 and Certificate.

ENTRY FEE: None.

DEADLINES: Open.

| 130 |

Sainte-Marie Prize
Sainte-Marie Among the Hurons
Robert D. Kennedy, Public Information Coordinator
Huronia Historical Parks
P.O. Box 160
Midland, Ontario L4R 4K8 CANADA
Tel: (705) 526-7838

Spring

International; entry open to all; annual; established 1971. Sponsored by Ontario Ministry of Culture and Recreation, Huronia Historical Parks, and Sainte-Marie Among the Hurons' 17th-century French Jesuit mission (1639-1649) historic site and first European community in Ontario.

BOOK CONTEST: 17th-Century Canadian History, unpublished, 20,-000 words minimum; in French or English; typewritten, no publication pending, 2 copies. Concerned with 17th-century Canadian history and national or international circumstances, events influencing 17th-century Canadian exploration, colonization, politics, economics, individuals, relations between colonies, other matters. Require bibliography, resume.

AWARDS: $1649 Sainte-Marie Cash Prize for excellence in original research, interpretation. Winner published by Sainte-Marie Among the Hurons.

JUDGING: Other entries considered for publication. May withhold award.

ENTRY FEE: None.

DEADLINES: Entry, December. Award, Spring.

131

Rose Mary Crawshay Prizes for English Literature
The British Academy
Burlington House
Piccadilly
London W1V ONS, ENGLAND
Tel: 01-734-0457

Various

International; **entry restricted to women;** annual; established 1914. Sponsored by the British Academy. Supported by Byron, Shelley, Keats in Memoriam Yearly Prize Fund, founded 1888 by Mrs. Rose Mary Crawshay.

BOOK CONTEST: English Literature Historical-Critical, written or published in previous 3 years; any subject; preference to work regarding poets Byron, Shelley, Keats.

AWARDS: 2 Rose Mary Crawshay Prizes.

ENTRY FEE: None.

DEADLINES: Open.

BOOK (Language, Linguistics, Translation)

Book, Article, Essay Translation or In Foreign Language, including FRENCH, GERMAN, ITALIAN, JAPANESE, POLISH, PORTUGUESE, SPANISH, CASTILIAN. (Also see other BOOK.)

132

Friendship Fund Prize for Japanese Literary Translation
Japan-United States Friendship Commission (JSFC)
Francis B. Tenny, Executive Director
1875 Connecticut Avenue N.W.
Suite 709
Washington, District of Columbia
20009 U.S.A. Tel: (202) 673-5295

Summer

National; **entry open to U.S.;** annual; established 1979. Purpose: to encourage literary translation from Japanese to English; increase Japanese literature available in English. Sponsored by JUSFC, Japan Society, Inc. Recognized by Association of Asian Studies. Average statistics: 15 entries. Also sponsor Japan Exchange Fellowship Program. Second contact: Peter

Grilli, Japan Society, Inc., 333 East 47th Street, New York, New York 10017; tel: (212) 832-1155.

BOOK CONTEST: Japanese (Essay or Memoir) literature to English Translation, unpublished or newly published in previous 2 years; any period; book-length, 5 copies (if published), 5 photocopies (if unpublished). Translations in process considered if over half complete. No shorter works, other nonfiction translations.

ELIGIBILITY: U.S. translators with no book-length translation published or widely sold in U.S. more than 2 years previous.

AWARDS: $1000 Friendship Fund Prize for Best Translation (including fiction), assistance in finding publisher.

JUDGING: By editors, writers, established translators. Based on (in order of importance) literary merit of English, accuracy reflecting spirit of Japanese original, literary merit of Japanese original. All entries read in entirety. May withhold award.

ENTRY FEE: None. Entrant pays postage (include SASE).

DEADLINES: Entry, February. Judging, Spring. Winner announced, June. Award, Summer.

133

Modern Language Association (MLA) of America Prizes
Judith Teply
62 Fifth Avenue
New York, New York 10011 U.S.A.
Tel: (212) 741-7854

December

National; entry restricted to MLA members (or nomination by members); annual (biennial, Howard R. Marraro Prize). James Russell Lowell Prize, Citation, $1000 to Literary-Linguistic Study, or Critical Edition-Biography Book. William Riley Parker Prize, Citation, $500 for Article Published by MLA. Howard R. Marraro Prize, Citation, $750 to Italian Literature, Scholarly Book or Essay. Mina P. Shaughnessy Medal, one year MLA membership, $500 for Teaching of English Language-Literature Research Book or Article. Kenneth W. Mildenberger Medal, MLA membership, $500 for Teaching of Foreign Languages-Literature Research Book or Article. Sponsored by MLA. Awards, December.

134

PEN Translation Prizes
PEN American Center
Karen Kennerly, Executive Secretary
47 Fifth Avenue
New York, New York 10003 U.S.A.
Tel: (212) 255-1977

Spring

International; entry open to all; annual (PEN Translation, Goethe, Poggioli), biennial (Gulbenkian). Purpose: to recognize translations for English-speaking public. Sponsored by 1800-member PEN American Center (founded 1922) of the 10,000-member, 80-country International PEN (Poets-Playwrights-Essayists-Editors-Novelists), founded 1921 as independent, nonprofit world association of writers. Also sponsor PEN Writing Award for Prisoners, PEN Literature Awards, PEN Fund for Writers; Lucille J. Mednick Memorial Award ($500, annual) for distinguished service to the literary community and commitment to serve the young, unrecognized, unpopular (candidates by nomination only).

BOOK CONTEST: Into English Translation *(PEN Translation Prize),* published in U.S. during previous calendar year by established publishing house, translated from any language, 2 copies. No technical, scientific, reference books.

German to English Translation *(Goethe House Prize)*, published during previous year by established publishing house, 2 copies.

Portuguese to English Translation *(Calouste Gulbenkian Prize)*, published during previous 2 calendar years by established publishing house, 2 copies.

Italian to English Translation *(Renato Poggioli Award)*, published during previous calendar year by established publishing house. Require curriculum vitae, translation sample, original text.

AWARDS: $1000 PEN Translation Prize. $500 Goethe House Prize. $500 Calouste Gulbenkian Prize. $3000 Renato Poggioli Award.

JUDGING: By panel.

ENTRY FEE: None.

DEADLINES: Entry, December (for Poggioli Award, January). Awards, Spring.

| 135 |

South Atlantic Modern Language Association (SAMLA) Studies Award
Donald Kay, Executive Director
Drawer CA
100 Manly Hall
University, Alabama 35486 U.S.A.
Tel: (205) 348-7165

November

International; **entry restricted to SAMLA members;** annual; established 1958. $500 Award for **Literature-Language of America Scholarly Manuscript** (60,000-100,000 words in English; no dissertations, editions).

Winner published by University of Georgia Press (previously by University of Kentucky Press). Purpose: to promote outstanding literary and linguistics scholarship. Sponsored and supported by 4300-member SAMLA and University of Georgia Press. Recognized by Modern Language Association. Average statistics: 20-25 entrants, 4 countries, 4 finalists, 1 award. Held at SAMLA annual convention. Second contact: Paul Zimmer, Director, University of Georgia Press, Athens, Georgia. Winners announced, November.

| 136 |

French Studies Review Prize
Pierre Filion
University of Montreal Press
Case Postale 6128
Montreal, Quebec H3C 3J7 CANADA
Tel: (514) 343-6931

Fall

International; **entry restricted to French-speaking country or territory residents;** annual; established 1968. Purpose: to encourage literary works in French (representative of cultural spheres other than France). Sponsored and supported by University of Montreal Press, Therien Freres (printers).

BOOK CONTEST: French Nonfiction (Literary Essay, Narrative), unpublished, original; written in French; about cultural domains outside France; 100 pages minimum; typed double-spaced.

ELIGIBILITY: 7-consecutive-year resident of French-speaking country, territory (having lived outside France half of life or more).

AWARDS: $2000 (Canadian) French Studies Review Prize and publication by University of Montreal Press.

JUDGING: By jury selected by University of Montreal Press. Sponsor has exclusive publishing rights for 2 years. Nonwinners returned.

ENTRY FEE: None.

DEADLINES: Entry, May. Awards, Fall.

| **137** |

Translators Association Prizes
84 Drayton Gardens
London SW10 9SD, ENGLAND
Tel: 01-373-6642

Spring

International; **entry restricted to British publishers;** annual. Sponsored by The Translators Association. Supported by Arts Council of Great Britain, British publishers, Italian Institute and British Italian Society (Florio), French Government (Moncrieff Prize), West German Government (Tieck Prize). Recognized by Society of Authors.

BOOK CONTEST: **Italian to English Translation** *(Florio Prize)*, 3 proof and 3 original copies.
French to English Translation *(Moncrieff Prize)*, 3 proof and 3 original copies.
German to English Translation *(Tieck Prize)*, 3 proof and 3 original copies.

ELIGIBILITY: Translations of twentieth-century works of literary merit-general interest published in United Kingdom during current year by British publisher.

AWARDS: 500 pound John Florio Prize. 1000 pound Scott Moncrieff Prize. 1600 pound Schlegel-Tieck Prize.

JUDGING: By 3 judges, each award. May withhold, divide awards.

ENTRY FEE: None.

DEADLINES: Entry, December. Awards, Spring.

| **138** |

German Academy of Language and Literature Prizes
Dr. Gerhard Dette, General Secretary
Alexandraweg 23
6100 Darmstadt, WEST GERMANY
(FRG) Tel: 06151-44823

Fall

International; **entry restricted (nomination by Academy members);** annual. 10,000 DM Johann-Heinrich-Voss Prize for **Literary Translation into German** (established 1958); 10,-000 DM Friedrich-Gundolf Prize for **Foreign Achievements in Germanistics** (established 1964); 10,000 DM Johann-Heinrich-Merck Prize for **Literary Essay and Criticism** (established 1964); 10,000 Sigmund-Freud Prize for **Scientific Prose** (established 1964). Sponsored by German Academy of Language and Literature. Also sponsor fiction awards. Awards, Fall.

| **139** |

Hermann-Hesse Prize
Forderungsgemeinschaft der Deutschen Kunst
E. Hoenselaers
Kantstrasse 6
7500 Karlsruhe 1, WEST GERMANY
(FRG) Tel: 721-385751

June

International; entry open to all; triennial; established 1956. Named after Hermann Hesse, 1946 winner of Nobel Prize for Literature. Purpose: to promote writers. Sponsored by Forderungsgemeinschaft der Deutschen Kunst, City of Karlsruhe. Average statistics: 100 entries, 6 countries, 10 semifinalists, 3 awards. Held in Karlsruhe, West Germany. Also sponsor Fiction Book, Short Story Contests.

BOOK CONTEST: In German Language, published or unpublished, 1 entry, 3 copies.

ESSAY CONTEST: In German Language. Requirements same as for Book.

MONOGRAPH-PAPER CONTEST: In German Language. Requirements same as for Book.

AWARDS: (Including Fiction Contests) DM 10,000 Hermann-Hesse Prize, 2 DM 5000 Promotion Awards.

JUDGING: By 5 German writers-literature critics. May withhold awards. All entries reviewed in entirety. Entrants retain all rights. Not responsible for loss or damage.

ENTRY FEE: None. Sponsor pays return postage.

DEADLINES: Entry, July. Winners announced, May. Awards, June. Materials returned, July.

140

Polish PEN Club Literary Prize
Juliusz Zulawski, President
Palac Kultury i Nauki
00-901 Warsaw, POLAND
Tel: 26-39-48

Annual

International; entry open to all; annual; established 1929. Purpose: to award excellent literary translations from Polish language. Sponsored by Polish PEN Club. Recognized by PEN International. Held in Warsaw. Also sponsor prizes for Polish translators, poets, fiction writers, editors.

BOOK CONTEST: Polish Literature Translation.

AWARDS: Not specified.

ENTRY FEE: Not specified.

DEADLINES: Not specified.

141

Royal Spanish Academy Prizes
Real Academia Espanola
Felipe IV, 4
Madrid, SPAIN Tel: 239-46-05

Various

International; entry open to various; annual (Cartagena, Rivadeneira Prizes), biennial (Pidal Prize), every 9 years (Alba Prize); established 1905 (Alba), 1929 (Cartagena), 1940 (Rivadeneira), 1958 (Pidal), 1973 (Lopez). Sponsored by Royal Academy of Spain, founded 1713. Publish world-famous dictionaries, literary works, scholarly journals. Also sponsor Fastenrath Prize (annual, founded 1909) of 70,000 pesetas for Critical Literature, History-Biography by Spaniards in Castilian; Castillo de Chirel Prize (every 4 years, founded 1916) of 31,300 pts. for Newspapers-Magazines; XVII Marques de Cerralbo Prize (every 4 years, founded 1922) of 5800 pts. for Spanish Language-Literature; and San Gaspar Aid to Writers (annual, founded 1895), grants to writers, widows or families of writers.

BOOK CONTEST: Theme in Castilian *(Alba, Cartagena Prizes),* original, unpublished, in Spanish Castilian language *(Alba);* unpublished, by Spaniards or Spanish-Americans in Castilian *(Cartagena);* various yearly themes.
Spanish Linguistics in Castilian *(Rivadeneira Prizes),* unpublished.
Spanish Linguistics *(Pidal Prize),* in language of Spanish region-district studied.
Spanish Language *(Lopez Prize),* open to Spaniards, Spanish-Ameri-

cans.

AWARDS: Duke of Alba Prize, 12,-000 pesetas. 2 Count of Cartagena Prizes, 60,000 pts. each. 2 Rivadeneira Prizes, 20,000 pts. each. Ramon Menendez Pidal Prize, 30,000 pts. Nieto Lopez Prize, 150,000 pts.

ENTRY FEE: None.

DEADLINES: Various.

BOOK (Nonfiction)
General Nonfiction Book, Article, Script, including ACADEMIC, BIOGRAPHY, BIBLIOGRAPHY, BUSINESS, CHILDREN'S, GRAPHICS, HISTORY, MEDICAL, REFERENCE, SCHOLARLY, SCIENTIFIC, SMALL PRESS, TECHNICAL, TRANSLATION, TRAVEL BOOKS. (Also see other BOOK.)

| 142 |

American Book Awards
Association of American Publishers (AAP)
Joan Cunliffe, Director
One Park Avenue, 20th Floor
New York, New York 10016 U.S.A.
Tel: (212) 689-8920

Spring

National; **entry open to U.S. citizens (by publishers' submission);** annual; established 1979. Formerly called NATIONAL BOOK AWARD to 1979, TABA (The American Book Award) to 1980. Purpose: to recognize books of distinction, exemplary achievement, literary merit; select, honor, promote these books; generate public awareness. Motto: "Books make a difference." Sponsored by AAP. Supported by AAP, other book-related organizations. Average statistics: 1300 entries, 85 finalists, 18 awards. Held at Carnegie Hall, New York, for 1 day. Tickets: $50. Also sponsor National Medal for Literature ($15,000 and Bronze Medal for distinguished, continuing contribution to American Letters). Second contact: Laura Brown, Ingram Book Company, 347 Reedwood Drive, Nashville, Tennessee 37217.

BOOK CONTEST: United States Nonfiction, written or translated by U.S. citizen; published during previous calendar year by U.S. publisher; 1 category maximum per entry, either hardcover or paperback, 12 copies; 6 copies of translations. No reprints, newly edited or revised books previously published in same format, anthologies, compendiums. Categories: Autobiography-Biography, General Nonfiction, History, Science, Children's Nonfiction (Hardcover, Paperback); Translation (Hardcover or Paperback).

United States Book Graphics, by U.S. citizen, manufactured and published in U.S. during previous calendar year with minimum 1000-copy printing. Separate entry fee each category; 1 copy book, 2 covers, 2 jackets per entry. Categories: Book Design (Typographical, Pictorial), Illustration (Original, Adapted-Collected), Jacket Design (Hardcover), Cover Design (Paperback).

AWARDS: $1000 and Louise Nevelson Wall Sculpture to Best Translation (either hardcover or paperback), Best Hardcover, Best Paperback (each remaining book category). Nevelson Wall Sculpture to Best Design or Illustration, Best Jacket, Best Cover. Recognition Certificates. Promotion materials for winners distributed to over 10,000 bookstores, libraries.

JUDGING: Panel of 11 authors, critics, librarians, booksellers, editors, publishers choose 5 nominees and winner each category. For Translations and Graphics, separate 5-member panels choose 5 nominees, winner each category. All jurors selected by Awards Administration Council. Graphics based on originality, aesthetic value, manufacturing. Not responsible for loss or damage.

ENTRY FEE: $25 per entry per category.

DEADLINES: Entry, November (Books), February (Graphics). Awards, Spring.

143

American Library Association (ALA) Awards and Citations Program (Reference)
Andrew M. Hansen, Executive Director
50 East Huron Street
Chicago, Illinois 60611 U.S.A.
Tel: (312) 944-6750

Winter

National; **entry restricted (nomination by ALA);** annual. Dartmouth Medal for **Reference Works** (writing, compiling, editing, publishing of books). Isadore Gilbert Mudge Citation for **Reference Librarianship** (for constructive-imaginative library program, reference book-article writing, reference service instruction). Eunice Rockwell Oberly Memorial Award, Cash, Citation to American Citizen for **Agricultural or Related Science Bibliography** (biennial, odd years; administered by College and Research Libraries, Science and Technology Section). Outstanding Reference Sources of the Year to **U.S. Published Reference Books** and other sources (30-40 per year). Sponsored by ALA. Also sponsor Awards and Citations

for Librarianship, Children's Works. Awards, Winter.

144

American Society of Journalists and Authors (ASJA) Awards
Dorothy Stearn, Executive Director
1501 Broadway, Suite 1907
New York, New York 10036 U.S.A.
Tel: (212) 997-0947

Spring

National; **entry restricted to U.S. professionals;** annual; established 1978. Purpose: to recognize, encourage excellence in nonfiction writing-editing. Sponsored by ASJA. Held at ASJA Annual Writer's Conference in New York City. Also sponsor Mort Weisinger Award (for article by ASJA member).

BOOK AWARD: Nonfiction Any Subject, published.

MAGAZINE AWARD: Nonfiction Any Subject.

AWARDS: Author of the Year Award to writer whose book or body of work has made significant contribution to American society. Magazine of the Year Award to magazine showing innovation and excellence within last 5 years.

JUDGING: By Committee. May withhold awards.

ENTRY FEE: None.

DEADLINES: Entry, February. Awards, Spring.

145

Broome Agency Literary Contest
Larry Parr, President
3080 North Washington Blvd.
Sarasota, Florida 33580 U.S.A.
Tel: (813) 355-3036

April

International; entry open to all; annual; established 1970. Purpose: to encourage, attract more and better writing. Sponsored by Broome Literary Service, authors' representatives and editorial service. Average statistics: 10,000 entries (both nonfiction and fiction). Also sponsor fiction book, short story contest.

BOOK CONTEST: Nonfiction, unpublished, original, 50,000 words minimum. No carbons, photocopies, plays, scripts, or for children age 12 and under.

AWARDS: $1250 Best Book. Salable manuscripts considered for commission marketing.

JUDGING: By Sherwood and Mary Ann Broome. All entries read in entirety. Sponsor may use names, titles in advertising, publicity. Not responsible for loss or damage.

ENTRY FEE: None. Entrant pays postage (include SASE).

DEADLINES: Entry, December. Award, April.

[146]

Choice Outstanding Academic Books of the Year
Jay Martin Poole, Editor
100 Riverview Center
Middletown, Connecticut 06457
U.S.A. Tel: (203) 347-6933

Annual

National; entry restricted (nomination by Choice editors); annual. Magazine acknowledgement of U.S. Published Academic Books for college-university and public libraries. Sponsored by Choice, monthly journal published by Association of College and Research Libraries, a division of the ALA.

[147]

Editors' Book Award
Pushcart Press
P.O. Box 380
Wainscott, New York 11975 U.S.A.

Fall

International; entry restricted (nomination by U.S., Canadian editors); annual. Purpose: to encourage writing distinguished books of uncertain financial value; support editors' enthusiasm for literary merit. Sponsored by Pushcart Press. Also sponsor Fiction Book Contest.

BOOK CONTEST: Nonfiction, unpublished. Submit 1 copy (photocopy OK), nomination letter from editor. Only book-length manuscripts making rounds of commercial publishers without acceptance will be considered.

AWARDS: $1000, publication on standard royalty contract, and national advertising-promotion (including fiction entries).

JUDGING: By panel of editors. Not responsible for loss or damage.

ENTRY FEE: Not specified. Entrant pays postage (include SASE).

DEADLINES: Entry, May-August. Award, Fall.

[148]

Gordon J. Laing Book Prize
University of Chicago Press (UCP)
Ann Barret, Advertising and Publicity Manager
5801 Ellis Avenue
Chicago, Illinois 60637 U.S.A.
Tel: (312) 753-2594

Spring

Regional; **entry restricted to University of Chicago faculty authors (nomination by UCP staff);** annual; established 1963. $1000 and Certificate to **Author or Translator of Book Published by UCP** in previous 2 years. Named after Gordon J. Laing, Dean of Humanities and UCP General Editor. Purpose: to honor books published by UCP having greatest distinction. Sponsored by UCP. Event, Spring.

149

Houghton Mifflin Literary Fellowship
Houghton Mifflin Company
2 Park Street
Boston, Massachusetts 02107 U.S.A.

Continuous

National; **entry open to U.S.;** continuous; established 1935. Considered oldest publisher-sponsored award of its kind. Purpose: to help American authors complete projects of outstanding literary merit. Sponsored by Houghton Mifflin Company (book publishers). Also sponsor semiannual Houghton Mifflin New Poetry Series Poetry Competition.

BOOK CONTEST: Nonfiction, to unpublished book author for finished manuscript or work in progress; typed double-spaced; in English. Require 50 pages minimum, theme-intention description, biography. Authors published by private press, regional publisher, or university press are considered.

AWARDS: Houghton Mifflin Fellowships, $2500 cash and $7500 advance against publication royalties (10% of retail price on first 5000 copies, 12 1/2% on 5000-10,000, 15% on over 10,000; 90% of net proceeds of first serial, dramatic, motion picture, radio, television rights sale; 80% of net proceeds of British rights; 75% of net proceeds of translations; 50% of net proceeds of second serial rights, selections or abridgements, reprint publisher, book club, similar organization sale).

JUDGING: Sponsor may publish any book written under fellowship; has publishing option on winner's next book. Non-award winners also considered for publication. May withhold award.

ENTRY FEE: None. Entrant pays postage (include SASE).

DEADLINES: Open throughout year.

150

Professional and Scholarly Publishing (PSP) Awards Program
Association of American Publishers (AAP) PSP Division
Saundra L. Smith, Staff Director
One Park Avenue
New York, New York 10016 U.S.A.
Tel: (212) 689-8920

March

National; **entry restricted to AAP-PSP members;** annual; established 1977. R. R. Hawkins Award, Honorable Mentions, Certificates for **Technical, Scientific, Medical, Business, or Scholarly Publication.** PSP Book Awards for **Technology, Engineering, Architecture-Urban Planning, Physical Sciences, Life Sciences, Health Sciences, Social-Behavioral Sciences, Business-Management, Humanities Books.** PSP Journal Award for **New Journal.** PSP Looseleaf Award for **Looseleaf Publication.** PSP Awards for **Publishing Project (any medium-media)** and **Publication Design-Production.** Honorable Mentions, Certificates. Sponsored by AAP and PSP. Average statistics: 14 awards. Judging based on contribution to professional and scholarly community, high editorial, design and production standards, and publishers' ability to overcome special publication problems. Awards, March.

151

San Francisco Arts and Letters Foundation Award
Bay Area Small Press Bookfair
Todd S. J. Lawson, Director
P.O. Box 99394
San Francisco, California 94109
U.S.A. Tel: (415) 771-3431, 771-6711

Summer

International; entry open to all; annual; established 1971. Purpose: to bring together small presses with poets, writers, journalists; display wares and provide forum. Theme: International Arts for All. Sponsored and supported by San Francisco Arts and Letters Foundation (formerly called Peace and Pieces Foundation; nonprofit grass-roots arts agency), California Arts Council, NEA, COSMEP, City of San Francisco. Average statistics: 2000 entries, 20 countries, 50,000 attendance. Bookfair held at Fort Mason Center (Building D, San Francisco) for 2 days. Have room for 300 displays, 3 stages. Tickets: $.50-$3; free to handicapped, deaf, elderly, exhibitors. Also sponsor Video Prose and Poetry for Hearing and Deaf, photo displays.

BOOK AWARD: **Small Press Any Subject,** published material only. Categories: Prose, Journalism, Mixed Media, Magazines.

AWARDS: Plaques and $250 First, $100 Second, $50 Third Place Best Small Press. 20 Honorary Award Plaques. TV promotion as part of bookfair coverage.

JUDGING: By 3 judges from Arts and Letters Foundation board; 3 selected by attending presses; 1 city or state official involved in mixed-media arts. Not responsible for loss or damage.

ENTRY FEE: $25 all exhibitors. (Display space $100 per table; or $20 per book in combined exhibit.) Entrant pays all shipping.

DEADLINES: Entry, December. Acceptance, February. Materials, March. Event, award, June.

152

Fellowship of Australian Writers (FAW) National Literary Awards
Victorian Fellowship of Australian Writers
J. S. Hamilton, President
1-317 Barkers Road
Kew 3101, Victoria, AUSTRALIA
Tel: 03-805243

March-April

National; **entry restricted to Australia;** annual; established 1965 (considered largest literary awards program in Australia). FAW Barbara Ramsden Award of Plaque for **Literature Book** (fiction-nonfiction). $1000 C. J. Dennis Award for Book on **Australian Flora-Fauna.** 2 $150 Australian Natives' Association Literature Awards for **Literary Work with Australian Theme.** $500 Con Weickhardt Award for Biography, Autobiography, Memoir, Local History. $100 FAW **Local History** Award. $250 Wilke Literary Award for **Nonfiction Book** published and wholly manufactured in Australia. $100 Patricia Weickhardt Award to an **Aboriginal Writer.** Trophy for **Shell Book** of the Year. Alan Marshall Award for Best Manuscript with Strong **Narrative** Element (winning entry offered to publisher). $140, $40, $20 State of Victoria

Awards. $80, $55 (4) FAW **Play, Radio, TV Script** Award. Sponsored and supported by Victorian Fellowship of Australian Writers. Recognized by Literature Board of Australia Council, state governments. Held at National awards dinner in Melbourne. Publish *FAW Bulletin* (monthly). Also sponsor workshops, conferences, seminars. Awards, March-April.

153

Canadian Authors Association (CAA) Awards
24 Ryerson Avenue
Toronto, Ontario M5T 2P3 CANADA
Tel: (416) 868-6916

Spring

National; **entry open to Canadians;** annual; established 1975; originally established 1937 as GOVERNOR-GENERAL'S MEDALS FOR LITERATURE. Purpose: to honor literary excellence without sacrificing popular appeal. Sponsored by CAA. Supported by Harlequin Enterprises Ltd of Toronto. Publish *Canadian Author & Bookman* (quarterly). Also sponsor Vicki Metcalf Award, Fiction Book, Poetry, Play-Script Contests.

BOOK CONTEST: **Nonfiction,** published during current calendar year, 5 copies.

AWARDS: Silver Medal and $1000.

JUDGING: By trustees appointed by CAA National Executive. May withhold award.

ENTRY FEE: None.

DEADLINES: Entry, December. Awards, Spring.

154

National Book League Literary Prizes
B. A. Buckley, Publicity Officer
Book House, 45 East Hill
London SW18 2QZ, ENGLAND
Tel: 01-870-9055

October-January

International; **entry restricted to U.K. publishers of British Commonwealth, Eire, Pakistan, South African citizen authors;** annual; established 1942 (Rhys), 1976 (Jewish Chronicle), 1980 (Cook Travel). Sponsored by National Book League and Booker McConnell Ltd (founded 1969). Also sponsor Fiction Book Contests. Second contact (Jewish Chronicle): G. D. Paul, 25 Furnival Street, London EZ4A 1JT England.

BOOK CONTEST: **Young Author Nonfiction** *John Llewelyn Rhys Prize),* published during previous calendar year; by British Commonwealth author under 30; 5 copies.
Jewish Theme Nonfiction *(Jewish Chronicle-Harold H. Wingate Prize),* published before March current year; by author living in British Commonwealth, Eire, South Africa, Israel.
Irish-European Theme *(Christopher Ewart-Biggs Prize).* Requirements, restrictions, not specified.
Social Concern Nonfiction *(Manchester Oddfellows Prize),* first published in English August previous to July current year; by British Commonwealth, Eire, Pakistan, South African citizen. Book pamphlet of 10,-000 words minimum.
Travel Nonfiction *(Thomas Cook Travel Prizes),* published November previous to October current year. Categories: Travel Book, Guide Book.
Journalism *(George Orwell Memorial Prize).* Requirements, restrictions, not specified.

AWARDS: In English pounds: Rhys, 500. Jewish Chronicle-Wingate, 1500. Ewart-Biggs, 1500. 2 Oddfellows, 500 each. Cook Travel Book, 500 and touring exhibition. Cook Guide Book, 500 and touring exhibition. Orwell Memorial, 750.

JUDGING: By 3-5, each award.

ENTRY FEE: None.

DEADLINES: Entry, March (Jewish Chronicle-Wingate), June (Rhys), September (Cook), others not specified. Awards, October (Oddfellows), December-January (Cook, Jewish Chronicle-Wingate), others not specified.

155

Yorkshire Post Book of the Year
Yorkshire Post
Richard Douro
P.O. Box 168
Leeds LS1 1RF, ENGLAND
April

National; **entry restricted to U.K. publishers;** annual; established 1964 (Book of the Year), 1965 (First Work), 1972 (Art-Music). Held at Literary Luncheon in Leeds. Sponsored by Yorkshire Post Newspapers Ltd. Also sponsor Fiction Book Contests and Literary Luncheons for Yorkshire writers.

BOOK CONTEST: Nonfiction (Book of the Year).
First Nonfiction (First Work), by new author.
Art-Music (Art-Music).

ELIGIBILITY: Published (or due for publication) by publisher based in United Kingdom during previous-current year. 3 entries maximum per publisher. Submit review cuttings. No translations, reissues, scientific or technical books.

AWARDS: Yorkshire Post Book of the Year, 400 pounds First, 250 pounds Second Prize (one to be Fiction). Best First Work, 350 pounds First, 150 pounds Runner-up Prize. Music, 350 pounds. Art, 350 pounds.

JUDGING: By panel.

ENTRY FEE: None.

DEADLINES: Entry, November (Book of the Year), January (First Work, Art-Music). Winners announced, April.

156

Wattie Book of the Year Award
Book Publishers Association of New Zealand (BPANZ)
Gerard E. Reid, Director
P.O. Box 78-071
Grey Lynn, Auckland 2, NEW ZEALAND Tel: 09-767-251
September

National; **entry restricted to New Zealand BPANZ members;** annual; established 1968. Wattie Book of the Year Award of $4000 First, $2500 Second, $1000 Third to **New Zealand Fiction-Nonfiction Book** authors; scrolls to publishers. Named after Sir James Wattie, prominent industrialist, philanthropist, founder of Wattie Industries. Purpose: to recognize, award authorship and production of quality New Zealand books. Sponsored and supported by Wattie Industries and BPANZ. Recognized by New Zealand Book Publishers Association, Booksellers Association, Book Trade Organisation. Average statistics: 65 entries, 10 semifinalists, 3 awards, 200 attendance. Held in Auckland, Wellington, Christchurch, or Hastings (by rotation). Tickets: $20. Awards, September.

| 157 |

**Central News Agency (CNA)
Literary Award**
M. Jennings, Secretary
P.O. Box 9380
Johannesburg, REPUBLIC OF
SOUTH AFRICA Tel: 838-8161

April

National; **entry restricted to South African citizens, residents (nomination by publishers);** annual; established 1961. R3500 award each to **English and Afrikaans Books,** including Biography, History, Travel published during calendar year. Publishers submit 4 copies each entry, brief biography. Purpose: to foster creative writing by South African authors. Sponsored by CNA. Average statistics: 60 entries. Awards, April.

BOOK (Regional)

About or from a region. Book and Writing, including APPALACHIA, CALIFORNIA, LOUISIANA, NEW JERSEY, NEW ENGLAND, NEW YORK, OHIO, TEXAS, WISCONSIN, WESTERN, MIDWESTERN, ALBERTA, MONTREAL, QUEBEC, AUSTRALIA, SCOTLAND. (Also see other BOOK CATEGORIES.)

| 158 |

Banta Award
Wisconsin Library Association (WLA)
Literary Awards Chairman
1922 University Avenue
Madison, Wisconsin 53705 U.S.A.

Open

State; **entry restricted to Wisconsin authors;** annual; established 1974.

Named after George Banta Company. Purpose: to recognize literary achievement by Wisconsin author. Sponsored by WLA. Supported by George Banta Company, Menasha, Wisconsin. Held at WLA annual conference.

BOOK CONTEST: **Literature-Ideas,** published in previous calendar year by current or previous resident of Wisconsin; 50 pages minimum, copyrighted, contributing to world of literature-ideas. No texts, specialized or technical works.

AWARDS: Banta Award Medal for outstanding literary achievement by Wisconsin author.

JUDGING: By WLA.

ENTRY FEE: None.

DEADLINES: Open.

| 159 |

**Commonwealth Club of California
Literature Medal Award**
Michael J. Brassington, Executive Director
681 Market Street
San Francisco, California 94105
U.S.A. Tel: (415) 362-4903

Spring

State; **entry open to California residents;** annual; established 1931. Purpose: to honor books with exceptional literary merit. Sponsored by Commonwealth Club of California, founded 1903 as public-spirited organization offering educational perspective on important regional, national, international affairs (14,000 members). Have newsmaker luncheons, study sections.

BOOK CONTEST: **Nonfiction,** original, published during previous year, authored by California resident at time of delivery to publisher. Submit 3 copies per entry. Categories: Nonfiction, Children's Nonfiction, California-Related Nonfiction, Any Classification.

AWARDS: Gold Medal: Best Nonfiction. Silver Medals: 2 next best entries, Best Nonfiction for Children Under Age 16, Best California-Related Nonfiction.

JUDGING: By jury. No entries returned.

ENTRY FEE: None.

DEADLINES: Entry, January. Awards, Spring.

160

Friends of American Writers Awards
Mrs. Gene F. Lederer, Chair
755 North Merrill
Park Ridge, Illinois 60068 U.S.A.
Tel: (312) 823-5433

April

Regional; **entry restricted to publishers of Midwestern authors, books;** annual; established 1928. Purpose: to recognize beginning authors in adult and juvenile writing. Sponsored and supported by Friends of American Writers (Chicago, Illinois), founded 1922 to study American literature; encourage, promote high standards among new authors. Held at awards luncheon in Chicago. Second contact: Mrs. William Wiener, 2650 Lakeview Avenue, Chicago, Illinois 60614; tel: (312) 871-5143.

BOOK CONTEST: Midwestern Adult, Juvenile, published during previous year; 2 copies.

ELIGIBILITY: By author of not over 6 books (who has not received monetary award of $1000 or more), and is native, current resident, or previous 5-year resident of Arkansas, Illinois, In-

diana, Iowa, Kansas, Kentucky, Michigan, Minnesota, Missouri, North Dakota, Nebraska, Ohio, Oklahoma, South Dakota, Tennessee, Wisconsin; or author of book whose locale is Midwestern.

AWARDS: Adult: $1000 First, $600 Second Place (may divide) to authors. Juvenile: $500 First, 2 $250 Second Places to authors. 2 $250 or more Distinguished Recognition Award Certificates to publishers.

JUDGING: By 16 judges.

ENTRY FEE: Not specified.

DEADLINES: Entry, December. Awards, April.

161

Golden Spur Awards
Western Writers of America (WWA)
Rex Bundy, Secretary-Treasurer
Route 1, Box 35-H
Victor, Montana 59875 U.S.A.
Tel: (406) 961-3612

June

International; entry open to all; annual; established 1954. Purpose: to encourage high achievement in Western writing. Sponsored and supported by WWA (founded 1951). Held 3-4 days in June at annual WWA Convention, location varies. Publish *The Round-Up* (monthly) about Western writing.

BOOK CONTEST: Western, published in English in previous calendar year, 40,000 words minimum. No anthologies, collections of photographs, drawings, maps, diagrams with limited test. Categories: Nonfiction, For Young People.

SCRIPT CONTEST: Western Motion Picture, Television, first released for public viewing during current calendar year.

ELIGIBILITY: Living authors. Enter one category only, 3 copies each. No subsidized vanity publications.

AWARDS: Golden Spur Award, outstanding each category. Scrolls to 3 finalists, each category. Duplicate awards, if tie.

JUDGING: By 3 judges, each category; based on written text only. No award if less than 10 entries in category. No entries returned.

ENTRY FEE: None.

DEADLINES: Entry, December. Judging, March. Awards, June.

162

John Ben Snow Prize
Syracuse University Press
1011 East Water Street
Syracuse, New York 13210 U.S.A.
Tel: (315) 423-2596

Spring

International; entry open to all; annual; established 1978. Purpose: to encourage books about New York State's unique physical, historical, cultural characteristics. Sponsored by Syracuse University Press.

BOOK CONTEST: About Upstate New York, unpublished; typed double-spaced, notes on separate pages; include any illustrations. Query before submission, stating subject, scope, significance, length, biographical information. No poetry, children's books, theses or dissertations on microfilm, simultaneous submissions, manuscripts under consideration by another publisher.

AWARDS: $1000 John Ben Snow Prize advance to winner against royalties and publication by Syracuse University Press. May accept other meritorious manuscripts for publication.

JUDGING: By selection committee. Based on authenticity, accuracy, readability, importance, rather than formal academic treatment. Direct, personal experience will receive same consideration as scholarly research. May withhold or divide awards.

ENTRY FEE: Not Specified.

DEADLINES: Entry, December. Winner announced, Spring.

163

Joseph Henry Jackson and James D. Phelan Awards
San Francisco Foundation
Martin A. Paley, Director
425 California Street, Suite 1602
San Francisco, California 94104
U.S.A. Tel: (415) 392-0600

June

Regional; **entry restricted to residents of Northern California, Nevada age 20-35 (Jackson); age 20-35 born in California (Phelan);** annual; established 1957 (Jackson), 1936 (Phelan). Named for Joseph Henry Jackson, reviewer-critic-author-editor, and James Duval Phelan, banker-San Francisco mayor-U.S. Senator, who contributed to promoting, aiding the arts. Purpose: to encourage types of writing Jackson was most interested in (Jackson); develop California talent (Phelan). Sponsored and supported by San Francisco Foundation. Also sponsor James D. Phelan Award in Art. Second contact: San Francisco Foundation, 1100 Larkspur Landing Circle, Suite 250, Larkspur, California 94939; tel: (415) 499-1555.

BOOK CONTEST: Nonfiction Prose *(Jackson Award),* unpublished, partly completed; by Northern California, Nevada resident for 3 consecutive years immediately prior to entry date; typed on 8 1/2x11-inch paper.

Require proof of age, residence.

WRITING CONTEST: Nonfiction Prose *(Phelan Award).* unpublished, incomplete, by authors born in California. Other requirements same as for Book.

ELIGIBILITY: Entrants may enter both contests but are eligible for one award.

AWARDS: $2000, each award. Honorable Mentions.

JUDGING: By 3 judges. May withhold awards. Manuscripts become property of sponsor after July. Not responsible for loss or damage.

ENTRY FEE: None. Entrant pays postage (include SASE).

DEADLINES: Entry, January. Winners announced, June.

| 164 |

Louisiana Literary Award
Louisiana Library Association (LLA)
Chris Thomas, Executive Director
P.O. Box 131
Baton Rouge, Louisiana 70821
U.S.A.

Periodic

International; **entry restricted (selection by LLA);** periodic. Medallion to **Book about Louisiana.** Sponsored by LLA.

| 165 |

New Jersey Authors Awards
New Jersey Institute of Technology
Dr. Herman A. Estrin, Director
315 Henry Street
Scotch Plains, New Jersey 07076
U.S.A. Tel: (201) 889-7633

April

Regional; **entry restricted to New Jersey, New York, Pennsylvania au-**thors **(nominated by New Jersey publishers);** annual; established 1967. Purpose: to award New Jersey authors for their published work. Sponsored by New Jersey Institute of Technology, Division of Continuing Education and Department of Humanities. Average statistics: 100 entrants, 100 awards, 400 attendance. Held at annual New Jersey Authors Luncheon. Tickets: $10-$15. Also sponsor New Jersey Writers Conference, Annual Poetry Contest, and Technical Communications Skills Workshop.

BOOK AWARD: New Jersey Author, published.

ELIGIBILITY: Publishers complete nomination for each New Jersey author.

AWARDS: Citation. Winners serve as consultants during New Jersey Writers Conference.

JUDGING: By publishers and director of New Jersey Writers Conference.

ENTRY FEE: None.

DEADLINES: Entry, June. Judging, September-March. Awards, April.

| 166 |

North Carolina Literary and Historical Association Literary Competition
109 East Jones Street
Raleigh, North Carolina 27611
U.S.A. Tel: (919) 829-7442

November

State; **entry open to North Carolina;** annual. Purpose: to stimulate interest in North Carolina literature. Sponsored by North Carolina Literary and Historical Association, founded 1900 to foster, encourage literary activity in literature, history of North Carolina. Supported by Society of Mayflower Descendants in North

Carolina (Mayflower Cup), Historical Book Club of North Carolina (Raleigh Award; Margaret Hites, President, 1008 Bradbury Drive, Greensboro, North Carolina 27410), Roanoke-Chowan Group (Roanoke-Chowan Award), North Carolina Division of American Association of University Women (AAUW Award). Also sponsor annual Culture Week, Christopher Crittenden Memorial Award (for preservation of North Carolina history), Tar Heel Junior Historian Contest (for local history projects), R.D.W. Conner Award (for article in *North Carolina Historical Review),* Undergraduate Student Award (for research paper on North Carolina history). Publish *Carolina Comments* and *North Carolina Historical Review* (quarterly).

BOOK CONTEST: Nonfiction *(Mayflower Award),* published June previous to July current year, original, 3 copies. No technical, scientific works.

Juvenile *(AAUW Award).* Requirements same as for Book.

ELIGIBILITY: Authors maintaining North Carolina legal, physical residence for 3 years preceding entry date.

AWARDS: Mayflower Cup Award for Nonfiction. AAUW Award for Juvenile Literature.

JUDGING: Based on creative, imaginative quality, style excellence, universality, relevance to North Carolina.

ENTRY FEE: None.

DEADLINES: Entry, July. Awards, November.

167

Ohioana Book Awards

Martha Kinney Cooper Ohioana Library Association
James P. Barry, Director
Room 1105 Ohio Department Building
65 South Front Street
Columbus, Ohio 42315 U.S.A.
Tel: (614) 466-3831

Fall

International; **entry restricted to Ohioan authors-subjects;** annual; established 1929. Purpose: to honor books by Ohio Authors or about Ohio-Ohioans (Nonfiction). Sponsored by 1400-member Martha Kinney Cooper Ohioana Library Association, established 1929 to preserve-promote Ohio literary, musical, cultural heritage. Also sponsor Distinguished Service Citations, Career Medals for Ohio authors, artists, composers, Fiction-Poetry Book Contest. Publish *Ohioana Quarterly* magazine. Held during Ohioana Day Luncheon in Fall.

BOOK CONTEST: Ohio Nonfiction, published by Ohioan (born or lived 5 years in Ohio) on any subject, or by non-Ohioan about Ohio-Ohioans; 2 copies.

AWARDS: Ohioana Book Awards. Florence Roberts Head Memorial Book Award. Awards are certificates and medals.

JUDGING: Committee of 4-5.

ENTRY FEE: None.

DEADLINES: Judging, Spring. Awards, Fall.

168

Sarah Josepha Hale Award
Richards Library
Jean Michie, Librarian
58 North Main Street
Newport, New Hampshire 03773
U.S.A. Tel: (603) 863-3430

August

Regional; **entry restricted to New England (nomination by Library);** annual; established 1956. Bronze Medal to Individual for **Literature-Letters associated with New England.** Named after Sarah Josepha Hale, native of Newport and editor. Sponsored and supported by Friends of Richards Library (founded 1888). Award, August.

169

Texas Institute of Letters Literary Awards
Marshall Terry, Secretary-Treasurer
SMU Box 3143
Dallas, Texas 75275 U.S.A.

March-April

International; **entry restricted to Texas authors-subjects;** annual; established 1946 (Collins), 1960 (Dallas Library). Sponsored by Texas Institute of Letters, founded 1936. Also sponsor Fiction Book and Short Story Contests.

BOOK CONTEST: **Texas Various,** 3 copies. Categories: Nonfiction, General Knowledge, Journalism, For Children, Book Design.

NEWSPAPER-MAGAZINE CONTEST: **Texas Journalism,** 3 copies.

ELIGIBILITY: Published during previous year, by Texas author (born, present resident, or spent formative years in Texas) or on Texas subject.

AWARDS: $1000 Carr P. Collins

Award, Best Nonfiction. $500 Friends of Dallas Public Library Award, Contribution to General Knowledge. $500 Stanley Walker Journalism Award. $200 Steck-Vaughn Award, Book for Children (including fiction entries, formerly known as Cokesbury Book Store Award). $250 Collectors' Institute Award, Book Design (including fiction entries).

JUDGING: By 3 judges each category. Preference to books on Texas or Southwest.

ENTRY FEE: None.

DEADLINES: Entry, January. Awards, March-April.

170

W. D. Weatherford Award Competition
Berea College
Thomas Parrish, Chairman
Appalachian Center
College P.O. Box 2336
Berea, Kentucky 40404 U.S.A.
Tel: (606) 986-9341, ext. 513,453

April

National; **entry open to U.S.;** annual; established 1970. Named for Dr. W. D. Weatherford, Appalachian author. Sponsored by Appalachian Center, Hutchins Library of Berea College. Also sponsor Appalachian Studies Fellowships.

BOOK CONTEST: **Appalachia,** published during previous year; single or series, any length; 1 copy.

WRITING CONTEST: **Appalachia,** published during previous year (article, story); any length; 1 copy.

ELIGIBILITY: Writing of any kind, tone, point of view.

AWARDS: $500 to book, shorter

piece illustrating problems, personalities, unique qualities of Appalachian South. $200 Special Award to work or ongoing works making special contribution to region.

JUDGING: By 7 judges.

ENTRY FEE: None.

DEADLINES: Entry, December. Awards, April.

171

Western Heritage Awards
National Cowboy Hall of Fame and Western Heritage Center
1700 Northeast 63rd Street
Oklahoma City, Oklahoma 73111
U.S.A. Tel: (405) 478-2250

April

International; entry open to all; annual; established 1961. Purpose: to honor drama and heritage of Old West. Sponsored by and held at National Cowboy Hall of Fame and Western Heritage Center (world's largest Western lore exhibit), founded 1965 to perpetuate Western traditions in authentic, artistic exhibits. Also sponsor music category, Western Performer's Hall of Fame Awards (to 1 living, 1 deceased Western contributor).

BOOK CONTEST: Western Non-fiction, published in previous 2 years, 6 copies. One category per entry. Categories: Nonfiction, Juvenile, Art Book.

MAGAZINE CONTEST: Western Article. Requirements same as for Book.

AWARDS: Wrangler Trophies (replica of Charles Russell sculpture) for Excellence in Western Achievement, each category.

JUDGING: By panel, based on artistic merit, integrity, achievement in portraying spirit of Western pioneers. May change categories, withhold awards. Sponsor retains all winners for permanent collection.

ENTRY FEE: None. Entrant pays postage.

DEADLINES: Entry, February. Event, April.

172

"The Age" Book of the Year Award
Stuart Sayers, Literary Editor
250 Spencer Street
P.O. Box 257C G.P.O.
Melbourne 3001, AUSTRALIA
Tel: (03) 600421, ext. 2232

November

National; **entry restricted to Australian citizens;** annual; established 1974. Award to **Australian Identity-Concerns Book,** including Biography, Historical, Scholarly works, published November-October award year. No children's books, natural history, anthologies. Submit 4 copies each entry, 4 maximum per publisher. Purpose: to encourage, promote Australian writing of literary merit. Sponsored by *The Age.* Awards, November.

173

Alberta Culture Literary Awards
Alberta Culture, Film and Literary Arts
John Patrick Gillese, Director
12th Floor, CN Tower
1004-104 Avenue
Edmonton, Alberta T5J 0K5
CANADA Tel: (403) 427-2554

Spring

Regional; **entry restricted to Alberta residents;** annual; established 1972 (Nonfiction, Regional History),

1980 (For Young People). Purpose: to find, launch outstanding Alberta authors. Sponsored and supported by Alberta Culture, General Publishing, Clarke Irwin Publishing (For Young People). Have writers' workshops, correspondence courses, consultative and financial services to Alberta authors-publishers. Publish *Alberta Authors Bulletin* (bimonthly newsletter). Also sponsor Play and First Novel Contests, Literary Grants.

BOOK CONTEST: **Alberta for Young People,** unpublished; any subject; 1 entry; typed double-spaced. Categories: For Young Adults (to age 16; 40,000 words average); For Younger Readers (age 8-12; 12-20,000 words).
Alberta Nonfiction, published during current calendar year; of general interest (human drama, personalized adventure, biography, autobiography, history, animal-nature lore, humor); 50,000 words minimum; in English; 2 copies. No textbooks, educational or highly specialized books.
Alberta Regional History, published during current calendar year; 1 or group of authors; 25,000 words minimum; in English; 2 copies.

ELIGIBILITY: Canadian citizens or landed immigrants, living minimum 18 months in preceding 2 years in Alberta. Cannot enter both Nonfiction and Regional History Competitions.

AWARDS: $1500   Nonfiction Award. $1000 Regional History Award. $2500 Writing for Young People Award (including fiction-nonfiction). $500 award, $500 advance to other For Young People entries accepted for publications.

JUDGING: By 3 judges. Regional History based on readability, human interest, story-telling success, general literary excellence. May withhold awards. 1 Regional History copy kept

for Cultural Development Library (other returned).

ENTRY FEE: None. Sponsor pays return postage (registered mail).

DEADLINES: Entry,   December. Awards, Spring.

174

Grand Prize for Literature of the City of Montreal
Greater Montreal Council of Arts
Ferdinand F. Biondi, Secretary General
2, Complexe Desjardins
C.P. 129
Montreal, Quebec H5B 1E6 CANADA
Tel: (514) 872-2074, 866-4114

April

International; **entry restricted to Montreal published authors;** annual; established   1965.   Sponsored   by Greater Montreal Council of Arts, established 1956 to subsidize nonprofit artistic groups in Montreal (communication-film, literature, theater, music, visual-plastic art, ballet). Held during Montreal International Book Fair at Centre Pierre Charbonneau in the Olympic Complex. Also sponsor Fiction Book Contest.

BOOK CONTEST: **Montreal Published,** first published during previous year in Montreal, 5 copies. No directories, encyclopedias, index compilations, travel guides, instructional or self-help books, cookbooks, industrial or business histories, books containing advertising or previously published contents, educational texts, exhibit catalogs. Categories: Memoirs, Biographies, History; Philosophy, Essays, Science; English Language.

AWARDS: $3000 Grand Prize for Literature (includes fiction).

JUDGING: Preliminary by 3 judges,

each category; final by 7 judges. Judges keep entries.

ENTRY FEE: Not specified.

DEADLINES: Entry,   January. Award, April.

| 175 |

Delegation General of Quebec Prizes Association
France-Quebec Association
54 Avenue de Saxe
75015 Paris, FRANCE Tel: 783-31-34

November

National; **entry restricted (selection by sponsors);** annual; established 1961 (France-Canada, 1965 (Jean-Hamelin). France-Canada Prize of 2000 francs to **Book Published in France-Canada by Quebec-French Canadian Author** (sponsored by France-Canada Association). Jean-Hamelin France-Quebec Prize of 4000 francs to **Book Published in Quebec-France by Quebec Author** (sponsored by French Language Writers Association). Supported by Quebec Government, City of Paris. Awards, November.

| 176 |

Scottish Arts Counci; Literature Awards
Tim Mason, Director
19 Charlotte Square
Edinburgh EH2 4DF, SCOTLAND
Tel: 031-226-6051

January

International; **entry restricted to publishers;** annual. Sponsored by Scottish Arts Council. Also sponsor biennial Neil Gunn International Fellowship (established 1973) to international fiction writers (not open to entry, selection by Council); 4000 pound one-year Writers Fellowships at Dun-

dee, Glasgow Universities.

BOOK CONTEST: Scottish-Scotland, published November of previous to October of current year; of Scottish interest or by Scottish citizen, resident author; 1 copy. Require biography. Categories: By Established Author, First By New Author.

AWARDS: Scottish Arts Council Book Awards, 500 pounds each.

JUDGING: By writer-critic reading panel. Based on literary merit.

ENTRY FEE: None.

DEADLINES: Awards, January.

BOOK (Religious, Religious History, Humanitarian)

Book, Article, including CATHOLIC, CHRISTIAN, CHURCH, MARIOLOGY, HUMAN VALUE, SOCIAL EQUALITY. (Also see other BOOK.)

| 177 |

American Catholic Historical Association (ACHA) Writing Prizes
Rev. Robert Triscc, Secretary
Mullen Library 305
Catholic University of America
Washington, District of Columbia
20064 U.S.A. Tel: (202) 635-5079

December

International; **entry open to U.S., Canadian citizens, residents;** annual; established 1944 (Shea Prize), 1973 (Marraro Prize). Purpose: (Shea) to stimulate research, writing on history of Catholic Church; (Marraro) recognize, support historians of Italy, Italo-

American relations. Sponsored by ACHA, established 1919 to promote deeper, widespread knowledge of Catholic Church history, advancement of historical scholarship among American Catholics. Average statistics: 25 entries. Held during ACHA and AHA general meeting.

BOOK CONTEST: Catholic Church History *(Shea Prize)*, published during 12 months ending September; in English; by citizens, residents of U.S., Canada.
Italian History, Italo-American History-Relations *(Marraro Prize)*. Requirements, restrictions same as for Book.

ARTICLE CONTEST: Catholic Church History *(Guilday Prize,* first-published article of author's career, accepted for publication in *Catholic Historical Review* during 12 months ending September; 30 typed pages maximum. No historical book or learned journal article published authors.

AWARDS: $300 John Gilmary Shea Prize. $500 Howard R. Marraro Prize. $100 Peter Guilday Prize.

JUDGING: By 3 judges, each category. No entries returned.

ENTRY FEE: None.

DEADLINES: Entry, October (Shea), September (Marraro). Awards, December.

| 178 |

Blue Ridge Christian Writers Conference Award for Excellence in Literature
Yvonne Lehman, Director
Walker Cove Road
P.O. Box 188
Black Mountain, North Carolina
28711 U.S.A. Tel: (704) 669-8421

August

International; **entry restricted to former Conference students;** annual; established 1975. Plaque, free conference tuition for **Christian Book or Article.** Formerly called NORTH CAROLINA CHRISTIAN WRITERS CONFERENCE to 1977. Purpose: to bring writers together with editors, publishers; encourage, instruct writers; realize all talents are from God. sponsored by Blue Ridge Christian Writers Conference. Average statistics: 70-80 entrants, 3-4 countries, 1-5 winners. Held at YMCA Blue Ridge Assembly, Black Mountain for 5 days. Have workshops, group sessions, lodging, meals, classrooms, chapel, bookstore. Tuition: $80. Awards, August.

| 179 |

Brewer Prize Contest
American Society of Church History
William B. Miller, Secretary-Treasurer
305 East Country Club Lane
Wallingford, Pennsylvania 19086
U.S.A.

Spring

International; entry open to all; annual. Sponsored by American Society of Church History (founded 1888).

BOOK CONTEST: **Church History,** unpublished, preference to Congregationalism history.

AWARDS: Frank S. and Elizabeth D. Brewer Prize, $2000 for publication of winning manuscript.

ENTRY FEE: None. Entrant pays postage (include SASE).

DEADLINES: Entry, December. Award, Spring.

| 180 |

Bross Prize
Bross Foundation
Ron Miller, Department of Religion
Lake Forest College
Lake Forest, Illinois 60045 U.S.A.
Tel: (312) 234-3100, ext. 477

December

International; entry open to all; awarded every 10 years; established 1879. Named for William Bross, pioneer Chicago churchman, businessman who helped found Lake Forest College. Purpose: to recognize talent that illustrates relationship of science or knowledge to Christianity. Average statistics: 19 entries, 4 countries. Held at and sponsored by Lake Forest College (Sheridan and College Roads, Lake Forest, Illinois 60045), chartered 1857. Supported by Bross Foundation, founded 1879.

BOOK CONTEST: Christian Religion, unpublished, 50,000 words minimum; on Christianity or related discipline; in English or English translation; 3 copies.

AWARDS: Bross Prize, $20,000 for best book, treatise on relationship of any discipline (science, literature, history, modern life) and Christian religion. Winner asked to give lecture.

JUDGING: By 3 judges. Sponsor owns copyright.

ENTRY FEE: None. Entrant pays postage (include SASE).

DEADLINES: Entry, award, December.

| 181 |

Christopher Awards
The Christophers
Peggy Flanagan, Coordinator
12 East 48th Street
New York, New York 10017 U.S.A.
Tel: (212) 759-4050

January

International; entry open to all; annual; established 1949. Purpose: to recognize individuals producing works promoting sound values, with realistic, hopeful view of man and world; replace fault-finding with positive action. Motto: "Better to light one candle than to curse the darkness." Sponsored by The Christophers, founded 1945 as nonprofit mass media organization based on Judeo-Christian concept of service to God and humanity. Average statistics: 8 adult, 5 juvenile awards. Held in New York City. Sponsor publications, nationally syndicated TV-radio series, daily and weekly newspaper columns.

BOOK CONTEST: Human value adult, juvenile, published in previous year; original; 2 copies.

AWARDS: Bronze Medallions.

JUDGING: By 2-level panel of "grass-roots" judges and experts. Based on affirmation of human spirit, artistic or technical proficiency, public acceptance. All entries reviewed in entirety. Not responsible for loss or damage.

ENTRY FEE: None.

DEADLINES: Entry, open. Awards, January.

| 182 |

Conference on Christianity and Literature (CCL) Book of the Year Award
Editor of Christianity and Literature
Calvin College
Grand Rapids, Michigan 49506
U.S.A. Tel: (616) 949-4000, ext. 264

December

International; **entry restricted (nomination by members);** annual; established 1970. Sponsored by CCL, founded 1956 as international organization for understanding relationship between Christianity and creation, study, teaching of literature. Also sponsor CCL Student Writing Contest. Second contact: Roy Battenhouse, English Department, Indiana University, Bloomington, Indiana 47401.

BOOK CONTEST: Christian Scholarly, published previous August-September; dealing with relationship of Christian faith to literature.

AWARDS: CCL Book of the Year Award Certificate.

ENTRY FEE: None.

DEADLINES: Entry, September. Award, December.

183

Marian Library Medal
Marian Library
Rev. Theodore A. Koehler, S.M.
University of Dayton
300 College Park Avenue
Dayton, Ohio 45469 U.S.A. Tel: (513) 229-4214

Periodic

International; entry open to all; quadrennial; established 1954. Formerly annual award to best book on Virgin Mary in English (to 1967). Purpose: to encourage original research, publishing in Mariology (study of Blessed Virgin Mary) on highest scientific level. Sponsored by Marian Library, University of Dayton. Publish *Marian Library Newsletter* (irregular, free).

BOOK CONTEST: Mariology (Blessed Virgin Mary), published in any language, any length.

ARTICLE CONTEST: Mariology, series of scientific articles, published, in any language, any length.

AWARDS: Gold Medal, Best Book or Article Series, to author whose work has done most to advance scientific study of Mariology.

JUDGING: By panel of scholars and library director.

ENTRY FEE: Not specified.

DEADLINES: Not specified.

184

National Religious Book Awards
Religious Book Review
Charles A. Roth, Publisher
P.O. Box 1331
Roslyn Heights, New York 11577
U.S.A. Tel: (516) 621-7242

March

National; **entry open to U.S.;** annual. Formerly called RELIGIOUS BOOK AWARDS. Purpose: to acknowledge contribution religious book publishing makes to American society. Sponsored by Religious Book Review, Omni Communications.

BOOK CONTEST: Religious, published during previous year, original; 4 copies (Scholarly), 3 copies (other categories). Categories: Inspirational, Scholarly, Community Life (Social Awareness), Children-Youth.

AWARDS: Omni Trophy to author, publisher (translator, illustrator if applicable), each category. Seals for book covers. NRBA Plaques to Runners-Up.

JUDGING: By 3-4 reviewer, educator, editor, author judges, each category.

ENTRY FEE: $15 each.

DEADLINES: Entry, December. Finalists announced, February. Awards, March.

185

Religious Arts Guild Frederic G. Melcher Book Award
Unitarian Universalist Association (UUA)
Barbara M. Hutchins, Executive Secretary
25 Beacon Street
Boston, Massachusetts 02108 U.S.A.
Tel: (617) 742-2100

Summer

National; **entry restricted to U.S. publishers;** annual. Purpose: to promote religious liberalism. Sponsored by UUA. Have Anthem loan library. Publish *UU World* (130,000 circulation) religious drama, worship services. Also sponsor $100 Try Works Prize for creative performable Unitarian Universalist Church service celebrating great occasion.

BOOK CONTEST: Religious Liberalism, published in U.S. during previous year, submission by publishers only.

AWARDS: $1000, Bronze Medallion for Best Contribution to Religious Liberalism.

ENTRY FEE: None.

DEADLINES: Entry, January. Awards, Summer.

186

Robert F. Kennedy Book Awards
Coates Redmon, Executive Director
4014 49th Street N.W.
Washington, District of Columbia
20016 U.S.A. Tel: (202) 362-2410

May

National; **entry open to U.S.;** annual; established 1981. Purpose: to honor author whose work faithfully and forcefully reflects Robert Kennedy's purposes. Sponsored by RFK Journalism Awards Committee. Supported by Arthur Schlesinger, Jr., endowment from his *Robert Kennedy and His Times.* Also sponsor Robert F. Kennedy Journalism Awards.

BOOK CONTEST: Social Equality, published in U.S. previous year. Require 3 copies, description letter.

AWARDS: $2500 First Prize.

JUDGING: By 5 authorities in social affairs.

ENTRY FEE: None.

DEADLINES: Entry, February. Event, May.

187

Collins Biennial Religious Book Award
William Collins Sons & Company, Ltd
Lady Collins
14 St. James's Place
London SW1, ENGLAND Tel: (01) 493-7070

November

National; **entry open to British Commonwealth and Eire;** biennial; established 1969. Purpose: to reward distinguished contribution to relevance of Christianity in modern world. Sponsored and supported by William Collins Sons & Company, Ltd, Publishers. Held in London.

BOOK CONTEST: Modern Chirstianity, published between July of previous 2 years and June of current year by citizen of United Kingdom, the Commonwealth, Republic of Ireland, or South Africa. Categories: Science, Ethics, Sociology, Philosophy, Psychology, Other Religions.

AWARDS: 1000 pounds Religious Book Award.

JUDGING: By 4 judges. Based on scope, scholarship, provocative ideas and readability to laypersons. Not responsible for loss or damage.

ENTRY FEE: None.

DEADLINES: Entry, June. Judging, September. Award, November.

| 188 |

Thomas-Mann Award
Lubeck Office of Culture
Rathaushof
2400 Lubeck 1, WEST GERMANY
(FRG) Tel: 0451-1224102
Triennial

International; **entry restricted (nomination by judges)**; triennial; established 1975. 10,000 DM to Author for **Humanitarian Literary Works.** Sponsored by Hansestadt Lubeck.

BOOK (Scientific, Technical, Medical, Science History)

Book, Article, Essay, Monograph, including AERONAUTICS-ASTRONAUTICS, CARTOGRAPHY, CHILDREN'S SCIENCE, GEOGRAPHY, NATURE, PHARMACY, PHYSICS-ASTRONOMY, TECHNOLOGY. (Also see other BOOK.)

| 189 |

American Institute of Aeronautics and Astronautics (AIAA) Literature Awards

Robert Shapiro, Manager, Honors & Awards Program
1290 Avenue of the Americas
New York, New York 10019 U.S.A.
Spring

International; entry open to all; annual; established 1950 (Pendray Award), 1969 (History Award). Purpose: to give professional recognition for contribution to aeronautics-astronautics history, literature. Pendray named for past president of American Rocket Society, predecessor of AIAA. Sponsored by AIAA. Also sponsor National Student Awards (1 undergraduate, 1 graduate) to AIAA members; AIAA Publications Awards.

BOOK CONTEST: Aeronautics-Astronautics History *(History Award)*, unpublished as book; in English; typed double-spaced; 75,000 words maximum; dealing with science, technology impact of aeronautics-astronautics on society. May by multiauthored (but only 1 award given).

Aeronautical-Astronautical Literature *(Pendray Award)*. Prefer completion in previous 3 years. Submit 5 copies. Require biographical data, publications-patent list, literature references, 3-5 recommendation letters.

AWARDS: History Manuscript Award, Pendray Aerospace Literature Award. Each get AIAA Bronze Medal, Citation Certificate, possible publication.

JUDGING: By AIAA-member specialists. May withhold awards. Not responsible for loss or damage.

ENTRY FEE: Not specified. Entrant pays postage (include SASE).

DEADLINES: Entry, June (History), July (Pendray). Awards, Spring.

190

American Institute of Physics (AIP)-U.S. Steel Foundation Science Writing Award in Physics and Astronomy
Public Relations Division
335 East 45 Street
New York, New York 10017 U.S.A.
Tel: (212) 661-9404, ext. 522

Spring, Fall

International; **entry restricted to U.S., Canadian, Mexican citizen-resident journalists, scientists, and AIP members;** annual. Purpose: to stimulate, recognize distinguished writing improving public understanding of physics-astronomy. Sponsored by AIP and U.S. Steel Foundation. For Journalists: held at National Association of Science Writers Washington Group Luncheon during American Physical Society spring meeting. For Scientists and AIP members: held during Corporate Associates of American Institute of Physics fall meeting.

BOOK CONTEST: Physics-Astronomy, published, in English, for general public. Require 9 copies (not photocopies).

BOOKLET CONTEST: Physics-Astronomy. Requirements same as for Book.

ARTICLE CONTEST: Physics-Astronomy. Requirements same as for Book.

ELIGIBILITY: Published in U.S., Canada, Mexico between June previous, May current year for scientists and AIP members; between January previous, December current year for journalists; by citizens, permanent residents of U.S., Canada, Mexico. 3 entries maximum per author (series considered single entry). No professional scientific, technical, trade publications. No AIP, U.S. Steel Corporation or Foundation employees.

AWARDS: $1500, Certificate, Moebius Strip Trophy. Travel-accommodation expenses paid to winner. Certificate to publisher.

JUDGING: By committee.

ENTRY FEE: Not specified.

DEADLINES: Entry, January (for journalists), June (for scientists, AIP members). Awards, Spring, Fall.

191

American Institute of the History of Pharmacy Writing Awards
John Parascandola, Director
Pharmacy Building
Madison, Wisconsin 53706 U.S.A.
Tel: (608) 262-4939

Spring

International; **entry open to all (Urdang), to U.S. citizens (Kremers);** annual; established 1953 (Urdang), 1962 (Kremers). Sponsored by American Institute of the History of Pharmacy. Also sponsor Certificates of Commendation (founded 1966) for contributions to pharmacy history.

BOOK CONTEST: Pharmacy History, published or unpublished, original, about historical-historicosocial aspects of pharmacy. Categories: International *(Urdang Medal),* by U.S. Citizens *(Kremers Award).*

ARTICLE CONTEST: Pharmacy History, single or series, included in book categories.

AWARDS: George Urdang Medal, Edward Kremers Award.

JUDGING: Based on research, skill of interpretation, presentation.

ENTRY FEE: None.

DEADLINES: Entry, November. Awards, Spring.

192

American Medical Writers Association (AMWA) Medical Book Awards
Harold F. Osborne
5272 River Road, Suite 370
Bethesda, Maryland 20016 U.S.A.
Tel: (301) 986-9119

September-October

International; entry open to all; annual; established 1973. Purpose: to improve medical communication by review, recognition of outstanding medical literature. Sponsored by AMWA, international organization dedicated to advancement, improvement of medical communications. Held in various U.S. cities at AMWA annual meetings. Have workshops, seminars. Publish *Medical Communication*, freelance directory.

BOOK CONTEST: Medical, published first editions only (possibly substantially reorganized subsequent editions); 2 copies. No annually updated or series volumes. Categories: For Physicians, Allied Health Professionals, Trade Books.

AWARDS: AMMY Plaque, Best each category. Honorable Mentions. Winners invited to awards luncheon.

ENTRY FEE: None.

DEADLINES: Entry, March. Meetings, September-October.

193

Dexter Prize
Society for the History of Technology
Dr. Carroll Pursell, Secretary
History Department
University of California, Santa Barbara

Santa Barbara, California 93106
U.S.A. Tel: (404) 894-3198

Annual

International; entry open to all; annual. Sponsored by Society for the History of Technology (Brooke Hindle, President). Also sponsor Leonardo da Vinci Medal for career service to field, Usher Prize for article *Technology and Culture Quarterly Journal* (Melvin Kranzberg, Editor-in-Chief, Department of Social Sciences, Georgia Institute of Technology, Atlanta, Georgia 30332; tel: (404) 894-3198).

BOOK CONTEST: History of Technology, published in past 3 years.

AWARDS: $1000 Dexter Prize.

ENTRY FEE: None.

DEADLINES: Open.

194

Geographic Society of Chicago Publication Awards
Mildred F. Mitchell, Executive Secretary
7 South Dearborn Street
Chicago, Illinois 60603 U.S.A.
Tel: (312) 726-5293

Spring

International; entry open to all; annual; established 1951. Purpose: to encourage broader public interest in geography. Sponsored by Geographic Society of Chicago.

BOOK CONTEST: Geography, published.

MONOGRAPH CONTEST: Geography, published.

ARTICLE CONTEST: Geography, published.

ELIGIBILITY: Published during previous calendar year, of popular nature about geography.

AWARDS: 1-3 hand-made Scroll Awards.

JUDGING: By committee. Based on scientific merit, popular appeal.

ENTRY FEE: None.

DEADLINES: Entry, January. Awards, Spring.

195

History of Science Society (HSS) Writing Awards
Prof. Sally Gregory Kohlstedt
History Department, Maxwell School
Syracuse University
Syracuse, New York 13210 U.S.A.

December

International; **entry open to U.S., Canada;** annual; established 1955 (Schuman), 1958 (Pfizer). Sponsored by HSS. Supported by Charles Pfizer & Company. Held at annual HSS meeting.

BOOK CONTEST: Science History *(Pfizer Award)*, published in previous year.

ESSAY CONTEST: Science History *(Schuman Award)*, original; based on cultural influences; approximately 5000 words by graduate, undergraduate student in American, Canadian college, university or institute of technology; 1 entry maximum. No medical subjects.

AWARDS: Pfizer Award, $1500 and Medal. Schuman Award, $500.

ENTRY FEE: None.

DEADLINES: Entry, April (Pfizer), June (Schuman). Awards, December.

196

Hugo Science Fiction Achievement Awards
Howard DeVore
4705 Weddel Street
Dearborn, Michigan 48125 U.S.A.

Annual

International; **entry restricted (selection by SF fans);** annual; established 1953. Hugo Awards to **Science Non-Fiction Book, Professional Editor, Fan Writer, Fanzine.** Voted by Science Fiction fans prior to annual convention in September.

197

John Burroughs Medal Award
John Burroughs Memorial
Association
Farida A. Wiley, Secretary-Treasurer
American Museum of Natural History
79 Street at Central Park West
New York, New York 10024 U.S.A.

April

International; entry open to all; annual; established 1926. Named after John Burroughs, naturalist-writer. Sponsored and supported by John Burroughs Memorial Association, founded 1921.

BOOK CONTEST: Nature, published in previous 6 years, in English. No compilations of other's work.

AWARDS: Burroughs Bronze Medal.

JUDGING: Based on originality of observation, conclusion combined with literary quality, statement accuracy. May withhold award.

ENTRY FEE: None.

DEADLINES: Award, April.

| 198 |

Nebenzahl Prize
Hermon Dunlap Smith Center for the
History of Cartography
David Buisseret, Director
Newberry Library
60 West Walton Street
Chicago, Illinois 60610 U.S.A.
Tel: (312) 943-9090

Continuous

International; entry open to all; continuous; established 1978. Purpose: to encourage original work in history of cartography. Sponsored and supported by Mr. and Mrs. Kenneth Nebenzahl. Recognized by Newberry Library. Publish *Mapline* (quarterly journal). Have workshops, conferences.

BOOK CONTEST: Cartography (Map-Chart-Making), original, unpublished, in English; typed double-spaced on 8 1/2x11-inch paper, separately organized notes at end of manuscript. Author responsible for selecting illustrations, obtaining necessary permissions before submitting manuscript.

AWARDS: $1500 and publication by University of Chicago Press in Hermon Dunlap Smith Center for History of Cartography series.

JUDGING: By 5 judges. All entries read in entirety. Smith Center claims exclusive publication right. Not responsible for loss or damage.

ENTRY FEE: None.

DEADLINES: Entry, open. Judging, within 3 months.

| 199 |

New York Academy of Sciences Children's Science Book Awards
Ann E. Collins, Public Relations Director
2 East 63rd Street
New York, New York 10021 U.S.A.
Tel: (212) 838-0230

March

International; entry open to all; annual; established 1972. Purpose: to encourage writing, publishing of science books for children. Sponsored by 28,000-member, 85-country New York Academy of Sciences, founded 1817 to exchange, disseminate scientific information.

BOOK CONTEST: Children's Science, published December previous to November current year. Categories: Younger (for under age 10), Older (age 10-16).

AWARDS: $500 Awards for best general, trade books on science for children, each category. Honorable Mentions. Gold, Silver Seals for dust jackets.

JUDGING: By 10 judges.

ENTRY FEE: None.

DEADLINES: Entry, November. Judging, January. Awards, March.

| 200 |

Robert Troup Paine Prize
Harvard University Press
79 Garden Street
Cambridge, Massachusetts 02138
U.S.A.

Spring

International; entry open to all; quadrennial (next award 1986); established 1962 under will of Dr. Martyn Paine in memory of his son. Theme:

Natural, Social Sciences (varies quadrennially). Sponsored by Harvard University Press. Supported by Robert Troup Paine Publication Fund.

BOOK CONTEST: Natural-Social Science, original, unpublished manuscript, on award-year theme in natural and social sciences; may be single or multiple authored.

AWARDS: $3000, publication by sponsor with royalties.

ENTRY FEE: None.

DEADLINES: Entry, December. Awards, Spring.

| 201 |

Kalinga Prize for the Popularization of Science
UNESCO
7 Place de Fontenoy
75700 Paris, FRANCE
Tel: 331-577-1610

Spring

International; **entry restricted (nomination through official science or science writers organizations in each country);** annual; established 1951 by B. Patnaik (of Cuttack, Orissa, India), named for ancient Kalinga empire of India. Monetary award (for travel to India) to **Science Writer, Editor, Speaker, Television-Radio Program Director,** for distinguished career in interpreting science, technology, research for public; limit 1 per country; recipient expected to visit Indian universities, deliver addresses. Sponsored by UNESCO. Supported by Kalinga Trust Foundation of India. Also have Architecture Prize. Event, Spring.

BOOK (Other)
Book, Article, Script, Newspaper-Magazine Journalism, including ANIMAL RIGHTS, DOG, COOKBOOK, GARDEN, HUMOR, JOURNALISM.

| 202 |

Animal Rights Writing Award
Society for Animal Rights (SAR)
Helen Jones, Chair, Reviewing Committee
421 South State Street
Clarks Summit, Pennsylvania 18411
U.S.A. Tel: (717) 586-2200

October

International; entry open to all; annual (at discretion of sponsor); established 1974. Award honors memory of Richard Martin (Member of Parliament for Galway), author of first successful Parliamentary Bill concerning cruelty to animals; and Henry Bergh, author of first anticruelty laws in U.S., founder of American Society for the Prevention of Cruelty to Animals (ASPCA), and first child protection society in America. Sponsored and supported by SAR. Have circulating film library. Also sponsor seminars, bills in Congress concerning animals' rights, rallies.

BOOK CONTEST: Animal Rights, published.

ARTICLE CONTEST: Animal Rights, published.

AWARDS: $300, Plaque, for best book or article.

JUDGING: By SAR Board of Directors.

ENTRY FEE: None.

DEADLINES: Entry, open. Awards, October.

| 203 |

Dog Writers' Association of America (DWAA) Writing Competition
Susan Jeffries, Second
Vice-President
1616 13th Avenue S.W.
Great Falls, Montana 59404 U.S.A.
Tel: (406) 761-1871
February

International; entry open to all; annual; established 1940s. Purpose: to promote, honor excellence in writing about dogs. Sponsored and supported by DWAA, founded 1935. Average statistics: 300 entries, 50 awards. Held at DWAA annual banquet, New York City. Also sponsor grants to college students with background in dog activities; special Public Service Awards for educational or promotional efforts.

BOOK CONTEST: Dog, first published between November previous year and October current year, 3 entries maximum each category. Categories: Technical-Instructional; Single Breed; Multi-Breed; General.

NEWSPAPER-MAGAZINE CONTEST: Dog, published, mounted on 8 1/2x11-inch paper. Other requirements same as for Book. Categories: Newspapers, including Sunday magazines (circulation over 150,000, under 150,000, weekly or less); Column or News Report (3 examples); Single Feature Story (3 maximum examples); Syndicated Column (3 examples). Magazines not club-affiliated: All-Breed, Multi-Breed, Single Breed, General Interest, Canine Newspaper Articles (3 examples maximum); Any Magazine or Canine Newspaper Series (3 issues); Single-Breed, Multi-Breed, All-Breed, Make-Up or Art Design of Magazine or Canine Newspaper (3 monthly issues or 2 quarterly, bimonthly issues); Canine Newspaper (3 issues).

PUBLICATION CONTEST: Dog Club Bulletin, Newsletter, Magazine. Categories: National Club, Local Club Articles (3 maximum); National Club, Local Club Series (3 issues); National Club, Local Club, Make-Up or Art Design of Club Publications (3 monthly issues or 2 quarterly, bimonthly issues); Special (yearbook).
Dog Welfare Brochure, Pamphlet, Booklet. Requirements same as for Newspaper-Magazines.

AWARDS: Certificates for "Best", Certificates of Merit, Honorable Mentions.

JUDGING: All entries read in entirety by dog journalism experts. May withhold awards. No entries returned. Not responsible for loss or damage.

ENTRY FEE: $5 each.

DEADLINES: Entry, October. Winners notified, January. Awards, February.

| 204 |

Frank Luther Mott-Kappa Tau Alpha Research Award in Journalism
Kappa Tau Alpha
Dr. William H. Taft, Chief, Central Office
School of Journalism
Box 838, University of Missouri
Columbia, Missouri 65205 U.S.A.
April

International; **entry restricted to publishers;** annual; established 1944. Sponsored by Kappa Tau Alpha (National Journalism Scholarship Society).

BOOK CONTEST: Journalism Research, published during previous year, 5 copies.

AWARDS: $300 and Certificate for Best Researched. Certificates to Top Five.

JUDGING: By 5 judges.

ENTRY FEE: None.

DEADLINES: Entry, not specified. Winners announced, April.

205

Garden Writer's Award
American Association of Nurserymen (AAN)
230 Southern Building
Washington, District of Columbia
20005 U.S.A. Tel: (202) 737-4060

July

National; **entry open to U.S.;** annual. Purpose: to recognize contributions to public understanding-appreciation of environmental plants, landscape beautification through popular journalism over period of time. Sponsored by AAN.

BOOK CONTEST: Garden, popular for amateurs.

NEWSPAPER-MAGAZINE CONTEST: Garden, popular for amateurs, including daily-weekly press, home garden magazines, syndicated columns.

SCRIPT CONTEST: Garden Television-Radio, popular for amateurs.

AWARDS: Walnut Plaque, coach travel expenses and 1-night accommodation at AAN Convention.

ENTRY FEE: None.

DEADLINES: Entry, December. Judging, January-February. Awards, July.

206

R. T. French Tastemaker Award for Cook Book Excellence
Harshe-Rotman & Druck
Maryellen Conroy, Account Executive
300 East 44th Street
New York, New York 10017 U.S.A.
Tel: (212) 661-3400

Spring

National; **entry open to U.S. publishers;** annual; established 1966. Purpose: to honor authors whose high standards and creativity have advanced U.S. food culture. Sponsored and supported by R. T. French Company. Average statistics: 500 entries. Held at annual luncheon in New York City. Have cookbook library for home economics students at Syracuse University. Also sponsor Cookbook Hall of Fame, founded 1976 at Syracuse University College for Human Development. Second contact: Laura Weill, Vice President; Charles Chadwick, Director of Public Relations, One Mustard Street, P.O. Box 23450, Rochester, New York 14692; (716) 482-8000.

BOOK CONTEST: Cookbook, original, published, copyrighted, placed on sale in U.S. in previous calendar year; hard or soft cover; major portion consisting of recipes (including number of servings, all ingredients in order of use); unlimited entries. Submission by publisher only. No revisions, updates, reprints, cards, entries sponsored by brand-name products. Categories: Basic, General; Europe and Americas; International; Oriental; Natural Foods and Special Diet; Specialty; Single Subject; Original Soft Cover.

AWARDS: $500   Tastemaker Award to Best Overall Cookbook. Awards each category, author's first.

JUDGING: Nominations Committee (food editors, authors, publishers) operates independently of sponsor, sets standards, determines eligibility, validates ballots. 1200 voters elect winners by majority vote. Based on text and recipe quality, presentation suitability.

ENTRY FEE: None.

DEADLINES: Entry, December. Awards, Spring.

207

Stephen Leacock Medal For Humor
Stephen Leacock Associates
Jean Bradley, Chair, Awards Committee
P.O. Box 854
Orillia, Ontario L3V 3K8 CANADA
Tel: (705) 325-6546

June

National; **entry open to Canadians;** annual; established 1946. Named after Stephen Leacock, Canadian humorist and founder of Canadian Authors' Association. Purpose: to serve as memorial to Leacock; encourage writing-publishing of Canadian humor. Sponsored by Stephen Leacock Associates, Hudson's Bay Company. Average statistics: 20 entries. Held at Awards dinner in Orillia, Ontario. Tickets: $28 (nonmembers). Publish *Newspacket* (quarterly newsletter). Also sponsor Student Award for Humor for essays by Simcoe County high school students.

BOOK CONTEST: Humor, any form; published in previous calendar year; 6 copies.

AWARDS: Stephen Leacock Memorial Silver Medal and $2000 Hudson's Bay Company Prize (including Fiction-Nonfiction entries).

JUDGING: By 5 Canadian judges. May withhold awards. Sponsor keeps entries.

ENTRY FEE: None.

DEADLINES: Entry, February. Winner announced, May. Awards, June.

BOOK, ARTICLE, ESSAY
Nonfiction Book, Article, Essay, Script, including CHILDREN'S, HISTORY, HUMOR, MASS MARKET, RELIGIOUS, SMALL PRESS. (Also see other BOOK, ARTICLE, ESSAY.)

208

Deep South Writers' Competition
Deep South Writers' Conference
John Fontenot
USL Box 4691
University of Southwestern Louisiana
Lafayette, Louisiana 70504 U.S.A.

September

International; entry open to all; annual; established 1960. Purpose: to discover, develop, promote literary and artistic talent. Sponsored by and held at Deep South Writers' Conference. Have workshops, panels, speakers. Tickets: $30 registration fee, $7.50 awards banquet. Also sponsor Fiction Books, Short Story, Poetry, One-Act Play Contests.

BOOK CONTEST: Nonfiction, unpublished; typed double-spaced; limit 3 entries. Submit synopsis and 30-page sample; biographical sketch.

ARTICLE CONTEST: Feature, Inspirational, Humorous, Historical,

Personality Profile. Requirements same as for Book.

AWARDS: $25 Prize. In case of tie, awards duplicated.

JUDGING: By professional writers. No entries returned. Not responsible for loss or damage.

ENTRY FEE: None. Entrant pays postage (include SASE).

DEADLINES: Entry, July. Awards, September.

209

National Writers Club (NWC) Annual Writing Competition
Donald E. Bower, Director
1450 South Havana
Aurora, Colorado 80012 U.S.A.
Tel: (303) 751-7844

October

International; entry open to all; annual; established 1937. Purpose: to increase interest in writing. Sponsored and supported by NWC. Average statistics: 1000 entries. Publish *Authorship* (bimonthly), *NWC Newsletter.* Also sponsor annual national and regional workshops; Novel, Short Story, Poetry Contests.

BOOK CONTEST: Nonfiction, any subject, any length.

ARTICLE CONTEST: Any Subject, 5000-word limit.

AWARDS: Cash prizes and certificates, each contest: $800 (Book, including fiction), $500 (Article).

JUDGING: By professionals, each category. All entries reviewed in entirety. Entrants retain all rights. Not responsible for loss or damage.

ENTRY FEE: $15 (Book), $10 (Article). Entrant pays postage (include SASE).

DEADLINES: Entry, May. Judging, June-October. Awards, October.

210

Pacific Northwest Writers Conference (PNWC) Creative Writing Contests
Gladys Johnson, Executive Secretary
1811 N.W. 199th
Seattle, Washington 98155 U.S.A.
Tel: (206) 364-1293

July

International; entry open to all; annual; established 1956. Sponsored by PNWC, Pacific Lutheran University. Held during PNWC annual conference at Pacific Lutheran University (122nd and Park Avenue, Tacoma, Washington). Have seminars, workshops, personal meetings. Also sponsor High School Writing Contest for Northwest U.S.-Canada students (short story, poetry).

BOOK CONTEST: Nonfiction, original, unpublished; 10,000-word maximum, 1 entry; 1 photocopy (no originals); typed double-spaced. Submit first chapter and maximum 5-page synopsis (plus additional chapters or excerpts).

ARTICLE CONTEST: Any Type, original, unpublished; 4000-word maximum; 1 photocopy (no originals); typed double-spaced.

AWARDS: $200 First, $100 Second, $50 Third Prize, each contest. $300 Memorial Grand Prize for Best Manuscript Overall (including fiction).

JUDGING: By panel. Comments included when material returned. May withhold awards. Not responsible for loss or damage.

ENTRY FEE: $5 per entry plus $10 Conference dues ($5 senior citizens). Entrant pays postage (include SASE).

DEADLINES: Entry, April. Awards, July.

211

Pushcart Prize
Pushcart Press
Bill Henderson, Editor
P.O. Box 845
Yonkers, New York 10701 U.S.A.
Tel: (212) 228-2269

Spring

International; **entry restricted to small press publishers;** annual. Purpose: to publish best of small press literary work. Sponsored by Pushcart Press. Statistics: 4000 entries, 325 authors from 197 presses published to date. Also sponsor Fiction Book, Poetry, Short Story, Writing Contests. Second contact: P.O. Box 320, Stone Ridge, New York 12484.

BOOK CONTEST: **Small Press Any Subject,** published.

ESSAY CONTEST: **Small Press Any Subject,** published.

WRITING CONTEST: **Small Press Any Type,** published.

ELIGIBILITY: Published during current calendar year; 6 entries maximum per small press publisher-editor.

AWARDS: Published in *Pushcart Prize: Best of the Small Presses* (clothbound copy to each reprinted author, press). $100 to lead essay.

JUDGING: By panel.

ENTRY FEE: None. Entrant pays postage (include SASE).

DEADLINES: Entry, October. Selection, January. Publication, Spring.

212

Southwest Writers' Conference Awards
University of Houston, Continuing Education Center
Marilyn R. Nerem
4800 Calhoun
Houston, Texas 77004 U.S.A.
Tel: (713) 749-4182

July

Regional; **entry restricted to Southwestern U.S. Conference participants;** annual; established 1952. $50 Golden Pen or Golden Palette Awards to **Conference Nonfiction Books, Short Articles, Children's Books, Juvenile Writing, Television Scripts.** Purpose: to create opportunity for writers to meet editors-publishers, have manuscripts critiqued. Sponsored by University of Houston Continuing Education Center, Houston Writers' Workshop. Average statistics: 200 entries, 10 finalists, 375 attendance. Held at Continuing Education Center, University of Houston for 3 days. Have workshops, discussions. Tickets: $85 (before July), $95 (after). Awards, July.

213

Author's Awards for Mass Market Writing
Periodical Distributors of Canada
Sheryll Reid, Coordinator
322 King Street West, 4th Floor
Toronto, Ontario M5J 1J2 CANADA
Tel: (416) 977-9977

October

National; **entry open to Canadians;** annual; established 1977. Purpose: to recognize outstanding Canadian writers, artists. Sponsored by Foundation for the Advancement of Canadian Letters, Periodical Distributors of Canada.

BOOK CONTEST: Mass Market Paperback, published. Categories: Nonfiction, Cover Design.

MAGAZINE ARTICLE CONTEST: Mass Market. Categories: Public Affairs, Personality Feature, Humor, Cover Design.

ELIGIBILITY: By Canadian citizens or landed immigrants, published in mass market form and distributed in Canada July previous to June current year. Hardcover reprints acceptable if original published not prior to second calendar year previous. Submit 1 category only; 4 copies each. No weekend newspaper supplements, free distribution publications. Request entrant photograph. Publisher submits nominations (with reasons) for Author of the Year, maximum 2 titles for Book of the Year.

AWARDS: $600 First, $300 Second Place, Best Nonfiction Book; $400, $200, Best Public Affairs Article; $300, $150, Best Humor and Personality Feature Articles. $300 each First Place, Book and Magazine Cover Designs (including Fiction entries). Book of the Year Award to author with greatest impact on Canadian publishing industry. Author of the Year Award to Outstanding Canadian Paperback author of past year.

JUDGING: By 3 independent judges. Cover Design based on artistic skill, aesthetics, effectiveness. Judging by wholesalers' panel for Book of the Year. No materials returned.

ENTRY FEE: Not specified.

DEADLINES: Entry, July. Awards, October.

BOOK-PUBLICATION DESIGN

Book, Newspaper, Magazine, Publication and Periodical Design, including BOOKMAKING, COVER, GRAPHICS, ILLUSTRATIONS, JACKET, TYPOGRAPHY and EDITORIAL DESIGN.

| 214 |

Art Directors Club Annual Exhibition
488 Madison Avenue
New York, New York 10022 U.S.A.

March

International; **entry restricted to U.S., Canada;** annual; established 1922. Purpose: to search for new expressions, techniques, breakthroughs, talents, directions. Sponsored by New York Art Directors Club. Publish Art Directors Club Annual. Also sponsor Newspaper-Magazine Advertising, Promotion-Graphic Design, Poster, Art-Illustration, Photography, and Television Contests.

BOOK DESIGN CONTEST: Book-Jacket Design. Categories (Book, Jacket): Trade, Children's, Text.

NEWSPAPER-MAGAZINE DESIGN CONTEST: Editorial Design, tearsheets or proofs, unmounted, trimmed. Divisions: Single, Campaign (3-5 pieces as series). Newspaper categories: Full Page; Less Than Full Page; Section, Insert, Supplement (submit as campaign). Magazine categories: Consumer, Business or Trade (1 page or spread, b/w); Consumer, Business or Trade (1 page or spread, minimum 2 colors); Consumer Business or Trade (section or insert, submit as campaign); Consumer, Business or Trade Cover; Consumer, Business Magazine.

ELIGIBILITY: First produced in U.S.

or Canada, in current calendar year. No foreign market publications.

AWARDS: Gold, Silver Medals (1 per entry), Distinctive Merit Awards, each category. Merit Award and publication in Annual for each accepted for exhibition.

JUDGING: May withhold awards. No entries returned. Not responsible for loss or damage.

ENTRY FEE: $12 Single, $25 Campaign. $55 (Single), $85 (Campaign) Hanging Fee for entries accepted.

DEADLINES: Entry, November. Winners notified, March.

215

Communication Arts Magazine CA Design and Advertising Exhibition
Jean A. Coyne
410 Sherman Avenue
P.O. Box 10300
Palo Alto, California 94303 U.S.A.
Tel: (415) 326-6040

January

International; entry open to all; annual; established 1959. Sponsored by *Communication Arts Magazine* (bimonthly design publication, 52,000 circulation), considered largest juried competition. Average statistics: 19,000 entries.

BOOK DESIGN CONTEST: Design, printed between July previous and July current year, unmounted. Request English translation. No originals. Divisions: Single, Campaign (5 maximum). Categories: Complete Unit, Cover-Jacket.

NEWSPAPER-MAGAZINE DESIGN CONTEST: Graphic Design, published between July previous and July current year, unmounted. Request English translation. No originals. Divisions: Single, Campaign (5

maximum). Categories: Consumer or Trade Magazine, Newspaper (page, spread, or section).

AWARDS: Award of Excellence Certificates, publication in *CA Annual* (November-December issue).

JUDGING: By designers, art directors, writers. No entries returned. Not responsible for loss or damage.

ENTRY FEE: $6 (single), $12 (campaign, series). Entrant pays postage (include SASE).

DEADLINES: Entry, June. Winners notified, October. Awards, January.

216

Creativity Awards Show
Art Direction Magazine
Ray Morrison, Director
10 East 39th Street, 6th Floor
New York, New York 10016 U.S.A.
Tel: (212) 889-6500

Fall

International; **entry restricted to professionals;** annual; established 1969. Purpose: to record trends in advertising design, art illustration, photography, TV commercials; reward, publicize talented art directors. Sponsored by *Art Direction Magazine,* founded 1949. Average statistics: 15,-000 entries, 800 winners. Have Creativity Show (annual 1-week showcase at New York Coliseum for best work), exhibitions in major cities. Publish *Creativity* (international annual of awards show), *Advertising Techniques Magazine, Graphic Arts Buyer.*

BOOK-MAGAZINE DESIGN CONTEST: **Cover Design,** printed between May previous and May current year; unmounted; copies only. Categories: Book Cover Design; Magazine Cover Design.

AWARDS: Creativity Certificate of Distinction, exhibition at Annual Creativity Show.

JUDGING: Art Directors judged on concept, design. Artists, illustrators, photographers judged on excellence of various fields. No entries returned.

ENTRY FEE: $5 (single spread), $10 (3 or more). $9 (single), $18 (3 or more) Hanging Fee for winners.

DEADLINES: Entry, April. Winners notified, July.

217

DESI Awards Competition
Graphics Design: USA Magazine
Louis J. Boasi, Director
32 Gansvoort Street
New York, New York 10014 U.S.A.
Tel: (212) 675-5867

Spring

National; **entry open to U.S. citizens;** annual; established 1977. DESI is derived from "Design." Purpose: to showcase excellent professional-academic graphic design. Sponsored by *Graphics Design: USA.* Exhibition held in New York City for 2 weeks. Publish awards issue of *Graphics Design: USA.* Second contact: Valerie Stewart, *Graphics Design: USA,* 120 East 56th Street, New York, New York 10022.

BOOK-PUBLICATION DESIGN CONTEST: **Design, Cover,** printed previous calendar year. Categories: Book Design, Cover; Publication Design, Cover.

AWARDS: DESI Certificates, each winner. Exhibition at Graphics Design Show.

JUDGING: By 4 judges in graphic design. No entries returned (unless requested). Not responsible for loss or damage.

ENTRY FEE: $8 (single piece, slide). 50 (single), $30 (slide) Hanging Fee required from winners. Entrant pays postage (include SASE).

DEADLINES: Entry, January. Judging, February-March. Awards, April.

218

Graphic Arts Awards Competition
Printing Industries of America
Katherine W. Rose, Assistant to Director
1730 North Lynn Street
Arlington, Virginia 22209 U.S.A.
Tel: (703) 841-8154

November

International; entry open to all; annual; established 1953. Purpose: to promote high standards in printed material production-design. Sponsored by Eastman Kodak Company, Harris Corporation, Printing Industries of America. Average statistics: 4500 entrants. Held in Arlington, Virginia. Have folder-broadside, booklet, catalog, direct mail, business-annual report, point-of-purchase, business form, greeting-pictorial postcard, carton-container, label-wrap, stationery, calendar, miscellaneous specialty, poster categories.

BOOK DESIGN CONTEST: **Graphics-Design,** published. Categories: Juvenile, Trade-Other, Yearbooks-School Textbooks, Book Jackets.

MAGAZINE DESIGN CONTEST: **Graphics-Design,** published. Categories: Magazines-House Organs (1-2 colors, 3 or more colors), Magazine Inserts.

ELIGIBILITY: Printed March previous to April current year. Divisions: National (U.S., Canada, Mexico), International (other countries).

AWARDS: Best of Category Plaque Award, each category. Award Certificates to Runners-Up.

JUDGING: By graphic arts experts. Based on technical reproduction quality, design, art, typography, general layout. May reclassify entries. No entries returned.

ENTRY FEE: $10 each. $35 additional, each winner.

DEADLINES: Entry, May. Judging, June. Awards, November.

| 219 |

Maggie Awards Program
Western Publications Association (WPA)
Jan Nathan, Executive Director
505 North Sepulveda Blvd., Suite 14
Manhattan Beach, California 90266
U.S.A. Tel: (213) 772-4796

Spring

Regional; **entry restricted to publications in 14 western states;** annual; established 1948. Named after Magazines (Maggie). Formerly called EDDIE to 1976 (for editorial excellence). Purpose: to recognize overall graphic, editorial excellence in western magazines, monthly tabloids. Sponsored and supported by WPA. Average statistics: 600 entries, 150 semifinalists, 40 winners, 1000 attendance. Held in Southern California for 3 days. Have seminars, exhibits during Conference. Tickets: $50 (members), $70 (nonmembers). Publish monthly newsletter. Also sponsor Western Publishing Conference.

MAGAZINE DESIGN CONTEST: **Graphics, Editorial,** published in (or solely for distribution in) 14 western states. 40 categories.

AWARDS: Maggie Award, each category.

JUDGING: Each publication read in entirety by 30 judges (15 graphic, 15 editorial). Based on submitted editorial description of readership. Tabulation of results by Touche Ross & Company. No entries returned. Not responsible for loss or damage.

ENTRY FEE: Not specified.

DEADLINES: Entry, January. Judging, February. Winners announced, Spring banquet.

| 220 |

Midwestern Books Competition
University of Kentucky
Lawrence S. Thompson, Project Director
Department of Classics
Lexington, Kentucky 40506 U.S.A.
Tel: (606) 266-4056

January

Regional; **entry restricted to Midwestern book publishers, printers, designers;** annual; established 1955. Purpose: to recognize outstanding typography and design of Midwest books. Sponsored by Department of Classics, University of Kentucky. Average statistics: 400 entries, 40 entrants.

BOOK-PERIODICAL   DESIGN CONTEST: **Midwestern Design, Typography,** published in current year; pamphlet-periodical in paper covers acceptable, 1 copy each. Published or printed and designed in Ohio, Indiana, West Virginia, Illinois, Kentucky, Michigan, Minnesota, Wisconsin, Iowa, Missouri, Kansas, Nebraska, North and South Dakota, Pittsburgh (no other part of Pennsylvania). Submit (in triplicate) full production information.

AWARDS: Various Midwestern Books of the Year, exhibited internationally.

JUDGING: Based on typography, design, production quality; content considered only as design has aided in conveying spirit of books, aims of author. All entries kept in University of Kentucky Library. Winning publishers furnish additional copies for exhibition.

ENTRY FEE: $4 first, $2 each additional.

DEADLINES: Entry before Christmas. Awards, January.

221

Society of Illustrators Annual Exhibition
Terry Brown, Curator
128 East 63rd Street
New York, New York 10021 U.S.A.
Tel: (212) 838-2560

January-April

International; entry open to all; annual; established 1959. Purpose: to present best in illustration art. Sponsored by Society of Illustrators. Held in Society's gallery in New York. Have advertising, institutional illustration categories. Also sponsor Student Scholarship Competition; Film and Video contests.

BOOK DESIGN CONTEST: Illustrations, published (submit proofs or tearsheets); unpublished (submit 35mm cardboard-mounted slides); 1 per entry. No stats, photos, original art. Categories: Paperback, Hardbound (Books and Covers).

NEWSPAPER-MAGAZINE DESIGN CONTEST: Editorial Illustrations. Requirements same as for Book. Categories: Newspaper, Magazine, House Organs.

ELIGIBILITY: Published or created October previous to October current year. Foreign entries submit slides only. Require original art work for exhibition and awards (except foreign entries).

AWARDS: Gold Medal, Silver Medals, Excellence Certificates to illustrators, art directors for Best, each category, and Best Unpublished in Show. Merit Certificates and reproduction with credit in *Illustrators Annual Book,* each exhibited.

JUDGING: By 6-9 judges, each category. Black and white, limited color, judged separately from full color. No entries returned.

ENTRY FEE: $8 per illustration or slide ($10 per slide, foreign entries). $25 Hanging Fee ($20 members) if accepted (except foreign).

DEADLINES: Entry, September. Exhibition, January-April.

222

Society of Publication Designers Competition
Liz Wilbur
Room 501
3 West 51st Street
New York, New York 10019 U.S.A.
Tel: (212) 582-4077

Spring

International; entry open to all; annual; established 1966. Purpose: to evaluate and recognize designer, photographer, art director, illustrator creative efforts. Sponsored by Society of Publication Designers, founded 1964. Have exhibitions. Publish *Publication Design Awards Annual.*

NEWSPAPER-MAGAZINE DESIGN CONTEST: Publication Design, published during previous calendar year; unmounted proofs and tearsheets; text attached to each entry. No catalogs, advertising, promotional publicity materials. Divisions: 1 or 2 colors, 3 or more colors, each category except Total Unit Design (1 or 2 colors). Categories: Total Unit Design (Overall Design of 3 different issues, Single Issue); Page Design, Illustration, Photography (Cover, Single Page, Story Presentation of 2 or more pages). Classes: Consumer Publications (General Interest, Women's, Men's, News-Business, Shelter, Food, Beauty-Fashion, Travel-Entertainment-Art, Sports, Outdoors, Technical, Educational); trade-Professional; Institutional Publications Without Advertising (Institution-Company, Museum, Annual Reports, School, Newsletters-Journals); Newsprint Publications (Daily, Weekly, Magazine Supplement); New Publications.

AWARDS: Merit Award, inclusion in exhibition and book, each finalist. Gold Award of Excellence, Silver Award of Distinctive Merit to Art Director at judges' discretion. Jerome Snyder Award for Exceptional Art Direction, Best of Show, at judges' discretion.

JUDGING: Judged against like publications. Based on aesthetics, relationships of aesthetics to editorial requirements. Consider illustrative material only in relation to editorial text. Evaluation by secret ballot. May withhold awards. No entries returned.

ENTRY FEE: $10 (members), $15 (nonmembers), each entry. $45 (members), $60 (nonmembers) hanging fee and mounted entry required from finalists.

DEADLINES: Entry, February. Finalists notified, April.

| 223 |

Southern Books Competition
Southeastern Library Association
Frank J. Anderson, Project Director
Sandor Teszler Library, Wofford College

Spartanburg, South Carolina 29301
U.S.A. Tel: (803) 585-4821, ext. 355

Spring

Regional; **entry restricted to Southern publishers;** annual; established 1952. Purpose: to recognize excellence in book design, production. Sponsored and supported by Southeastern Library Association. Average statistics: 114 entries, 36 entrants, 19 awards. Publish Southern Books of the Year Handlist of winners.

BOOK DESIGN CONTEST: **Southern Bookmaking, Design,** published during previous calendar year by Southern publishers (Alabama, Arizona, Arkansas, Florida, Georgia, Kentucky, Louisiana, Mississippi, New Mexico, North Carolina, Oklahoma, South Carolina, Tennessee, Texas, Virginia, Washington, D.C., West Virginia, Puerto Rico). Submit 1 copy.

AWARDS: Recognition Certificate and national 1-year exhibition.

JUDGING: By publishers, printers, booksellers, librarians. Based on design, typography, materials, production quality. Request additional copies of winners for exhibition. Winners kept at University of Kentucky Library. Winning publishers furnish additional copies for traveling exhibit. No entries returned.

ENTRY FEE: $4 first, $2 each additional.

DEADLINES: Entry, January. Awards, Spring.

| 224 |

Type Directors Club (TDC) Search for Typographic Excellence
12 East 41st Street
New York, New York 10017 U.S.A.

Summer

International; entry open to all; annual; established 1954. Purpose: to recognize typographic excellence. Sponsored by TDC. Held in New York City. Have traveling exhibitions (U.S., Europe, Far East).

BOOK-PUBLICATION DESIGN CONTEST: Typography, printed in previous calendar year, 1 copy (photographic prints but not slides), credits. Submit 4 copies if winner. Categories: Booklets, Book Jackets, Books, Brochures, Catalogs, House Organs, Manuals.

AWARDS: Typographic Excellence Certificates to Type Director, Typographic Supplier, Calligrapher, Agency, Client, each winning entry. Winners exhibited, reproduced in published catalog.

JUDGING: By panel. Based on typographic excellence in type, type techniques, design, paper, print.

ENTRY FEE: $6 each (U.S., Canada), $3 each (foreign). Hanging Fee, $50 each (U.S., Canada), $25 (foreign).

DEADLINES: Entry, January. Event, Summer.

GRANTS (Aid, Emergency Assistance)

For Aid, Assistance to Writers in Financial Emergency. (Also see GRANTS.)

225

Carnegie Fund for Authors Emergency Grants-in-Aid
W. L. Rothenberg
330 Sunrise Highway
Rockville Centre, New York 11570
U.S.A.

Continuous

International; entry open to all; continuous. Sponsored by Carnegie Fund for Authors.

WRITING GRANT: Writing Emergency Assistance, up to $500 to author with at least 1 book of reasonable length published commercially (which has received reader acceptance), for financial emergency due to illness or injury to self, spouse, dependent child, or other misfortune. Require published books listed in standard reference source, or commercial publication confirmation. No loans or project, publication grants.

DEADLINES: Open.

226

Change Inc. Emergency Assistance Grants
Susan Lewis, Secretary
Box 705, Cooper Station
New York, New York 10276 U.S.A.
Tel: (212) 473-3742

Continuous

National; entry open to U.S.; continuous; established 1970. Purpose: to award emergency grants to professional artists in all fields. Sponsored by Change Inc., P.O. Box 489927, Los Angeles, California 90048.

WRITING GRANTS: Writing Emergency Assistance, $100-$500 to professional writers in need of emergency assistance resulting from utility turn-off, eviction, unpaid medical bills, fire, illness. Require detailed letter, proof of professional status, recommendation letters (2 people in applicant's field), outstanding bills substantiating amount needed.

JUDGING: By Board of Directors.

DEADLINES: Open.

| 227 |

Mary Roberts Rinehart Foundation Grants-in-Aid
The Directors
516 Fifth Avenue, Room 504
New York, New York 10036 U.S.A.
Tel: (212) 840-6378

Continuous

National; **entry open to U.S. residents (nonnationals included);** continuous; established 1958. Named for writer Mary Roberts Rinehart. Purpose: to help creative people with no means to complete projects; encourage contributions to biography, autobiography, fiction, history, poetry, drama. Sponsored and supported by nonprofit Mary Roberts Rinehart Foundation.

WRITING GRANT: Creative Writing Aid, up to $500 (tax-free), payable in equal installments at quarterly intervals, to creative writer as financial assistance to complete work definitely projected; preference to new, relatively unknown writers. Require project plan-outline in English, 25% project sample (if already started), writing samples, evidence of financial need and ability; progress reports from recipients. No pedantic scholarship, experimental research, applicants with vague yearning to write but who cannot produce. No grants for criticism, instruction, printing, publishing.

JUDGING: All entries read in entirety by Foundation Directors and specialists. Entrant retains all rights. Not responsible for loss or damage.

ENTRY FEE: None. Entrant pays postage (include SASE).

DEADLINES: Open.

| 228 |

PEN Fund for Writers
PEN American Center
Karen Kennerly, Executive Secretary
47 Fifth Avenue
New York, New York 10003 U.S.A.
Tel: (212) 255-1977

Continuous

International; entry open to all; continuous. Sponsored and supported by 1,800-member PEN American Center (founded 1922) of the 10,000-member, 80-country International PEN (Poets-Playwrights-Essayists-Editors-Novelists), founded 1921 as independent, nonprofit world association of writers. Also sponsor PEN Writing Award for Prisoners, PEN Literature Awards, PEN Translation Awards; Lucille J. Mednick Memorial Award ($500, annual) for distinguished service to the literary community and commitment to serve the young, unrecognized, and unpopular (candidates by nomination only).

WRITING GRANTS: Writing Emergency Assistance, up to $500 to help established writers through financial emergency. Require professional, financial information.

ENTRY FEE: None.

DEADLINES: Open.

GRANTS (General)

Primarily for RESEARCH, WRITING, and PUBLISHING, including Book, Newspaper, Magazine, Script, Translation, and RESIDENCE GRANTS and TRAINING. (Also see RESIDENCE GRANTS, SCHOLARSHIPS, FELLOWSHIPS.)

229

Corporation for Public Broadcasting (CPB) Program Fund
Lewis Freedman, Director
1111 Sixteenth Street N.W.
Washington, District of Columbia
20036 U.S.A. Tel: (202) 293-6160
July

National; **entry restricted to U.S. independent producers and writers, public TV stations;** periodic; established 1980. Purpose: to stimulate television dramas that express emotions, ideas of American people. Sponsored by CPB, private, nonprofit corporation founded 1967 by Public Broadcasting Act. Supported by NEA, federal, private funds. Also sponsor media grants.

SCRIPT-WRITING GRANT: Public Television Script Development, up to $10,000 to public TV stations, independent writers, producers, for developing ideas, not yet in dramatic form, for 60-120 minute programs. Require proposal including basic information sheet, 5-page (or less) synopsis, samples on request, proof of rights, resume(s), script completion by 6 months after submission. Categories: Original, Literary Adaptation.

JUDGING: Program Fund staff checks for proposal completeness. Experts review, evaluate (deliberations confidential; names of panel members withheld until after final selections). Final selection by Program Fund Director. Based on audience appeal, value beyond entertainment, suitability for film or videotape, appropriateness for television. Not responsible for loss, damage, third-party use-misuse of proposal.

ENTRY FEE: None. Entrant pays postage (include SASE).

DEADLINES: Entry, April. Notification, July.

230

Eben Demarest Trust Fund Grant
Anne Shiras, Secretary
4601 Bayard Street, Apt. 807
Pittsburgh, Pennsylvania 15213
U.S.A.
Summer

International; **entry restricted (nomination by organizations);** annual. Purpose: to free artist from livelihood dependence upon sale, approval of work. Sponsored by Eben Demarest Trust.

WRITING GRANT: Literature, 1 $5500 grant to gifted writer, artist who has produced work of recognized worth, has no other income equal to grant; nominated by organizations, institutions, or by Demarest Advisory Council member. No applications from individuals.

JUDGING: By 5-member council.

DEADLINES: Application, May. Notification, Summer.

231

Ford Foundation Grants
320 East 43rd Street
New York, New York 10017 U.S.A.
Continuous

International; entry open to all; continuous; established 1978. Purpose: to support educational, developmental, experimental efforts to produce significant advances in selected problems of national, international importance. Sponsored and supported by Ford Foundation, private, nonprofit institution serving public welfare (founded 1936 as Michigan State Foundation; became national 1950).

Average statistics (all Ford Foundation programs): 22,000 applicants, 900 grants, 7% budget to Communications. Also sponsor Ford Foundation Arts Grants; Graduate Fellowships to Black Americans, Mexican-Americans, Native Americans (Aleuts, American Indians, Eskimos, Hawaiians), Puerto Ricans. Publish *Ford Foundation Letter.*

WRITING GRANT: **Communications,** most grants to institutions, limited grants to individuals. Categories: Communications Policy (including conflicts between freedom of the press and judicial process), International Communications (research on impact of mass media, especially effects on politics, children).

ELIGIBILITY: Require inquiry letter, proposal (with objectives, plans, present support means, applications to other funding sources), personnel qualifications, detailed budget, Internal Revenue classification (as charitable, educational, or scientific activity).

JUDGING: Final by 19-member board.

ENTRY FEE: None.

DEADLINES: Open.

| 232 |

Jo Caldwell Meyer Research Grant
Women in Communications (WIC)
Mary E. Utting, Executive Director
National Headquarters
P.O. Box 9561
Austin, Texas 78766 U.S.A.
Tel: (512) 345-8922

June

International; **entry restricted to WIC members;** annual; established 1964. $1000 1-year **Communications Research and Writing Grant** to paid

members. Sponsored by Women in Communications (8305-A Shoal Creek Blvd., Austin, Texas 78758). Awarded, June.

| 233 |

John and Mary R. Markle Foundation Mass Communications Grants
Dolores E. Miller, Assistant to President
50 Rockefeller Plaza
New York, New York 10020 U.S.A.
Tel: (212) 489-6655

March, June, November

National; **entry restricted to U.S. organizations;** triannual; established 1936. Purpose: to strengthen educational uses of mass media-communications technology; promote advancement, diffusion of knowledge and general good of mankind. Sponsored and supported by John and Mary R. Markle Foundation (Lloyd N. Morisett, President), founded 1927 by John Markle, coal millionaire. Average statistics: 748 entrants, 36 grants totaling $3,270,667.

WRITING-RESEARCH GRANT: **Mass Communications Improvement Newspapers, Magazines, Books.** For projects that expand research on mass communication role in society, analyze public policy questions and issues, improve professional performance, develop better media service to specialized groups (children, elderly, minorities), explore media-politics relationship, enrich print journalism quality, support publication of books and reports. Require project proposal, resources needed, personnel, timetable, budget, method descriptions; visit to, interview with finalists.

JUDGING: By staff and directors. Foundation works as active partner on projects.

DEADLINES: Open. Response within 2 weeks. Grants awarded, March, June, November.

| 234 |

Kaltenborn Foundation Grants for Scholarly Studies in Communications
Rolf Kaltenborn, Trustee
349 Seaview Avenue
Palm Beach, Florida 33480 U.S.A.
Tel: (305) 655-8024

Continuous

National; **entry open to U.S.**; continuous. Purpose: to promote scholarly studies in communications dealing with effectiveness of informing public through television, radio, press, magazines. Sponsored by Kaltenborn Foundation. Average statistics: 3-4 grants.

WRITING-STUDY GRANT: Press and Magazine Scholarly Studies. 3-4 grants, approximately $1500 each, given for scholarly studies in the field of communications. Require project proposal, background biographical material, 1-2 references.

DEADLINES: Open.

| 235 |

Ludwig Vogelstein Foundation Grants
Douglas Turnbaugh, Treasurer
Box 537
New York, New York 10013 U.S.A.

Semiannual

International; entry open to all; semiannual; established 1940. Purpose: to support original projects by individuals in arts and humanities. Average statistics: 33 awards per year, $3000 average. Also sponsor art, music, photography, drama grants.

WRITING GRANT: Any Type, $100-$5000 to individuals to support original project. Require evidence of achievement in field, importance of project to field; financial need.

DEADLINES: Open.

| 236 |

National Endowment for the Arts (NEA) Writing Fellowships and Grants
2401 E Street N.W.
Washington, District of Columbia
20506 U.S.A. Tel: (202) 634-6044

Various

National; **entry open to U.S. citizens-residents and nonprofit, tax-exempt organizations;** various; established 1965. Sponsored by NEA (independent agency of federal goverment) to encourage and assist U.S. cultural resources; make arts widely available; strengthen cultural organizations; preserve cultural heritage; develop creative talent. Supported by annual appropriations from U.S. Congress, private donations. Address inquiries to programs *italicized* in parentheses.

WRITING FELLOWSHIP GRANTS: Criticism, Literature Writing *(Literature Program),* $12,500 to writers for writing, research, general career advancement. Require previous publication of one of following: minimum 5 literary essays-articles or 5 short stories in 2 or more literary magazines; novel; volume of short fiction, poetry, or literary criticism; script publication or production. Submit samples. Application for only 1 genre. No playwrights. Application, December-February. Notification, following December.

Criticism of Art Writing *(Visual Arts Program),* $10,000 fellowships for specific projects (including travel), limited number of $3000 fellowships for travel only, to critical-theoretical writers for investigation, evaluation, analysis, travel projects concerning contemporary art. Submit articles, essays. Application, December. Notification, July.

Literature Translation *(Literature Program)*, $6250 or $12,500 (depending on project) to translators for translation-to-English projects. Require previous publication of book-length literary work or publication-production of play. Submit original work samples and translation. Preference to creative writers. Application, April-June. Notification, following June.

Museum Arts Research-Writing *(Museum Program)*, up to $20,000 (usually less) to museum professionals for arts-related study, travel, writing, community project participation. Application 7 months prior to notification.

WRITING GRANTS: Arts Development *(Challenge Arts Grants)*, $30,000-$1,500,000 on matching basis to media arts centers, public television-radio stations, cultural groups, groups consortia, for fund-raising, other activities contributing to organization's long-term financial stability. Application, June. Notification, February.

Folk Arts Documentation, Preservation *(Folk Arts Program)*, up to $50,000 (usually $5000-$25,000) on matching basis to organizations, Native American tribes, media centers, educational institutions, state-local arts agencies for documentation, preservation, presentation of traditional folk arts. Have limited grants, heritage awards, apprenticeships, short-term advanced learning opportunities ($1000-$5000) on nonmatching basis to individuals. Application 5-6 months prior to notification.

Literary Arts Education *(Expansion Arts Program)*, $5000-$30,000 on matching basis to professionally directed, community-based organizations offering participation-training in literary arts (workshops, poetry festivals). Application, October. Notification, June.

Special Interdisciplinary Arts Projects *(Inter-Arts Program)*, up to $50,000 on matching basis to organizations for collaborative projects, special events, career entry projects, services to field involving 2 or more arts ineligible for other NEA funding. Application 6 months prior to notification.

Special Literary Services *(Literature Program)*, limited assistance grants to organizations for services to writers not funded under other NEA Programs. Deadlines: Open.

ELIGIBILITY: Programs may require project summary, audience benefits, budget, secured sources of matching grants, schedules, fiscal reports, resumes-biographies, recommendation letters, reviews, other supplementary information, evidence of nonprofit, tax-exempt status. Special consideration often given to projects involving minorities, women. Other requirements vary by program.

JUDGING: Application review by Program Panel. Recommendation by National Council on the Arts. Final by NEA Chair.

DEADLINES: Vary by program.

| 237 |

National Endowment for the Arts (NEA) Publishing and Residence Grants
2401 E Street N.W.
Washington, District of Columbia
20506 U.S.A. Tel: (202) 634-6044
Various

National; **entry open to U.S. citizens-residents and nonprofit, tax-exempt organizations;** various; established 1965. Sponsored by NEA (independent agency of federal government) to encourage and assist U.S. cultural resources; make arts widely available; strengthen cultural organizations; preserve cultural heritage; develop creative talent. Supported by annual appropriations from U.S. Congress, private donations. Address inquiries to programs *Italicized* in parentheses.

PUBLISHING GRANTS: Contemporary Art Publications *(Visual Arts Program)*, up to $15,000 on matching basis to organizations, on nonmatching basis to individuals, for reference works, journals, publications, serving particular region or aesthetic and contributing to national dialog on contemporary art. Application, June (arts organizations), October (others). Notification, May (arts organizations), August (others).

Crafts Exhibition Catalog Publication *(Visual Arts Program)*, up to $50,000 to large, $15,000 to small crafts exhibitions, on matching basis, for catalog publication. Application, July. Notification, February.

Design Communication Publications *(Design Arts Program)*, up to $50,000 on matching basis to organizations for writing, design, printing of publications informing public about design issues, ideas. Application 6 months prior to notification.

Film-Video-Audio Publications *(Media Arts Program)*, up to $25,000 on matching basis to organizations, up to $10,000 on nonmatching basis to individuals, for newsletters, journals serving particular region or aesthetic and contributing to national dialog on media arts. Require 2 copies of 3 most recent issues. Application, May. Notification, December.

Museum Cataloging Documentation, Publication *(Museum Program)*, up to $100,000 on matching basis to organizations, museums for documen-

tation-publications in service of cataloging permanent collections of artistic significance. Application, June. Notification, December.

Photography Publication *(Visual Arts Program)*, up to $20,000 on matching basis to organizations for publication of contemporary photography, photography essays, research, criticism. Application, December. Notification, August.

WRITING RESIDENCE GRANTS: Artists' Colonies *(Inter-Arts Program)*, up to $50,000 (usually $10,000-$30,000) on matching basis to artists' colonies for residency cost of artist unable to pay, fund-raising, minority participation projects, colony's visibility. Application, December. Notification, June.

Translation Writer *(Literature Program)*, up to $10,000 on matching basis to organizations for fees, travel, per diem expenses of writers in residence. No playwrights. Application, January-March. Notification, October.

ELIGIBILITY: Programs may require project summary, audience benefits, budget, secured sources of matching grants, schedules, fiscal reports, resumes-biographies, recommendation letters, reviews, other supplementary information; evidence of nonprofit, tax-exempt status. Special consideration often given to projects involving minorities, women. Other requirements vary by program.

JUDGING: Application review by Program Panel. Recommendation by National Council on the Arts. Final by NEA Chair.

DEADLINES: Vary by program.

238

National Endowment for the Humanities (NEH) Writing and Publishing Grants
806 15th Street N.W.
Washington, District of Columbia
20506 U.S.A.

Various

National; **entry open to U.S. nonprofit organizations;** semiannual; established 1965. Sponsored by NEH (independent federal grant-making agency) to support research, education, public activity in the humanities (modern, classical languages; linguistics; literature; history; jurisprudence; philosophy; archaeology; comparative religion; ethics; art history, criticism, theory, practice; historical, philosophical, social sciences with humanistic content, methods; human environment, condition; national life). Supported by annual appropriations from U.S. Congress, private donations. Address inquiries to programs *italicized* in parentheses.

WRITING   FELLOWSHIP GRANTS: **Scholarly Humanities Writing** *(Division of Fellowships)*, $2000-$20,000 to teachers, scholars, interpreters of the humanities for 6-12-month or summer full-time study, research, writing and-or seminar participation. Categories: College Teacher-Scholar, Professional (including journalism). Deadlines: Various.

SCRIPT   GRANT: **Humanities Scriptwriting** *(Division of Public Programs, Humanities Projects in Media)*, on matching basis to nonprofit organizations for writing 1 or more scripts, documentary treatments, on thought-provoking topics using humanities themes-resources. NEH approves project distribution, publicity; grantee retains rights. Application, January, July. Notification, June, December.

PUBLISHING GRANT: **Humanities Research Publishing, Distribution** *(Division of Research Programs)*, up to $10,000 per volume to individuals, nonprofit organizations, and publishers for publication-dissemination of humanities works. Consider works resulting from previous NEH grants, others on limited basis. Application, November, May. Notification, March, September.

WRITING GRANTS: **Humanities Development** *(Challenge Grants Program)*, on 3 (nonfederal) to 1 (federal) matching basis to nonprofit institutions for fund-raising, other activities contributing to organization's long-term financial stability. Application, April. Notification, November.

Humanities Reference Material Writing *(Division of Research Programs)*, up to 3 years' support for preparation of Research Tools and Reference   Works   (dictionaries, atlases, encyclopedias, concordances, catalogues raisonnes, calendars, linguistic grammars, descriptive catalogs, data bases); Editions; Translations that fill need as defined by significant segment of learned community.

Humanities Research Writing support for wide range of scholarship in Basic   Research;   Archaeological Projects   (including   prepublication manuscript preparation); State-Local Regional Studies. Deadlines: Various.

Youth Humanities Project *(Division of Special Programs)*, $2500-$5000 (and over) to youth (teens, 20s), nonprofit organizations, to develop, conduct humanities projects. May include writing projects exploring humanities topics. Application, January. Notification, July.

ELIGIBILITY: U.S.   citizens-residents; nonprofit, tax-exempt organizations. Fresh approach to humanities subject, evidence of potential for new uses of humanities resources. Require statement of project need, summary, complete description, work plans, outreach-audience benefits; resumes, recommendations, reviews; budget, marketing plans; samples, manuscripts; other documentation, supporting materials.

JUDGING: By 4-stage review; NEH Panel (subject-area experts), Individual Review (external experts), National Council on the Humanites (26 presidential appointees), NCH Chair (makes final funding decisions). Based on proposal clarity, logic; use of humanities resources; interpretive nature; appeal to large audience (including English, Spanish speakers; blind; hearing-impaired); outreach potential to underserved social groups; feasibility, planning efficiency, budget.

DEADLINES: Vary by program.

239

National Historical Publications and Records Commission (NHPRC) Publications Grants and Fellowships
National Archives Bldg.
Washington, District of Columbia
20408 U.S.A.

Various

National; **entry open to U.S.;** various. Purpose: to preserve, publish documents-papers important to U.S. history understanding, appreciation. Sponsored by NHPRC. Also have Microform Publications Project (microcopying of nationally significant papers).

BOOK　　　PUBLICATIONS GRANTS: **U.S. History Book Edition,** up to $10,000 per volume, on matching basis to nonprofit organizations, institutions, federal-state-local government agencies for collecting, compiling, editing, publishing papers by outstanding U.S. citizens or other documents important to understanding U.S.. history. Require project description; copyrights-literary property rights involved; statement of facilities, equipment provided; personnel list; description of editorial principals; detailed budget.

PUBLICATIONS TRAINING FELLOWSHIPS: **U.S. Historical Document Editing,** 5 stipends of $13,000 each to individuals holding Ph.D. in American History-Civilization (or having completed degree requirements except dissertation) for one-year training with project in historical document editing. Require transcripts, resume, references. Categories of projects vary.

DEADLINES: Application, March (Fellowships); March, April, November (Grants). Notification, April (Fellowships); unspecified for Grants.

240

National Library of Medicine Publication Grant Program
National Library of Medicine
Extramural Programs
Dr. Jeanne L. Brand, Chief,
International Programs Branch
8600 Rockville Pike
Bethesda, Maryland 20209 U.S.A.
Tel: (301) 496-4195, 496-6131

September, January, May

International; entry open to all; triannual; established 1965. Purpose: to assist health professions by making available national health effort information. Sponsored by Department of Health and Human Services. Application kits from: Chief, Grants Inquiries Office, Division of Research Grants, National Institutes of Health, 5333 Westbard Avenue, Bethesda, Maryland 20205.

WRITING GRANT: Nonprofit Biomedical-Scientific Publication, financial assistance (salaries, consultant fees, equipment, supplies, travel, publication costs, promotion, distribution) to nonprofit organizations or individuals for preparation, publication of scientific works by biomedical research scientists-educators, health practitioners, medical librarians, health communications specialists; 3-year project maximum. Microfiche, computerized typesetting acceptable. Require written proposal, preparation, publication plan, type of financial need, sample chapter, manuscript; 5 copies (publications relating to project). Plans for new editions of previously published works considered (submit full publication-production data). No textbooks, curriculum materials, initial reporting of original health science research, scientific society meetings proceedings, local interest or commercially viable projects. Categories: Analytic-Critical Reviews, Biomedical Monographs on Present Status of Health Research, Practice (special emphasis on health care delivery, improvement); Scholarly Research Monographs in History of Medicine, Life Sciences, Development of Medical Research, Health Services (translations of classics accepted); Medical Librarianship, Health Information Science, Biomedical Communications; Secondary Periodical Publications; Secondary Health Science Literature Tools; English-Language Translations of Current Monographs; Scientifically Significant Symposia, Conferences on U.S. Priority Health Needs.

JUDGING: By panels of nonfederal consultants, based on scientific, technical merit. Final recommendations approved by Board of Regents. Preference to in-progress, ready for publication projects.

DEADLINES: Entry, February, June, October. Final review, September-October, January-February, May.

| 241 |

National Science Foundation Scientific Research Grants
National Science Foundation (NSF)
Central Processing Section
Washington, District of Columbia
20550 U.S.A.

Continuous

National; **entry open to U.S.;** continuous; established 1950. Purpose: to initiate, support scientific research and programs to strengthen scientific research potential. Sponsored by NSF. Supported by U.S. government. Also sponsor Public Understanding of Science Grants to groups-agencies-institutions for improving communication between scientific-nonscientific communities; Technological Innovation in Education Program Grants to innovative educational television-communication technology in science education institutions; AAAS Mass Media Intern Program.

WRITING-RESEARCH GRANT: Science Research Publication, standard (limited period) and continuing (tentatively ongoing) grants (including salary, fringe benefits, equipment, supplies, travel costs, other direct and indirect costs) with possible renewal-extension, to individuals or groups for projects partially resulting in research publication. Submit signed proposal typed single-spaced on one side, unbound, stapled, with 9-19 copies, including cover page, contents, summary, project description, bibliography, biographical sketches, budget, current and pending support, appendixes. Divisions: U.S. University-College, Nonprofit Nonacademic Research Institution, Private Profit Organization, Foreign Institution (depending on U.S. holdings of foreign currencies), Other Federal Agency, Unaffiliated Scientist in U.S. Categories: Astronomy, Atmospheric Sciences, Biological-Behavioral Sciences, Chemistry, Computer Sciences, Earth Sciences, Engineering and Applied Sciences, Information Science, Mathematics, Materials, Physics, Social Sciences, Interdisciplinary, Other. No arts, humanities, business, social work, clinical or security classification research.

JUDGING: By scientists, with advisory committees and senior NSF staff review. Based on creative performance of research, internal structure of science, relevance to national objectives, future scientific potential of U.S. No proposals returned.

DEADLINES: Application, open. Notification, 6-9 months.

242

Public Understanding of Science Grants
National Science Foundation (NSF)
G. Triml, Program Director
Science Education Directorate
1180 G Street N.W.
Washington, District of Columbia
20550 U.S.A.

Continuous

National; **entry restricted to U.S. organizations, academic institutions;** continuous. Purpose: to improve communication between scientific, nonscientific communities for increased public understanding of scientific, technological public policy issues, methods, activities of scientists, engineers. Sponsored by NSF Science Education Directorate, dedicated to understanding between scientific, technological communities and general society. Also sponsor NSF Scientific Research Grants; Technological

Innovation in Education Program Grants to innovative educational television, communication technology in science education institutions; Science for Citizens Program Grants.

WRITING GRANT: Science Communication Newspaper, Magazine, Writing. Require 3 copies of 5-page preliminary proposal, 20 copies formal proposal and budget; quarterly activity-progress reports; final fiscal and technical report; summary of completed project from grant recipients. Categories: Projects Improving Public Understanding of Science, Technology; Projects Increasing Communication Between Scientists, Nonscientists; Research, Analysis on Scientific, Technological Information Flow to General Public.

ELIGIBILITY: Open to colleges, universities, laboratories, museums, government agencies, professional associations-societies, citizens groups, profit and nonprofit organizations interested in improving public understanding of science. No long-term institutional support, communication among scientists, facility construction, equipment purchase, educational system course and curriculum development.

JUDGING: By scientists, engineers, professional and institutional leaders. Based on innovative communication modes, rationale, project design, impact, cost-effectiveness, monitoring and evaluation, personnel and institutional resources, budget, quality. Sponsor has royalty-free, irrevocable, worldwide, nonexclusive license in U.S. government to reproduce, perform, translate, use, authorize others to use for government purposes, and to sell any materials produced under grant.

DEADLINES: Entry, April, August,

December. Preliminary proposal response within 8 weeks.

243

Translation Center Fellowships and Grants
Columbia University
307A Mathematics Building
New York, New York 10027 U.S.A.
Tel: (212) 280-2305

Fall

National; **entry open to U.S. citizens;** annual; established 1972. Sponsored by Translation Center, Columbia University. Supported by NEA, NEH, NYSCA. Average statistics: 200 entries, 5 finalists, 1 award. Publish *Translation Magazine,* chapbooks, anthologies.

TRANSLATION GRANT: Literary Translation *(Work-in-Progress Translation of Literature Awards),* $500 for translation completion. Require work-in-progress details, 10-20 pages of translation and original text, option letter or statement from university or small press indicating publishing interest. Occasional larger grants to multiple-translator projects.

TRANSLATION FELLOWSHIP: Translation Language Training *(Translation Fellowships),* $10,000 for 1 year to American writers for training in lesser-known language as preparation for literary translation. Require 10-page minimum samples of original-translation work, proof of some knowledge of proposed language.

JUDGING: 5 judges read all entries in entirety. Not responsible for loss or damage.

ENTRY FEE: None. Entrant pays postage (include SASE).

DEADLINES: Entry, January (fellowship), February (grants). Awards, Fall.

244

U.S. Army Military History Institute Advanced Writing-Research Grants
Assistant Director for Historical Services
Carlisle Barracks, Pennsylvania 17013 U.S.A. Tel: (717) 245-3611

Continuous

National; **entry restricted to U.S. graduates, postgraduates;** continuous; established 1967. Purpose: to perpetuate history, traditions of U.S. Army, Army's role in development of United States and its people. Sponsored and supported by U.S. Army Military History Institute (USAMHI). Have library with largest collection of items relating to U.S. military history, staff assistance, research-study facilities, oral history program (interviewing retired U.S. Army Officials). Publish Bibliographies of research material, anthologies, newsletter. Also sponsor Student Internships.

WRITING-RESEARCH GRANT: Military History, 4-5 $500 advanced research stipends offered annually to assist scholars in conducting research at Institute in military history (organization, administration, policy, biography, civic affairs). Preference to areas where there is abundance of material available. Require subject, scope, character of project; estimated time for residency, how USAMHI will aid in research, estimate of expenses; 1 copy of completed research document at end of project.

JUDGING: Review by professional military professors, personnel. Final by Advisory Committee. Based on feasibility, competitiveness, usefulness to U.S. Army, historical value.

DEADLINES: Application, December.

245

Writers Guild of America East (WGA) Foundation Fellowship Program

Craig Fisher, Executive Director
555 West 57th Street
New York, New York 10019 U.S.A.
Tel: (212) 245-6180

Annual

National; **entry open to U.S.**; annual; established 1980. Purpose: to encourage young writers working in film and television. Sponsored by East WGA Foundation. Supported by NEA, NYSCA. Average statistics: 400 entries, 40 semifinalists, 20 finalists, 8 awards. Also sponsor seminars for young film, television writers.

SCRIPTWRITING FELLOWSHIP GRANT: **Film, Television Scriptwriting,** $3500 fellowship to writers (Guild members and nonmembers) to complete material by end of current year. Submit 2 copies previous scripts (produced or unproduced) showing understanding of film medium; 2 copies outline or treatment.

JUDGING: By WGA members. Judges assigned to guide and assist in script completion. Entrants retain all rights. No entries returned.

ENTRY FEE: Entrant pays postage (include SASE).

DEADLINES: Not Specified.

246

Phoenix Trust Grants

Society of Authors, Limited
84 Drayton Gardens
London SW10 9SD, ENGLAND
Tel: 01-373-6642

Continuous

National; **entry restricted to U.K. publishers;** continuous. 150-500 pound **Grants for Literature-Research Publication.** Purpose: to assist literature publication where publisher's advance does not cover research cost.

JOURNALISM (General)

General Newspaper-Magazine Journalism, including CONSERVATION, EDITORIAL, FIRST AMENDMENT, HUMAN INTEREST, JOURNALISM IMPROVEMENT, LOCAL-GOVERNMENT REPORTING, PUBLIC SERVICE. (Also see OTHER JOURNALISM CATEGORIES.)

247

By-Line Awards

Marquette University
College of Journalism
1131 West Wisconsin Avenue
Milwaukee, Wisconsin 53233 U.S.A.
Tel: (414) 224-7132

February

International; **entry restricted to Marquette Journalism College alumni (by nomination);** annual; established 1946. By-Line copper plaques to **Newspaper Journalists.** Purpose: to honor alumni who have attained distinction in journalism field for competence, acceptance, fulfillment of professional responsibility. Sponsor keeps entries. Sponsored by and held at College of Journalism, Marquette University. Event, February.

248

George Polk Awards in Journalism

Long Island University (LIU)
Sidney Offit, Curator
The Brooklyn Center
University Plaza
Brooklyn, New York 11201 U.S.A.
Tel: (212) 834-6170

March

International; entry open to all; annual; established 1949. Formerly called GEORGE POLK MEMORIAL AWARDS. Purpose: to recognize distinguished reporting, writing, editing, photography, production in newspaper, magazine, book, radio, and TV local, national, foreign coverage, community service, criticism. Sponsored by LIU Department of Journalism. Average statistics: 200 entrants, 20 awards.

NEWSPAPER-MAGAZINE CONTEST: **Journalism,** published; in scrapbook, with cover letter explaining, justifying entry.

BOOK CONTEST: **Journalism, Investigative Reporting,** published; 2 copies, with cover letter explaining, justifying entry.

AWARDS: George Polk Awards for Outstanding Achievement in Journalism.

JUDGING: By LIU journalism faculty. Based on initiative, coverage, perception, style, courage, resourcefulness, skill. No entries returned.

ENTRY FEE: None.

DEADLINES: Entry, January. Winners announced, February. Awards, March.

249

Headliner Achievement Awards in Journalism

Press Club of Atlantic City
Herb Brown, Director
Devins Lane
Pleasantville, New Jersey 08232
U.S.A. Tel: (609) 645-1234

Spring

International; **entry restricted to journalists;** annual; established 1934. Purpose: to recognize men-women who uphold responsibilities, traditions of journalism profession. Sponsored by Press Club of Atlantic City (membership in Headliners Club limited to Headliner winners, consultants, judges). Average statistics: over 1000 awards to date. Held during 3-day National Headliners weekend in Atlantic City.

NEWSPAPER-MAGAZINE CONTEST: **Journalism,** unlimited entries, one per category. Require biography, photo. Newspaper categories: News Reporting, Feature, or Series in Daily Newspaper (circulation under 50,000, 50-150,000); Local Interest Column (general subjects); Special, Feature Column (1 subject); Editorial Cartoons; Sportswriting; Sports Column (by individual); Newspaper-Published Magazine; Investigative Reporting; Public Service. Magazine, syndicate categories: Major News Event; Special Feature Column (1 subject).

ELIGIBILITY: Published in previous 2 years. Public Service, Investigative Reporting entries require background, accomplishments, results.

AWARDS: Headliner Medallions for Outstanding Achievements in Journalism. Winners are guests at National Headliners Club.

JUDGING: Entries become property of Headliners Club.

ENTRY FEE: $10 each.

DEADLINES: Entry,   February. Awards, Spring.

250

International Society of Weekly Newspaper Editors Award Competition
Irvan J. Kummerfeldt
Department of Journalism
Northern Illinois University
DeKalb, Illinois 60115 U.S.A.
Tel: (815) 753-1925

June

International; **entry restricted to newspapers of less than daily frequency;** annual; established 1961 (Golden Quill Award), 1975 (Cervi Award). Sponsored and supported by International Society of Weekly Newspaper Editors (ISWNE). Held at ISWNE Conference in Illinois. Publish *Grassroots Editor* (quarterly magazine); also monthly newsletter for members.

NEWSPAPER CONTEST: Editorial Writing *(Quill),* editorials or signed opinion pieces appearing in newspapers of less than daily frequency (less than 5 days per week). Published in previous calendar year, mounted on 8 1/2x11-inch white paper; 2 maximum per newspaper.
Local   Affairs-Government   Reporting *(Cervi),* recognizing outstanding lifetime public service through community journalism; consistently aggressive reporting, interpreting of local government affairs. By newspapers of less than daily frequency. Require nominating letter, biography, clippings from any point in nominee's career.

AWARDS: Golden Quill Award.

Eugene Cervi Award. Plaque, certificate, paid expenses to ISWNE Conference, each category. Top 12 finalists (Golden Dozen) published in annual award booklet.

ENTRY FEE: None.

DEADLINES: Entry,   February. Awards, June.

251

Lowell Mellett Award for Improving Journalism through Critical Evaluation
Mellett Fund for a Free and Responsible Press
Ellis T. Baker
Suite 835, 1125 15th Street N.W.
Washington, District of Columbia
20005 U.S.A. Tel: (202) 296-2990

Spring

National; **entry open to U.S., Canada;** annual; established 1979. Named after Lowell Mellett, distinguished Scripps-Howard editor, syndicated Washington columnist. Purpose: to improve journalism through critical evaluation without impairing press freedom; encourage innovative approaches to constructive criticism. Sponsored by Mellett Fund for a Free and Responsible Press. Supported by Philip L. Graham Fund. Recognized by The Newspaper Guild. Average statistics: 42 entries. Held in Washington, D.C.

NEWSPAPER-MAGAZINE AWARD: **Journalism Improvement,** published, completed, or continuing in previous year. Require 3 copies, descriptive letter, other documentation.

BOOK AWARD: **Journalism Improvement.** Requirements same as for Newspaper-Magazine.

AWARDS: Mellett Citation and-or Plaque for outstanding media-monitoring, press performance evaluation; significant contributions, current or cumulative.

JUDGING: By 3 journalists. Not responsible for loss or damage. Entries returned on request.

ENTRY FEE: None. Entrant pays postage.

DEADLINES: Entry, March. Event, Spring.

| 252 |

Scripps-Howard Foundation Journalism Awards
1100 Central Trust Tower
Cincinnati, Ohio 45202 U.S.A.

Various

National; **entry open to U.S.;** annual. Sponsored by Scripps-Howard Foundation, founded 1962 as charitable nonprofit corporation. Also sponsor Scripps-Howard Foundation Scholarships and Grants; Roy W. Howard Public Service Broadcasting Awards; Robert P. Scripps Graphic Arts Grants to colleges for newspaper journalism, graphic arts. Second contact (Roy W. Howard Awards only): Station WEWS, 3001 Euclid Avenue, Cleveland, Ohio 44115.

NEWSPAPER CONTEST: **Public Service** *(Roy W. Howard Awards)* to newspaper outstanding in public service (defined as exposure and contribution toward alleviation of corruption, crime, health, other problems inimical to general welfare). Require sponsoring letter from editor and history of endeavor. Category: Newspaper.

Conservation *(Edward J. Meeman Awards)* to educate public, public officials to understand-support conservation (including news, feature stories, campaigns, editorials, columns, cartoons, essays). Require tearsheets-clippings, mounted, with sponsoring letter. Categories: Over 100,000 Circulation, Under 100,000.

Human Interest *(Ernie Pyle Awards)* to honor warmth, style, craftsmanship of late Ernie Pyle. Require sponsoring letter, portfolio of work.

First Amendment *(Edward Willis Scripps Award)* to newspaper for public service in cause of First Amendment guarantee of free press. Require sponsoring letter, clippings.

Editorial *(Walker Stone Awards)* to honor late editor-in-chief of Scripps-Howard Newspapers. Require sponsoring letter, portfolio of work.

ELIGIBILITY: Open to U.S. and territories; published during previous year.

AWARDS: Roy W. Howard Public Service Awards, $2500 First Prize and Bronze Plaque, $1000 Runner-Up Prize (to newspapers). Edward J. Meeman Conservation Awards, 1 $2500 Grand Prize and Bronze Plaque, $2000 and $1000 Prizes, each category (to individuals). Ernie Pyle Memorial Human Interest Awards, $1000 First Prize and Bronze Plaque, possible $500 Second Prize (to individuals). Edward Willis Scripps First Amendment Award, $2500 First Prize and Bronze Plaque (to newspaper). Walker Stone Editorial Awards, $1000 First Prize and Bronze Plaque, $500 Second Prize (to individuals).

JUDGING: By 5 judges. Human Interest based on warmth, story-telling; Editorial on general excellence, writing quality, forcefulness, public interest importance. May withhold awards. Sponsor keeps entries.

ENTRY FEE: None.

DEADLINES: Entry, March (Public Service), February (Conservation,

First Amendment, Editorial), January (Human Interest).

253

Sigma Delta Chi Distinguished Service in Journalism Awards

Society of Professional Journalists
Kathy Lieberman, Information Director
35 East Wacker Drive, Suite 3108
Chicago, Illinois 60601 U.S.A.
Tel: (312) 236-6577

April-May

International; entry open to all; annual; established 1932. Purpose: to foster high ethics; safeguard flow of information; attract young people to journalism; raise prestige of journalists in community. Sponsored by Society of Professional Journalists (Sigma Delta Chi), international nonprofit voluntary professional journalist society with 154 campus, 130 professional chapters; founded 1909 as fraternity at Depauw University, Greencastle, Indiana. Average statistics: 1200 entries, 16 winners, 1000 attendance. Publish *The Quill* (monthly magazine).

NEWSPAPER-MAGAZINE CONTEST: **Journalism,** published in previous year, in 20x24-inch (maximum) scrapbook or notebook. Require typewritten summary, biography, photograph if nomination is for individual. Newspaper categories: General Reporting, Editorial (3 maximum; series or single topic counts as 1), Washington Correspondence, Foreign Correspondence, Editorial Cartoon (6 maximum), Public Service.

BOOK CONTEST: **Journalism Research,** original, published or unpublished in previous year; 5 copies (manuscript or galley proofs accepted). Other requirements same as for Newspaper-Magazine.

AWARDS: Bronze Medallions, Plaques for Distinguished Service in Journalism.

JUDGING: All entries reviewed in entirety by journalist jury. Based on completeness, readability, accuracy, interest, enterprise, resourcefulness of reporter, journalist. May withhold awards. Sponsor owns all entries.

ENTRY FEE: $10 each.

DEADLINES: Entry, January. Judging, February-March. Winners announced, April. Event, April-May.

254

William Allen White Foundation National Award for Journalistic Merit

William Allen White School of Journalism
Del Brinkman, Director
University of Kansas
Lawrence, Kansas 66045 U.S.A.

February

National; **entry open to U.S.;** annual. Sponsored by William Allen White Foundation. Also accept broadcast and photo journalism.

NEWSPAPER-MAGAZINE CONTEST: **Journalism,** require recommendation letter. Other requirements, restrictions not specified.

AWARDS: National Award for Journalistic Merit.

JUDGING: By 100 Foundation trustees.

ENTRY FEE: None.

DEADLINES: Award, February (on birthday of William Allen White).

255

British Press Awards
Mirror Group Newspapers
David H. Tyler, Awards Secretary
Orbit House
9 New Fetter Lane, Room 302
London EC4A 1AR, ENGLAND
Tel: 01-822-3504

April

National; **entry restricted to British journalists;** annual; established 1962. Formerly called HANNEN SWAFFER NATIONAL PRESS AWARDS to 1965; I.P.C. NATIONAL PRESS AWARDS to 1974. Purpose: to recognize British journalism. Sponsored and supported by Mirror Group Newspapers in collaboration with Associated Newspapers, Express Newspapers, *The Financial Times,* Guardian Newspapers, *The Observer,* Times Newspapers, United Newspapers, Westminster Press. Average statistics: 350 entrants. Second contact: Mirror Group Newspapers, Anthony Miles, Chairman, Editorial Director, P.O. Box 644, Athene House, 66-73 Shoe Lane, London, England EC4P 4AB.

NEWSPAPER CONTEST: British Journalism, original, published in daily (anytime), weekly newspaper, from January to December in year prior to contest in England, Scotland, Wales, Northern Ireland; unlimited entries. Require 5 examples of original published cuttings each entry (single byline, multi-byline), 8 additional copies of each cutting (photocopies OK); 5 examples on 1 subject considered 1 example. Categories: Reporter (general, investigative, news-feature); International Reporter (correspondent stationed abroad, journalist who has carried out major assignment abroad); Provincial Journalist; Young Journalist (not over 25 on December 31, year before entry deadline); General Feature Writer (specialist, columnist, critic); Specialist Writer (all fields except criticism); Sports Journalist; Columnist (columnist, regular commentator); Critic (all fields); Campaigning Journalist; Journalist Award (public interest service); David Holden Award (contribution to international understanding, selected from previous categories).

AWARDS: 1000 pounds, Journalist. 250 pounds, each category.

JUDGING: By 7-member panel. May change or withhold awards; change categories. No entries returned.

ENTRY FEE: None.

DEADLINES: Entry, January. Judging, February. Winners announced, March, Awards, April.

JOURNALISM (Business, Financial, Industrial)

Newspaper-Magazine Journalism, Script, incuding AMERICAN FREE ENTERPRISE, CITY-REGIONAL PLANNING, ECONOMICS, FIRE FIGHTING, HIGHWAY SAFETY, OIL-GAS INDUSTRY, REAL ESTATE, WOMEN IN BANKING. (Also see OTHER JOURNALISM.)

| 256 |

American Planning Association Journalism Award Competition
Sylvia Lewis, Dirctor of Publications
1313 East 60th Street
Chicago, Illinois 60637 U.S.A.
Tel: (312) 947-2108

April

International; **entry restricted to U.S., Canadian newspapers;** annual; established 1949. Purpose: to honor public service in newspaper coverage of city, regional planning. Sponsored and supported by American Planning Association (called American Society of Planning Officials to 1979). Average statistics: 50 entries, 2-4 awards.

NEWSPAPER CONTEST: City-Regional Planning Journalism, published in U.S. or Canadian daily or weekly newspapers in previous calendar year; single article or series; mounted in 15x24-inch maximum scrapbook. Require background statement, information about efforts to support, improve, initiate planning programs or inform public about issues, problems, choices in improving community; statements by planning agencies, public officials, civic associations on effect, public service of articles. Newspaper categories: Over 100,000 Circulation, Under 100,000 Circulation.

AWARDS: $100 and Certificate, each category.

JUDGING: In Chicago, by 3 judges from planning, journalism fields, or from citizens' groups. Based on public service in coverage, perspective, interpretation, impact. All entries read in entirety. Entries returned on request.

ENTRY FEE: None. Sponsor pays return postage.

DEADLINES: Entry, February. Judging, March. Awards, April. Materials returned, May.

| 257 |

Frank Kelley Memorial Award
American Association of Petroleum Landmen (AAPL)
Carolyn Stephens, Public Relations Director
2408 Continental Life Bldg.
Fort Worth, Texas 76102 U.S.A.
Tel: (817) 335-9751

June

International; **entry restricted to U.S., Canadian journalists;** annual; established 1967. Named after Frank Kelley, oil executive (died 1963). Purpose: to recognize journalistic excellence in reporting oil, gas, energy news. Motto: "Land is the basis of all wealth." Sponsored and supported by AAPL. Average statistics: 30-50 entrants, 1-2 awards.

NEWSPAPER CONTEST: Oil-Gas Industry Journalism, written and published in U.S., Canada, April previous to April current year; single article (submitted in tearsheet) or several mounted, bound in 12x14-inch scrapbook.

AWARDS: Frank Kelley Memorial Award, bronze plaque to publication, $250 and plaque to writer.

JUDGING: By journalism professor, working journalist, and AAPL member. Based on accuracy, style, subject matter, reader interest, overall quality, not volume.

ENTRY FEE: None.

DEADLINES: Entry, May. Awards, June.

258

Gerald Loeb Awards for Distinguished Business & Financial Journalism

University of California, Los Angeles (UCLA)
Rebecca Novelli, Communications Director
Graduate School of Management
405 Hilgard Avenue, Room 4250E
Los Angeles, California 90024 U.S.A.
Tel: (213) 825-3217

June

National; **entry restricted to U.S. writers, publications;** annual; established 1957. Considered Pulitzer prize of business, financial journalism; since 1974 sponsored by UCLA Graduate School of Management and Loeb Foundation. Purpose: to recognize writers for significant contributions to understanding of business, finance. Average statistics: 500 entries, 16 finalists, 4 awards.

NEWSPAPER-MAGAZINE CONTEST: **Business-Financial Journalism,** published in previous calendar year; may be single article or series (limit 8 stories per entry), 10 copies each, 11x14 inches maximum. Categories: Large Newspapers (circulation over 250,000), Small Newspapers (circulation under 250,000), Magazines, Editorial-Commentary.

AWARDS: $1000 and Plaque, each category. If multiple winners per category, prize money divided. $500 and Plaque to Honorable Mentions, each category. Winners receive transportation, lodging to attend Loeb Awards Banquet.

JUDGING: 2 professors, 1 journalist select 4 finalists per category. Final by 3 academicians, 3 journalists, 3 business representatives. Based on news value; ingenuity and-or exclusivity; reportorial, writing quality; analytical value.

ENTRY FEE: None. Entrant pays postage (include SASE).

DEADLINES: Entry, January. Judging, February-March. Winners announced, March. Awards, June.

259

Highway Safety Editorial Awards Contest

National Foundation for Highway Safety
William H. Veale, President
P.O. Box 3043 Westville Station
New Haven, Connecticut 06151
U.S.A. Tel: (203) 387-2977

Spring

International; entry open to all; annual. Purpose: to reach thousands of drivers, influence them to be courteous at the wheel, saving lives, preventing injuries. Theme: Driving Carries a Moral Responsibility. Sponsored by National Foundation for Highway Safety, founded 1951.

NEWSPAPER CONTEST: **Highway Safety Feature-Editorial.** Categories: Editors, Editorials, Sunday Editors, Reporters, Editorial Cartoonists; Letters to Editor in local newspaper.

SCRIPT CONTEST: **Highway Safety Television or Radio Editorial or Program.**

ELIGIBILITY: May depict any phase of theme (including drinking & driving, speedsters, tailgaters, bright lighters, thoughtless and careless operation of car). Require 3 clip sheets, typed copies of television or radio editorials or programs. Any number of entries.

AWARDS: $100 U.S. Savings Bond for Best Feature or Editorial, Best Cartoon. Bronze Plaques, Special Printed Awards. Foundation may reproduce entries without profit in interest of highway safety, certifying the source.

ENTRY FEE: None.

DEADLINES: Entry by January. Awards, Spring.

260

International Association of Fire Fighters (IAFF) International Awards Program
John A. Gannon, President
1750 New York Avenue N.W.
Washington, District of Columbia
20006 U.S.A. Tel: (202) 872-8484

April

International; **entry restricted (nomination by local U.S. and Canadian IAFF unions);** annual; established 1965. First, Second Place monetary awards and plaques, Honorable Mentions, Certificates for **Fire Fighting Newspaper and Magazine Writing;** news media reporting of U.S., Canadian fire fighters published in previous year. Sponsor may reproduce winners in IAFF publications. Sponsored by IAFF. Average statistics: 350 entries. Event, April.

261

John Hancock Awards for Excellence in Business and Financial Journalism
John Hancock Mutual Life Insurance Company (T-54)
John Hancock Place, P.O. Box 111
Boston, Massachusetts 02117 U.S.A.

Spring, Fall

National; **entry open to U.S.;** annual; established 1967. Purpose: to foster public knowledge of, interest in

business and finance; increase understanding of personal money management; clarify economic significance of sociopolitical developments. Sponsored by John Hancock Mutual Life Insurance Company. Held at a leading American university.

NEWSPAPER-MAGAZINE CONTEST: **Business-Financial Journalism,** appearing in U.S. publication during previous calendar year; single or series, 1 or more (selective) entries, 6 unmounted tearsheets with publication date (teletype copy and photocopies for wire service writers). Categories: Syndicated or News Service, National General Interest Magazine, Financial-Business Newspaper or Magazine, Newspaper (Circulation Above 300,000, 100-300,000, Under 100,000).

AWARDS: $2000 and expenses to attend awards presentation, each category. Additional permanent trophy to 3-time winners.

JUDGING: By press, business, educational panel. May withhold awards. No entries returned.

ENTRY FEE: None.

DEADLINES: Entry, December. Awards, Spring, Fall.

262

Media Awards for Economic Understanding
Amos Tuck School of Business Administration
Jan B. Bent, Program Administrator
Dartmouth College
Hanover, New Hampshire 03755
U.S.A. Tel: (603) 643-5596

Spring

National; **entry restricted to U.S. journalists, general media employees;** annual; established 1977.

Formerly called MEDIA AWARDS FOR THE ADVANCEMENT OF ECONOMIC UNDERSTANDING to 1978. Purpose: to recognize, improve quality, increase quantity of public economics reporting. Sponsored and supported by Champion International Corporation. Average statistics: 1400 entries. Held at Amos Tuck School of Business Administration.

NEWSPAPER-MAGAZINE CONTEST: Economics Journalism, published during previous calendar year. Submit 1 copy of published material, clipped and pasted up. Newspaper categories: (Circulation over 250,000; 100-250,000; 50-100,000; 10-50,000; under 10,000); Syndicate, Wire Service, Column. Magazine category: General Audience Publications.

AWARDS: First Place, $5000; Second Place, $2500, each category.

JUDGING: By 11 judges. Based on effectiveness, understanding of economic system. Sponsor has reproduction rights, keeps entries.

ENTRY FEE: None.

DEADLINES: Materials, March. Judging, April. Winners announced, May.

| 263 |

National Association of Bank Women (NABW) Distinguished Journalism Award
Public Relations Director
500 North Michigan, Suite 1400
Chicago, Illinois 60611 U.S.A.
Tel: (312) 661-1700

Summer

International; entry open to all; annual. Purpose: to recognize, honor writing contribution to better understanding of executive women in banking industry. Sponsored and supported by NABW.

NEWSPAPER-MAGAZINE CONTEST: Women in Banking journalism, published in year prior to June, about women's roles in banking; 800 words minimum, 3 articles or series maximum, 1 copy each. No reprints, NABW members or employees. Categories: U.S. Newspaper-Periodical, Bank-Sponsored Publication.

AWARDS: $300 and Certificate, each category. 3 Honorable Mention Certificates.

JUDGING: By journalists. May withhold awards. Sponsor keeps entries.

ENTRY FEE: None.

DEADLINES: Entry, June. Awards, Summer.

| 264 |

National Association of Real Estate Editors (NAREE) Writing Awards
Robert F. Brennan, Executive Secretary
901 Lakeside Avenue
Cleveland, Ohio 44114 U.S.A.
Tel: (216) 623-6721

November

National; **entry restricted to NAREE members;** annual; established 1948. $75, $50, $25 Awards to **Real Estate-Home Newspaper and Magazine Writing** in each of 5 categories. Purpose: to give incentive for better real estate journalism. Sponsored by NAREE. Average statistics: 15 awards. Awards, November.

265

National Association of Realtors (NAR) Real Estate Journalism Achievement Competition
Ilene DeBoissiere, Communications Division
430 North Michigan Avenue
Chicago, Illinois 60611 U.S.A.
Tel: (312) 440-8106

October

National; **entry restricted to U.S. real estate editors, freelance writers;** annual; established 1964. Purpose: to encourage real estate reporting, writing excellence. Sponsored and supported by NAR (745,000 members), founded 1908. Considered nation's largest trade and professional association.

NEWSPAPER-MAGAZINE CONTEST: **Real Estate Journalism,** published August previous to July current year; unfolded, mounted on 8 1/2x11-inch paper (series considered 1 entry). No editors, writers employed by state association or local board of realtors, NAR (publications, institutes, societies, councils) or freelance writers who submit articles to these publications; no illustration, photography layouts or entries in folders, notebooks. Daily, Weekly Newspaper categories (1 entry each maximum, as article, column, or series): Local Situation Involving Real Estate of National Concern, Consumer Information, Real Estate Columns (3 consecutive). Other categories: General Interest Magazine, Industry-Trade Publication (3 maximum each, written by 1 entrant).

AWARDS: $200 First, $100 Second, $50 Third Place each category (15 total). Plaques to all winners.

JUDGING: By writing specialists. Based on information quality, writing excellence, creativity, reporting skills, research. Entries returned by request.

ENTRY FEE: None. Entrant pays postage (include SASE).

DEADLINES: Entry, August. Winners notified, October.

266

United States Industrial Council (USIC) Educational Foundation Editorial Awards
Elizabeth Bennett, Editorial Assistant
P.O. Box 2686
Third Floor, Realtors Building
Nashville, Tennessee 37219 U.S.A.
Tel: (615) 256-5961

Spring

National; **entry open to U.S.;** annual; established 1978. Purpose: to encourage research, editorial writing on free enterprise. Sponsored and supported by USIC, founded 1933 to promote interest in free enterprise system. Average statistics: 100-150 entries, 35-40 awards. Publish booklet containing winning material. Also sponsor Editorial Cartoon "Dragonslayer" Contest (cartoon attacking collectivist "dragons" menacing free enterprise system).

NEWSPAPER-MAGAZINE CONTEST: **American Free Enterprise Editorial,** published in U.S. daily, weekly newspaper during previous calendar year, dealing with defending free enterprise system; unlimited entries. Require statement of work's originality, permission to USIC to publish.

SCRIPT CONTEST: **American Free Enterprise Television or Radio Editorial Broadcast,** broadcast on U.S. station during previous calendar year. Requirements same as for Newspaper-Magazine.

AWARDS: $500 First, $300 Second,

$200 Third, $150 Fourth, $100 Fifth Prize. $50 Honorable Mentions. Award Medallions to First, Second, Third Place. Winning entries published in awards booklet.

JUDGING: Based on interpretation of American free enterprise system spirit, goals, achievements. No entries returned.

ENTRY FEE: None. Entrant pays postage (include SASE) for acknowledgment of entry.

DEADLINES: Entry, February. Winners announced, April. Awards, Spring.

267

University of Missouri Business Journalism Awards
University of Missouri
James K. Gentry, Director
School of Journalism, Neff Hall
Columbia, Missouri 65211 U.S.A.
Tel: (314) 882-7862

November

National; **entry restricted to U.S. publications;** annual; established 1962. Purpose: to cultivate, encourage professionalism in business and economics reporting. Sponsored by University of Missouri School of Journalism. Supported by Interstate Natural Gas Association of America. Average statistics: 260 entries. Held during Business Journalism Workshop in Columbia, Missouri. Have business news writing-reporting workshops. Also sponsor 15 Herbert J. Davenport Fellowships in Economics Reporting to professional journalists for 1-month study at University of Missouri School of Journalism; scholarships to business-economic journalism students.

NEWSPAPER-MAGAZINE CONTEST: Business-Economics Journal-ism, published in U.S. from June previous to June contest year; about American business and its operation in present-day society; 3 articles or 1 series maximum per writer, 6 copies each. Require letter from editor about writer. No professional journals, company publications, annual reports. Categories: Daily-Weekly Newspaper Staff Member or Team (Circulation Under 100,000; Over 100,000 or syndicated columnist, wire service member, newspaper-distributed magazine); Outside Contributor (to General Circulation Magazine Staff Member or Team; to Controlled-Paid Circulation Publication Staff Member or Team).

AWARDS: $1000 and Silver Trophy to winner, Commemorative Plaque to publication, each category. $150 and Plaque to Runners-Up, Plaque to publication, each category.

JUDGING: By 4 business editors, reporters, business executives. Based on reporting skill-accuracy, exposition clarity, public interest contribution.

ENTRY FEE: None.

DEADLINES: Entry, June. Judging, September. Awards, November.

JOURNALISM (Children, Student, Youth)

Newspaper-Magazine Journalism, including COLLEGE. (Also see other JOURNALISM.)

| 268 |

Golden Press Awards
American Legion Auxillary (ALA)
Layton K. Hurst, Program
Coordinator
1698 K Street N.W.
Washington, District of Columbia
10006 U.S.A. Tel: (202) 861-2795

August

National; **entry restricted to U.S. newspapers;** annual; established 1968. Purpose: to recognize newspapers attaining high standards in interest of youth. Theme varies yearly. Sponsored and supported by ALA. Held at ALA national convention. Second contact: Miriam Junge, 777 North Meridian Street, Indianapolis, Indiana 46204.

NEWSPAPER CONTEST: **In Interest of Youth Journalism,** 1 copy, printed between May previous and May current year, on various yearly themes. Request letters showing reader reaction, letter from editor. Categories: Editorial, Feature Article (single or series on same subject).

AWARDS: Golden Press Award Trophy, best each category. Golden Press Award Certificate, best each state.

JUDGING: Preliminary by state public relations chair. Final by national committee of judges.

ENTRY FEE: None. Sponsor pays return postage.

DEADLINES: Entry, May. Awards, August.

| 269 |

Odyssey Institute Media Awards Competition
Jean S. Elahi, Vice President
Development
656 Avenue of the Americas
New York, New York 10010 U.S.A.
Tel: (212) 691-8510

December

International; **entry open to U.S., Australia, New Zealand;** annual; established 1977, added books 1981. Purpose: to recognize, encourage media productions of excellence on children's issues, programming. Theme: Concerns of Children. Sponsored by Odyssey Institute, international nonprofit organization committed to health care concerns, research, legislative action, child advocacy. Average statistics: 260 entries, 520 entrants, 70 finalists, 36 winners, 250 attendance. Held in New York City for 1 day. Have multimedia library. Publish *Odyssey Journal,* books. Also sponsor internships for fieldwork experience.

NEWSPAPER-MAGAZINE CONTEST: **Children's Issue Journalism, Journalism,** original; published by previous September. Category: Print.

BOOK CONTEST: **Children's Issue.**

AWARDS: Awards each category. Special Mentions. Winners displayed at ceremonies. Entries referenced in publications, appearances, legislative consultations prepared by sponsor.

JUDGING: Entries viewed in entirety by 15 judges from media schools, Congress, public relations firms, foundations. Entrants retain rights, institute keeps entries for Concerns of Children Multi-Media Library, New York City. Not responsible for loss or damage.

ENTRY FEE: $20.

DEADLINES: Entry, October. Judging, November. Event, December.

| 270 |

Quill and Scroll National Writing Contest
Quill and Scroll Society
Richard P. Johns, Executive Secretary
University of Iowa
School of Journalism
Iowa City, Iowa 52242 U.S.A.
Tel: (319) 353-4475

April-May

National; **entry restricted to U.S. junior-senior high school students** (selection by local schools); annual. Purpose: to provide exposure and critique for entrant; determine eligibility for journalism scholarship. Sponsored by Quill and Scroll Society (International Honorary Society for High School Journalists), American Newspaper Publishers Association (ANPA). Supported by Quill and Scroll Foundation. Average statistics: 3839 entries, 228 finalists. Publish *Quill and Scroll* (quarterly). Also sponsor 10 $500 Edward J. Nell Memorial Scholarships in Journalism (open to senior class Writing, Photography, Current Events Quiz contest winners); George H. Gallup Award Newsmedia Evaluations (for member high school news publications); Current Events Quiz and Photography Contest (both open to U.S. junior-senior high school students); Graduate Student Journalism Research Grants.

NEWSPAPER-MAGAZINE CONTEST: **High School Journalism,** by 1 student, published in high school or professional newspaper September previous to February of contest year; complete page; 2 entries maximum per category per school. No yearbook work. Categories: Editorial, Editorial Cartoon, News, Feature, Sports, Advertisement.

AWARDS: Quill and Scroll Na-
tional Award Gold Key to national winner, each division. Senior winners may apply for $500 Edward J. Nell Journalism Scholarships.

JUDGING: By professional and scholastic journalists; separate judge each division. Editorials judged on reader interest, appropriateness for high school newspaper, clarity of purpose, structure, effectiveness. Editorial Cartoons on originality, reader interest, appropriateness, clarity of purpose, effectiveness. Advertisements on enterprise, originality, student appeal, display-design, printed reproduction. All entries automatically eligible for ANPA Journalism Awards. No entries returned.

ENTRY FEE: None.

DEADLINES: Entry, February. Winners announced in April-May issue *Quill and Scroll.*

| 271 |

William Randolph Hearst Foundation Journalism Awards Program
Mary A. Argenti, Director
690 Market Street, Suite 502
San Francisco, California 94104
U.S.A. Tel: (415) 982-8551

October-May

National; **entry restricted to U.S. college undergraduate journalism students at AASDJ-member schools;** monthly, 6 times a year; established 1960. Scrolls, Medallions, $100-$1200 Scholarships to Students (similar Grants to Schools) for **College College Student Journalism Writing.** Various monthly themes. Purpose: to encourage excellence in journalism education at college level. Sponsored by William Randolph Hearst Foundation, founded 1948 as nonprofit educational and charitable organization, AASDJ. Average statistics: 600 entries, 162 awards totaling $103,650. Also sponsor photojournalism awards.

JOURNALISM (Health, Medical, Mental Health)

Newspaper-Magazine Journalism, Book, Monograph, including ARTHRITIS, CYSTIC FIBROSIS, HEART DISEASE, OSTEOPATHIC, PSYCHOLOGY. (Also see other JOURNALISM.)

| 272 |

American Psychological Foundation (APF) National Media Awards

Kathleen Holmay, Public Information Officer
1200 Seventeenth Street N.W.
Washington, District of Columbia
20036 U.S.A. Tel: (202) 833-7881

August

National; **entry open to U.S.;** annual; established 1956. Purpose: to recognize, honor, encourage outstanding, accurate psychology coverage to public. Sponsored by APF, American Psychological Association (APA). Average statistics: 345 entries, 6 winners, 15,000 attendance. Held at annual APA convention.

NEWSPAPER-MAGAZINE CONTEST: **Psychology,** published May previous to May current year; include references to psychology, psychologists, depict findings or applications of psychological science. Require 3 article clippings. May be submitted as series if billed and run as series.

BOOK-MONOGRAPH CONTEST: **Psychology.** Requirements same as for Newspaper-Magazine. No texts or reference books.

AWARDS: $1000 and Citation each category. Winner invited to 3-day convention, all expenses paid. Honorable Mentions. Special Citation. Sponsor distributes 45 copies winning book (author must supply).

ENTRY FEE: None. No entries returned.

DEADLINES: Entry, May. Winners announced, July. Awards, August.

| 273 |

Anson Jones Award Competition

Texas Medical Association (TMA)
Jon R. Hornaday
1801 North Lamar Blvd.
Austin, Texas 78701 U.S.A.
Tel: (512) 477-6704, ext. 120

May

State; **entry restricted to Texas Media;** annual; established 1956. Named after Anson Jones, pioneer Texas physician and last president of Texas Republic. Purpose: to award Texas news media for communicating health information to public; recognize journalism contributing to public understanding of Texas medicine and health. Sponsored and supported by TMA (founded 1853). Average statistics: 100 entries, 9 awards. Held at TMA annual meeting.

NEWSPAPER-MAGAZINE CONTEST: **Health Journalism,** published. Require tearsheets, scrapbook, or mounted and bound; entire magazine acceptable. Unlimited entry. Categories: Daily Newspaper in Dallas, Fort Worth, Houston, or San Antonio; Daily Newspaper in all other cities; Weekly, Biweekly, or Semiweekly; Company-Trade Magazine or Newsletter; Consumer-Oriented, General-Interest Magazine or Newsletter.

ELIGIBILITY: Published in previous calendar year. Not primarily for medical or allied professions. No entries from members of medical profession, associations or employees, health-related organizations.

AWARDS: Anson Jones Plaque and $250 for Excellence in Communicating Health Information to Public, each category. Merit Citations.

JUDGING: Preliminary by publishers, final by Texas physicians. Based on accuracy, significance, quality, public interest, impact. May withhold awards.

ENTRY FEE: None. Sponsor pays return postage.

DEADLINES: Entry, January. Judging, February-March. Winners announced, April. Awards, May.

274

Cystic Fibrosis Foundation (CFF) Communications Awards Competition
6000 Executive Blvd., Suite 309
Rockville, Maryland 20852 U.S.A.
Tel: (301) 881-9130

February

National; **entry open to U.S.**; annual; established 1975. Formerly called LEROY WOLFE COMMUNICATIONS AWARDS. Purpose: to recognize news and feature reports on cystic fibrosis, the disease and its consequences. Theme: Cystic Fibrosis. Sponsored and supported by CFF. Held at Spring Board of Trustees Meeting, Washington, D.C.

NEWSPAPER-MAGAZINE CONTEST: **Cystic Fibrosis, Children's Lung Disease,** published for U.S. general public in previous calendar year.

Require tearsheet and typewritten copy. No CFF personnel.

AWARDS: $1000 to top winners each category.

JUDGING: By professional communicators. Based on accuracy, quality, impact, ability to stimulate greater public knowledge and concern.

ENTRY FEE: None.

DEADLINES: Entry, February. Event, Spring.

275

Health Education Writers Awards
Dr. James Pahz, Awards Chairperson
Department of Health Education
Central Michigan University
Mt. Pleasant, Michigan 48859 U.S.A.
Tel: (517) 774-2541

August

International; entry open to all; annual; established 1979. Purpose: to recognize superior writing in health education; promote activities of health educators. Sponsored and supported by Upjohn Company. Recognized by Central Michigan University. Average statistics: 100-200 entries, 3 finalists.

NEWSPAPER-MAGAZINE CONTEST: **Health Education,** published during previous calendar year; any length, form; unlimited entries. Require 3 copies (reprints acceptable). Categories: Professional Articles; Consumer Magazines, Newspapers; Student Publications.

AWARDS: First Prize $250 and Plaque, each category.

JUDGING: By university committee of professionals. May withhold award. Entries become property of Central Michigan University Department of Health Education. Not responsible for loss or damage.

ENTRY FEE: None.

DEADLINES: Entry, May. Judging, Spring. Winners announced, August. Awards, September.

| 276 |

Health Journalism Awards
American Chiropractic Association (ACA)
Joann Ozimek, Thomas E. Blackett, Public Affairs
2200 Grand Avenue
Des Moines, Iowa 50312 U.S.A.
Tel: (515) 243-1121

Summer

International; **entry restricted to journalists;** annual; established 1976. Purpose: to recognize journalists who promote health, suggest problem solutions, motivate public health care, contribute to responsible reporting. Sponsored by ACA. Average statistics: 161 entries. Held at annual ACA conference.

NEWSPAPER-MAGAZINE CONTEST: **Health.** Published during previous calendar year, public-oriented. No chiropractic professionals, associations, employees. Categories: Newspaper, Consumer Magazine, Publications (trade, professional, special interest).

AWARDS: First Place Distinguished Journalism Gold Award and $200. Runners-Up, Bronze Medallions each category. Special Recognition Plaques.

JUDGING: By media professionals. Sponsor may withhold awards, display entries to public.

ENTRY FEE: None.

DEADLINES: Entry, March. Event, Summer.

| 277 |

Howard W. Blakeslee Awards
American Heart Association (AHA)
Howard L. Lewis, Chairman
7320 Greenville Avenue
Dallas, Texas 75231 U.S.A.
Tel: (214) 750-5340

December

National; **entry open to U.S.;** annual; established 1952. Named for Howard W. Blakeslee, founder of National Association of Science Writers. Purpose: to encourage mass communication reporting on heart and circulatory diseases. Sponsored by AHA. Held at AHA meeting.

NEWSPAPER-MAGAZINE CONTEST: **Heart Disease Publications,** 5 maximum per entrant. Require clippings, tearsheets, photocopies, or reprints; 8 1/2x12 inches maximum, not stitched or stapled; objectives, audience. Categories: Newspaper, Magazine, Scientific, Medical Publications.

BOOK CONTEST: **Heart Disease.** Require objectives, audience.

ELIGIBILITY: Published in U.S. or territories from March previous year to February current year. No employees or materials of AHA affiliates, local heart organizations.

AWARDS: Plaque and $500 for outstanding public reporting on heart and blood vessel diseases, each winner.

JUDGING: Based on accuracy, significance, skill, originality, achievements.

ENTRY FEE: None.

DEADLINES: Entry, May. Awards, December.

| 278 |

Mental Health Media Awards
National Mental Health Association (NMHA)
Lynn Schultz-Writsel, Coordinator
1800 North Kent Street
Arlington, Virginia 22209 U.S.A.
Tel: (703) 528-6405

November

National; **entry open to U.S.**; annual; established 1977. Purpose: to honor media representatives for outstanding contributions in fight against mental illness, promotion of mental health. Sponsored by NMHA. Held at NMHA annual meeting. Also sponsor NMHA Film Festival.

NEWSPAPER-MAGAZINE CONTEST: **Mental Health Journalism,** published within past year. Require standard scrapbook, 12x15 inches, including clippings or photostats of original articles. Categories: Daily Newspaper, Other Publication (including nondaily newspaper, magazine), Individual Reporter.

AWARDS: Mental Health Media Awards.

JUDGING: Sponsor keeps all entries.

ENTRY FEE: None.

DEADLINES: Entry, July. Awards, November.

| 279 |

Osteopathic Journalism Awards Competition
American Osteopathic Association (AOA)
Monica E. Lynch, Audio-Visual Coordinator
212 East Ohio Street
Chicago, Illinois 60611 U.S.A.
Tel: (312) 280-5857

Spring

International; **entry restricted to journalists;** annual; established 1956. Oldest journalism competition sponsored by a professional association. Purpose: to recognize journalists who report, interpret osteopathic medicine to scientific community, general public. Sponsored by AOA. Supported by Ross Laboratories (division of Abbott Laboratories).

NEWSPAPER-MAGAZINE CONTEST: **Osteopathic Medicine Journalism** (Newspaper, Magazine, Wire Service, Periodical), published during previous calendar year; 3 entries maximum, series may be submitted as single if it has continuity; mounted on white paper. No members of osteopathic profession, spouses, employees, AOA employees. Categories: Scientific Advances; College, Hospital Programs; Focus on Individuals.

AWARDS: $1000 to most outstanding article. 2 supplemental awards, $500 each.

JUDGING: By professional journalists. Based on good journalism, contribution to understanding of osteopathic profession. AOA keeps all entries, may print winners in AOA publications.

ENTRY FEE: None.

DEADLINES: Entry, March. Event, Spring.

| 280 |

Russell L. Cecil Arthritis Awards
Arthritis Foundation
Roy Scott, Communications Specialist
3400 Peachtree Road N.E.
Atlanta, Georgia 30326 U.S.A.
Tel: (404) 266-0795

Fall

National; **entry open to U.S.;** annual; established 1956. Named after R. L. Cecil, pioneer rheumatologist, former medical director of Foundation. Purpose: to recognize, encourage writing on arthritis, related diseases. Sponsored by Arthritis Foundation. Average statistics: 75-100 entries, 9 semifinalists, 4 winners, 150 attendance. Held for 1 day at site selected by Foundation. Tickets: free.

NEWSPAPER-MAGAZINE CONTEST: **Arthritis Journalism,** single story or series, published in U.S. general public media during previous calendar year. Require 5 copies from publication, unmounted. Categories: Newspaper, Magazine.

AWARDS: Cecil Medallions.

JUDGING: By 2 journalism professionals, 1 rheumatologist. Based on accuracy, concern for arthritic problems. No entries returned.

ENTRY FEE: None.

DEADLINES: Entry, January. Judging, Spring. Winners announced, Spring-Fall. Event, Fall.

JOURNALISM (Humanitarian, Religious, Social Concern)

Newspaper-Magazine Journalism, Book Script, including BROTHERHOOD, CATHOLIC, CURRENT-PUBLIC INTEREST, DISADVANTAGED, MINORITY PROBLEMS, And RACIAL-RELIGIOUS HATRED, INTOLERANCE, DISCRIMINATION, BIGOTRY. (Also see other JOURNALISM.)

| 281 |

Catholic Press Association (CPA) Journalism Awards
119 North Park Avenue
Rockville Centre, New York 11570
U.S.A. Tel: (516) 766-3400

May

International; **entry restricted to CPA member publishers;** annual. First, Second, Third, Honorable Mention Awards to **Catholic Newspapers, Magazines** in 60 categories. Sponsored by CPA of the United States and Canada. Publish *Catholic Journalist* (newspaper). Awards, May.

| 282 |

Clarion Competition
Women in Communications, Inc. (WICI)
Mary E. Utting, Executive Director
P.O. Box 9561
7719 Wood Hollow
Austin, Texas 78766 U.S.A.
Tel: (512) 345-8922

October

International; entry open to all; annual; established 1973. Named after Clarion, medieval trumpet noted for tonal clarity. Purpose: to recognize excellence in all areas of communications; provide incentive for achievement; demonstrate role of communications in current issues. Sponsored and supported by WICI. Average statistics: 680 entries. Have public relations category. Also sponsor Vanguard Award.

NEWSPAPER-MAGAZINE CONTEST: **Current Issue Journalism,** at least two-thirds published in previous year; any length; original preferred, mounted on paper in 10x12 folder or notebook. Require synopsis of rationale, research results. Divisions: Human Rights, World We Live In, Community We Serve. Categories: Magazine Article, Magazine Series (can be group effort), Newspaper Article (daily or weekly), Newspaper Series (can be group effort).

PUBLICATIONS CONTEST: Current Issue Public Relations. Requirements, divisions same as for Newspaper-Magazine. Also require samples, photos, other supporting material. Categories: Campaign (with stated goal), Annual Report (company or organization), External Newsletter (published at least 3 times a year), External Magazine (published at least 2 times a year), Special Event (promotion, contest, PR program).

AWARDS: Clarion Award Plaques and Honorable Mentions each category, each division.

JUDGING: By national communications professionals. Based on excellence, creativity, believability, effectiveness, thoroughness, depth of research, use of innovative techniques, achievement of stated objectives. May recategorize, disqualify entries; withhold, duplicate awards. Sponsor owns all entries.

ENTRY FEE: $25 WICI members, $50 nonmembers.

DEADLINES: Entry, February. Winners announced, July. Awards, October.

| 283 |

Heywood Broun Journalism Award
The Newspaper Guild
Yette Riesel, Research & Information Associate
1515 Fifteenth Street N.W. 8th Floor
Washington, District of Columbia
20005 U.S.A.

January

International; **entry restricted to U.S., Canadian, Puerto Rican journalists;** annual; established 1941. Named after Heywood Broun, crusading journalist and founder of The Newspaper Guild. Purpose: to encourage, recognize individual journalistic achievement, particularly in correcting injustice. Sponsored and supported by The Newspaper Guild. Average statistics: 100 entries.

NEWSPAPER-MAGAZINE CONTEST: Public Interest Journalism, News Magazine, News Service or Cartoons, published, submitted in scrapbook form with letter describing circumstances and results of work.

SCRIPT CONTEST: Public Interest Journalism Television or Radio. Requirements same as for Newspaper-Magazine.

ELIGIBILITY: Work done or completed during previous year by newspaper, news magazine, news service, radio, TV station employees in U.S., Canada, Puerto Rico Guild jurisdiction.

AWARDS: $1000 and Guild Citation for Outstanding Journalistic Achievement in spirit of Heywood Broun (devotion to public interest, concern for underdog). Citations, Honorable Mentions.

JUDGING: By 3 prominent journalists. All entries read in entirety, returned only on request. Not responsible for loss or damage.

ENTRY FEE: None. Sponsor pays postage.

DEADLINES: Entry, Winners announced, January.

284

Merit Awards for Religious Communication

Religious Public Relations Council (RPRC)
Marvin C. Wilbur, Executive Secretary
Room 1031
475 Riverside Drive
New York, New York 10115 U.S.A.
Tel: (212) 870-2013

April

International; entry open to all; annual; established 1929 (print media), 1959 (broadcasting). Purpose: to establish, raise, maintain high standards of religious public relations and communications. Sponsored by RPRC (Thomas J. Brannon, President), interfaith nonprofit 800-member international professional association. Average statistics: 188 awards to date, 55 in broadcasting. Held at RPRC annual conventions. Also sponsor membership-only Hinkhouse-Derose Awards.

NEWSPAPER-MAGAZINE CONTEST: Religious Journalism. Require tearsheets, work in previous calendar year by secular journalists. No RPRC members. Categories: Daily Newspaper, Weekly Newspaper, Wire Service, Magazine, Feature Syndicate.

AWARDS: RPRC Merit Awards for outstanding communication in religion.

JUDGING: By 18 judges. Based on excellence of general news, emphasis on special material, balanced and accurate reporting, outstanding coverage.

ENTRY FEE: None.

DEADLINES: Entry, January. Exhibits, February. Winners announced, March. Awards, April.

285

National Mass Media Brotherhood Awards

National Conference of Christians and Jews
Harry A. Robinson, Vice President
43 West 57th Street
New York, New York 10019 U.S.A.
Tel: (212) 688-7530

Various

National; entry open to U.S.; various throughout year. Purpose: to foster brotherhood and better understanding among people; pay tribute to outstanding creative work on behalf of brotherhood in mass communications. Sponsored by National Conference of Christians and Jews (Robert M. Jones, Executive Director, 3460 Wilshire Boulevard, Suite 1012, Los Angeles, California 90010).

NEWSPAPER-MAGAZINE AWARD: Brotherhood Journalism. Categories: Articles, Editorials, Cartoons.

BOOK AWARD: Brotherhood.

AWARDS: Gold Medallion and Recognition Certificates.

JUDGING: Executive Director reviews entries, submits finalists to New York committee. Based on mass impact, originality, creativity, integrity.

ENTRY FEE: None.

DEADLINES: Open.

286

Paul Tobenkin Memorial Award

Columbia University Graduate School of Journalism
Adelaide Katz, Director
Office of Special Programs, Room 706
Columbia University

New York, New York 10027 U.S.A.
Tel: (212) 280-3411

Spring

National; **entry open to U.S. newspaper reporters;** annual. Named after Paul Tobenkin, New York *Herald Tribune* reporter concerned with bigotry in U.S. Purpose: to honor fearless reporting in struggle against bigotry. Sponsored by and held at Columbia University Graduate School of Journalism. Also sponsor Maria Moors Cabot Prizes for journalistic contributions to inter-American understanding and freedom of information (open to U.S., Canadian, Latin American journalists); Mike Berger Awards for distinguished reporting (open to New York reporters only).

NEWSPAPER CONTEST: Racial-Religious Hatred, Intolerance, Discrimination or Bigotry Journalism, published in daily-weekly newspaper during previous calendar year, 10 clippings maximum, 4 copies (including original), in scrapbook, with summary letter from editor, brief biography-resume. About racial-religious hatred, intolerance, discrimination, and bigotry, reflecting spirit of Paul Tobenkin.

AWARDS: $250 and Certificate from Columbia University.

JUDGING: By committee. Not responsible for loss or damage. No entries returned.

ENTRY FEE: None.

DEADLINES: Entry, February. Awards, Spring.

287

Robert F. Kennedy Journalism Awards

Coates Redmon, Executive Director
4014 49th Street N.W.
Washington, District of Columbia
20016 U.S.A. Tel: (202) 362-0515

June

National; **entry open to U.S.;** annual; established 1968 by journalists covering Robert F. Kennedy's presidential campaign. Purpose: to encourage, recognize outstanding reporting on problems of disadvantaged in U.S. Sponsored by RFK Journalism Awards Committee (Paul Duke, Chairman). Average statistics: 740 entries. Also sponsor Robert F. Kennedy Book Awards.

NEWSPAPER-MAGAZINE CONTEST: Disadvantaged Journalism, single article or series; mounted 14x17 inches maximum; 3 copies each entry (students, 2 copies). Categories: Professional, Student Print.

ELIGIBILITY: Accounts of lifestyles, handicaps, potential of disadvantaged in U.S.; insights into causes, conditions, remedies, analysis of public policies, programs, attitudes, private endeavors. Published in U.S. first time previous calendar year. Students eligible all categories.

AWARDS: $2000 Grand Prize. $1000 First Prize, each category. 9 Honorable Mentions. 8 Citations. Winner may get 3-month internship in Washington, D.C.

JUDGING: By 24 judges. Sponsor keeps entries.

ENTRY FEE: Not specified.

DEADLINES: Entry, February. Awards, June.

288

Sidney Hillman Foundation Prize Awards

Joyce D. Miller, Executive Director
15 Union Square
New York, New York 10003 U.S.A.
Tel: (212) 242-0700

Spring

International; entry open to all; annual; established 1950. Theme: Contributions Relating to Sidney Hillman's Ideals, including protection of individual civil liberties, improved race relations, strengthened labor movement, social welfare-economic security advancement, greater world understanding. Sponsored by Sidney Hillman Foundation.

NEWSPAPER-MAGAZINE CONTEST: **Humanitarian Journalism,** published, unmounted, with accompanying letter.

SCRIPT CONTEST: **Humanitarian Television, Radio Broadcast,** final (produced) scripts, with accompanying letter. No films, tapes, records.

BOOK-WRITING CONTEST: **Humanitarian Nonfiction,** published, with accompanying letter.

ELIGIBILITY: Published or broadcast during previous calendar year.

AWARDS: Prizes of $750 each.

JUDGING: By 3 judges. Not responsible for loss or damage.

ENTRY FEE: None.

DEADLINES: Entry, January. Entries returned, May. Awards, Spring.

289

Unity Awards in Media

Lincoln University
Department of Communications
Jefferson City, Missouri 65102
U.S.A.

April

National; **entry open to U.S.;** annual; established 1949. Formerly called HEADLINER AWARDS to 1952. Purpose: to acknowledge U.S. media for reporting, covering minorities. Sponsored and supported by Lincoln University Department of Communications. Held during day-long symposium at Lincoln University. Tickets: $125 (registration fee). Also sponsor Missouri High School Journalism Awards Program (recognizing excellence in high school newspapers). Second contact: Connie Hudson; tel: (314) 751-4009; Warren G. Jackson, 280 North Central Avenue, Hartsdale, New York; tel: (914) 948-8144.

NEWSPAPER-MAGAZINE CONTEST: **Minority Problems,** published in previous year, 2 articles each entry (4 articles maximum per series), 1 or more tearsheets or reproductions per entry. Divisions: National Publications (Daily, Weekly, Monthly Newspapers and Magazines); Mid-State Regional Newspapers, Magazines. Categories: Investigative, Political, Economic, Educational Reporting, Editorial Policy, Excellence in Black Media (must deal with comment, interpretation, perspective relating to minority issues). Mid-State entries may also be entered in National division.

AWARDS: First, Second, Third Place, each category except Educational Reporting (First and Second only).

JUDGING: By journalists, journalism educators. Based on accuracy, clarity, significance. No entries returned.

ENTRY FEE: $35 each.

DEADLINES: Entry, February. Awards, April.

| 290 |

George Orwell Memorial Prize
National Book League
Barbara Buckley, Publicity Officer
Book House, 45 East Hill
London SW18 2Q2, ENGLAND
Tel: 01-870-9055

Fall

National; **entry restricted to British publications;** annual; established 1976. Purpose: to reward social, economic, political journalism. Sponsored and supported by Penguin Books. Average statistics: 60 entries, 1-2 awards. Second contact: Jenny Wilford, Penguin Books, 536 Kings Road, London SW10 0UH.

NEWSPAPER-MAGAZINE CONTEST: **Social, Economic, Political Journalism,** published in previous year in U.K. Must be sponsored by editor of journal in which work first appeared as article, essay, or series of articles on current cultural, economic, political issues in the world.

AWARDS: First Prize 750 pounds.

JUDGING: 5-6 judges see all submissions. Not responsible for loss or damage.

ENTRY FEE: None.

DEADLINES: Entry, May. Judging, September. Awards, September-October.

JOURNALISM (Legal,

Political, Freedom, International)
Newspaper-Magazine Journalism, Book, Essay, Script, including AMERICAN PATRIOTIC, FOREIGN AFFAIRS, FREEDOM OF INFORMATION, INTER-AMERICAN, LEGAL AID-DEFENDER, PENAL, DIPLOMATIC and WASHINGTON CORRESPONDENT. (Also see other JOURNALISM.)

| 291 |

American Penal Press Contest
Southern Illinois University
W. Manion Rice, Director
School of Journalism
Carbondale, Illinois 62901 U.S.A.

December

National; **entry restricted to U.S. penal institution newspapers, magazines, and their inmate staffs;** annual; established 1965. Sponsored by School of Journalism, Southern Illinois University at Carbondale. Also sponsor short story, poetry, art, cartoon, photo contests and periodic Charles C. Clayton Award for outstanding contribution to prison journalism (not open to entry).

NEWSPAPER-MAGAZINE CONTEST: **Penal Journalism,** published October previous to October contest year in U.S. penal institution newspaper-magazines. Sweepstakes divisions: Printed Newspaper, Printed Magazine, Mimeographed Publications (submit 3 issues each, 2 being consecutive). Individual categories: Column (excluding sports), Editorial, Feature Story, News, Sports Story-Column (3 entries per category, pasted, taped, or stapled to maximum 8 1/2x11-inch paper.

AWARDS: Sweepstakes First Place, Trophy (Newspaper, Magazine); Certificate (Mimeographed division). Sweepstakes Second, Third Place Certificates, Honorable Mentions, each division. Individual entry First, Second, Third Place Certificates, Honorable Mentions, each category.

JUDGING: Based on general excellence, coverage, make-up, appropriateness to prison media. May withhold individual awards.

ENTRY FEE: None.

DEADLINES: Entry, November. Winners announced, December.

| 292 |

Associated Press Freedom of Information Award
Associated Press Managing Editors (APME)
50 Rockefeller Plaza
New York, New York 10020 U.S.A.
Tel: (212) 262-4000

October

International; entry open to all; annual; established 1970. Sponsored by APME. Also sponsor AP Public Service Awards (open to Associated Press member-newspapers for service to community, state, nation).

NEWSPAPER CONTEST: Freedom of Information Journalism, for contributions to freedom of information standards, public information; published July previous to June contest year. Require narrative description of courageous act(s).

AWARDS: Freedom of Information Award. Citations for other distinguished efforts.

ENTRY FEE: None.

DEADLINES: Entry, August. Awards, October.

| 293 |

Elijah Parish Lovejoy Award
Colby College
Richard N. Dyer, Assistant to President
Office of the President
Waterville, Maine 04901 U.S.A.

Annual

National; entry restricted (nomination by college members); annual; established 1952. Award to Newspaper Editor, Reporter, Publisher for Journalistic Freedom. Named for Elijah Parish Lovejoy, Colby College graduate, and *St. Louis Observer* newspaper editor who died condemning slavery (1837). Sponsored by Colby College.

| 294 |

Emery A. Brownell Media Award
National Legal Aid and Defender Association (NLADA)
M. A. O'Donnell, Deputy Conference Director
1625 K Street N.W., 8th Floor
Washington, District of Columbia 20006 U.S.A. Tel: (202) 452-0620

Fall

National; entry restricted to U.S. newspapers, magazines; annual. Named after former executive director of NLADA (1940-1961). Purpose: to recognize news media for informing public of crucial role played by legal aid and defender offices in assuring equal justice under law. Sponsored and supported by NLADA. Average statistics: 20 entries, 1-2 awards. Held at annual NLADA Conference.

NEWSPAPER-MAGAZINE CONTEST: Legal Aid-Defender, published between August previous, August current year; 3 copies. Require summary letter (250 words maximum), biographical information, reader reaction, impact on legal services. Categories: News Article (single or series), Essay, Feature, Editorial. No legal publications.

AWARDS: Bronze Emery A. Brownell Media Award Medal.

JUDGING: By NLADA Committee (including attorneys, clients). Based on format, subject matter, educational value, courage in presenting controversial matter. May give more than 1 award, withhold award. Entries become property of sponsor.

ENTRY FEE: None.

DEADLINES: Entry, August. Awards, Fall.

| 295 |

Fourth Estate Award Program
American Legion (National)
Frank C. Momsen, Adjutant
P.O. Box 1055
Indianapolis, Indiana 46206 U.S.A.
Tel: (317) 635-8411

Fall

National; **entry restricted** (nomination by members); annual; established 1958. Up to 3 awards (plaque and $1000 travel-accommodation stipend) to **American Patriotic Newspaper-Magazine Communications Media.** Formerly called American Legion Mercury Award. Purpose: to recognize outstanding services to community, state, or nation which further American Legion policies, programs; contribute to preservation of American Way of Life. Sponsored by American Legion. Held in various U.S. cities at national convention. Event, Fall.

| 296 |

Freedoms Foundation National Awards
Freedoms Foundation at Valley Forge
Valley Forge, Pennsylvania 19481
U.S.A. Tel: (215) 933-8825

February

National; **entry open to U.S.**; annual; established 1949. Purpose: to recognize deeds that support America, contribute to citizenship, suggest solutions to problems. Sponsored by Freedoms Foundation at Valley Forge, nonprofit, nonpolitical, nonsectarian. Recognized by National Association of Secondary School Principals. Held during George Washington Birthday Celebration at Valley Forge and at local ceremonies. Have sermon, public-youth public addresses; college campus-community program; government-national activity; economic education; teacher, educator, individual contribution awards. Also sponsor other media contests; seminars; outreach programs; George Washington Plaque to Outstanding Individual; Principal School Award.

NEWSPAPER-MAGAZINE CONTEST: **Americanism Professional, Youth Journalism.** Individual efforts, no class assignments. Require tearsheets, date of publication (except youth category). Categories: Editorial, Letters to Editor, Editorial Cartoons, Articles, Youth.

PUBLICATIONS CONTEST: **Americanism Corporate, Nonprofit.** Submit minimum 3 different issues of company external or employee publications, union-trade association, nonprofit organization publications.

BOOK CONTEST: **Americanism.** Require comprehensive review or precis, 10 pages maximum.

ESSAY CONTEST: Patriotic Military, 100-500 words on selected theme. Restricted to U.S. Armed Forces personnel in active, reserve, ROTC, JROTC Components.

AWARDS: George Washington Honor Medals, Certificates; Valley Forge Honor Certificates. One award per person per category. Special Awards. $50, $75, $100 savings bond to Military-ROTC essays.

JUDGING: By national jury of state Supreme Court justices, patriotic, civic, service, veterans organization officers. May change classifications, amounts, withhold awards; retain or have access to winners for 3 years minimum for awards library research, display, convention, staff use.

ENTRY FEE: None.

DEADLINES: Entry, July (school), October (others). Judging, November. Awards, December. Event, February.

297

Gavel Awards
American Bar Association (ABA),
Division of Communications
Dean Tyler Jenks, Special Events
Director
77 South Wacker Drive
Chicago, Illinois 60606 U.S.A.
Tel: (312) 621-9249

August

National; **entry restricted to U.S. news and entertainment media;** annual; established 1958. Purpose: to recognize U.S. news, entertainment media that educate, increase public understanding of American legal and judicial system; promote correction, improvement of laws, courts, law enforcement, legal goals. Sponsored and supported by 270,000-member ABA. Average statistics: 378 entries, 235 entrants, 25 Gavel Awards, 42 Certificates. Held at ABA annual meeting. Tickets: $15-$20.

NEWSPAPER-MAGAZINE CONTEST: Legal and Judicial Journalism, published. Require 4 copies, scrapbook form, 12x15 inches. Sections: Newspaper Dailies (circulation under 50,000, 50-200,000, 200-500,000, over 500,000), Nondailies (under 50,000, over 50,000), Supplements (under 200,000, 200-500,000, over 500,000), Magazines (under 200,000, 200,000-1,000,000, over 1,000,000). Categories: Editorial, Feature, News, Interpretive Columns (or combinations). Other categories: Wire Services, News Syndicates.

BOOK CONTEST: Legal and Judicial, published. Require 4 copies, synopsis, subject summary (including book review comments), biography. No legal publications or text books.

ELIGIBILITY: Published January to December of previous year, 5 entries maximum. Entries should relate to work of the bench, bar, law enforcement, law itself; current, historical, or futuristic.

AWARDS: Silver Gavel Awards (Trophies and Plaques) for outstanding contribution to public understanding of American law and justice, top executives, each winning organization. Gavel Awards Merit Certificates to noteworthy examples of distinguished public service.

JUDGING: By lawyers, judges, teachers. Based on informational value, educational merit, creativity, thoroughness, reportorial and technical skills, impact. May withhold awards.

ENTRY FEE: None.

DEADLINES: Entry, February. Awards, August.

| 298 |

Maria Moors Cabot Prize
Columbia University Graduate School of Journalism
Adelaide Katz, Director
Office of Special Programs, Room 706
Columbia University
New York, New York 10027 U.S.A.
Tel: (212) 280-3411

Fall

International; **entry restricted to U.S., Canadian, Latin American reporters;** annual. Oldest international awards in journalism. Purpose: to encourage improved inter-American understanding. Sponsored by and held at Columbia University Graduate School of Journalism. Also sponsor Paul Tobenkin Memorial Award (open to U.S. newspaper reporters for articles concerned with bigotry); Mike Berger Awards for distinguished reporting (open to New York reporters only).

NEWSPAPER-MAGAZINE CONTEST: **Inter-American Understanding and Freedom,** preferably published in previous 15 months. Submission by editor with letter and representative clippings.

SCRIPT CONTEST: **Inter-American Understanding-Freedom Radio, Television Broadcast,** preferably produced in previous 15 months. Submit script(s) with nomination-recommendation letter.

AWARDS: Gold Medal, $1000 honorarium and round-trip air fare to Columbia University presentation ceremonies. At least 2 medalists selected each year (1 from U.S., 1 or more from other countries). Silver Plaque to news organization.

JUDGING: By committee headed by Dean of Graduate School of Jour-nalism. Based on single article or broadcast, series, or more extensive work. May also consider work done over several years. Materials returned upon request.

ENTRY FEE: None.

DEADLINES: Judging,   May. Awards, Fall.

| 299 |

National Press Club Edwin M. Hood Award for Diplomatic Correspondents
Rick Gordon, Vice Chairman
National Press Building
Washington, District of Columbia 20045 U.S.A. Tel: (202) 638-5300

March

National; **entry restricted to U.S. diplomatic news correspondents;** annual; established 1980. Named after Edwin M. Hood, distinguished diplomatic correspondent and founding member of National Press Club. Purpose: to recognize excellence in reporting on American foreign policy, related issues. Sponsored by National Press Foundation (nonprofit, tax-exempt). Held in Washington, D.C. Also sponsor Consumer Journalism Awards, Washington Correspondent Awards.

NEWSPAPER-PERIODICAL CONTEST: **Diplomatic Correspondent Journalism,** published in previous year; single entry or series of related articles (3 maximum). Require letter of work's merit, English translation. Categories: Foreign, American.

BOOK CONTEST: **Diplomatic Correspondent Journalism.** Requirements, categories same as for Newspaper-Periodical.

AWARDS: $1000 each Best Reporting to Foreign Audiences, American Audiences.

JUDGING: By panel. Based on awareness, clarity, insight.

ENTRY FEE: None. Entrant pays postage.

DEADLINES: Entry, event, March.

| 300 |

National Press Club Washington Correspondent Awards
Rick Gordon, Vice Chairman
National Press Building
Washington, District of Columbia
20045 U.S.A. Tel: (202) 638-5300

March

National; **entry restricted to U.S. Washington, D.C., news correspondents;** annual; established 1979. Purpose: to encourage excellence in reporting on events in Washington, D.C., affecting a community or region. Sponsored by National Press Foundation (nonprofit, tax-exempt). Held in Washington, D.C. Also sponsor Consumer Journalism Awards, Edwin M. Hood Award for Diplomatic Correspondents.

NEWSPAPER CONTEST: **Washington Correspondent Journalism,** published; single entry or series of related articles per category. Require clippings, wire copy, mounted on numbered pages; descriptive letter of work's merit (2 single-spaced pages maximum). Categories: Congressional, Justice (including courts, Department of Justice, FBI, issues of law), Executive Branch (including departments, agencies, White House), Commentary.

ELIGIBILITY: Normally, accredited resident Washington, D.C. correspondents.

AWARDS: $100 Best each category. Additional $100 Best Overall Entry.

ENTRY FEE: None.

DEADLINES: Entry, event, March.

| 301 |

Overseas Press Club Awards
Overseas Press Club of America
Norman A. Schorr, Chairman
52 East 41st Street
New York, New York 10017 U.S.A.
Tel: (212) 679-9650

April

International; entry open to all; annual; established 1941. Purpose: to recognize outstanding journalism by newspeople reporting overseas developments to American audiences. Sponsored by Overseas Press Club of America. Held in New York City.

NEWSPAPER-MAGAZINE CONTEST: **International Journalism,** published in previous calendar year. Require 3 copies of 200-word biography, 3 nominee photos, 2 copies published work. Categories: Daily Newspaper (wire service), Magazine, Reporting from Abroad, Foreign Affairs Interpretation, Business News from Abroad, International Humanity Reporting, Human Rights Editorial or Editorial Series from Abroad.

BOOK CONTEST: **Foreign Affairs.** Requirements, categories same as for Newspaper-Magazine.

AWARDS: Illuminated Scrolls for outstanding accomplishments in world journalism, each category. Humanity Reporting, $400.

JUDGING: By panel of newspeople.

ENTRY FEE: $20 each.

DEADLINES: Entry, February. Awards, April.

JOURNALISM (Lifestyle, Consumer, Women)

Newspaper-Magazine Journalism, Book, Script, including FASHION, FOOD, HOME APPLIANCE. (Also see other JOURNALISM.)

302

Association of Home Appliance Manufacturers (AHAM) Appliance Communications Award Program
Marian Johnson, Assistant General Manager
20 North Wacker Drive
Chicago, Illinois 60606 U.S.A.
Tel: (312) 984-5821

Various

International; **entry restricted to professionals;** various throughout year; established 1958. Formerly called ALMA AWARDS PROGRAM to 1980. Purpose: to encourage communication to public about home appliances; recognize excellence in consumer appliance communications. Sponsored and supported by AHAM. Average statistics: 55-100 entries. Held at National Home Appliance Conference.

NEWSPAPER-MAGAZINE CONTEST: Home Appliance Journalism. Original clips, tearsheets, or clean reproductions. May be total coverage articles, columns, series, features sections in daily or weekly press or periodicals. Categories: Newspaper, Magazine, Utilities, USDA Extension (state, country), Classroom Education (college or university, high school, junior high).

PUBLICATIONS CONTEST: Home appliance Newsletters, Bulletins, Brochures. Categories: Utilities, USDA Extension, Classroom Education.

SCRIPT CONTEST: Home Appliance. Categories: Radio-Television, Utilities, USDA Extension, Classroom Education.

ELIGIBILITY: Consumer information about small or large appliances (dehumidifiers, dishwashers, disposers, dryers, freezers, humidifiers, ranges, refrigerators, room air conditioners, trash compactors, washers). Completed August of previous to August of current year; 3 maximum. Require description and evaluation of activity, announcements, handouts, publications, other materials. No student projects.

AWARDS: AHAM Awards for imaginative consumer communications.

JUDGING: By home economists, journalism faculty of Iowa State University (Ames). Based on effectiveness, clarity, creativity, timeliness, practicality. May withhold some awards. Entries returned on request.

ENTRY FEE: None.

DEADLINES: Vary.

303

Fashion Journalism "Lulu" Awards
Men's Fashion Association of America (MFA)
Norman Karr, Executive Director
1290 Avenue of the Americas
New York, New York 10019 U.S.A.
Tel: (212) 581-8210

January-February

National; **entry open to U.S.;** annual; established 1960. Purpose: to award excellence in coverage of men's and boys' fashions. Sponsored by

MFA, Menswear Retailers of America. Held during 4-day MFA Spring-Summer Press Preview.

NEWSPAPER CONTEST: Men's and Boys' Fashion, published; minimum 12; maximum 24 pages, in plain scrapbook. Editorial (nonadvertising) published during previous calendar year. Categories: Daily (under 50,000 circulation, 50-100,000; 100-200,000; 200-400,000; over 400,000), Syndicated, Editorial Color, Newspaper Magazine.

AWARDS: Lulu and Runner-Up Awards for outstanding coverage of men's and boys' fashion, each category.

JUDGING: By panels of professionals. Newspaper based on originality, variety, layout, frequency.

ENTRY FEE: None.

DEADLINES: Entry, December. Event, January-February. Materials returned, April.

| 304 |

National Press Club Consumer Journalism Awards
Rick Gordon, Vice Chairman
National Press Building
Washington, District of Columbia
20045 U.S.A. Tel: (202) 638-5300

September-October

National; **entry restricted to U.S. professional journalists;** annual; established 1973. Purpose: to recognize outstanding journalism on consumer topics. Sponsored by National Press Foundation (nonprofit, tax-exempt). Supported by National Press Club. Average statistics: 150 entries, 6 winners. Held in Washington, D.C. Have scholarships. Also sponsor Edwin M. Hood Award for Diplomatic Correspondents, Washington Correspon-

dent Awards.

NEWSPAPER-PERIODICAL CONTEST: Consumer Journalism, published in previous year by professional journalist. Single entry or series of related articles (3 maximum). Require description letter, resources outline (including evidence of impact), clippings and reprints mounted on numbered pages. No house organs, pamphlets, theses, reports, special-interest publications. Categories: Wire Services or Print Syndicates, Newspapers (circulation over 100,000, under 100,000), Periodicals (circulation over 500,000, under 500,000).

BOOK CONTEST: Consumer Journalism, published in previous year. Single or series of related books (3 maximum). Require description letter, resources outline (including evidence of impact).

ELIGIBILITY: Professional journalists who receive no less than 50% of earned income from journalistic activity.

AWARDS: $1000 Best in Consumer Journalism. First Place Certificates, Best in Media categories. Merit Certificate at judges' discretion.

JUDGING: By panels. Not responsible for loss or damage.

ENTRY FEE: None. Entrant pays postage.

DEADLINES: Entry, May. Awards, September-October.

| 305 |

Penney-Missouri Magazine Awards
School of Journalism
University of Missouri, Columbia
Box 838
Columbia, Missouri 65205 U.S.A.
Tel: (314) 882-2721, 882-7771

October

National; **entry restricted to U.S. magazine journalists;** annual; established 1967. Purpose: to recognize, promote excellence in lifestyle journalism. Sponsored by University of Missouri School of Journalism. Supported by J. C. Penney Company. Also sponsor Penney-Missouri Newspaper Awards.

MAGAZINE CONTEST: Lifestyle Journalism, published previous calendar year in U.S. magazine; 1 entry maximum per category, 5 copies each (2 original, 3 may be photostats). 1 different entry maximum each category. Unsigned articles must be verified by editor. No mounted entries; no articles from fraternal magazines, company publications, books, excerpts, alumnae publications, newspaper magazine supplements; no winners of 3 awards in last 5 years. Categories: Contemporary Living (quality of living including arts contribution); Consumerism; Health and Medical Science; Personal Lifestyle (individual in contemporary society); Expanding Opportunities (women, minorities); Excellence in Smaller Magazines (100,000 circulation, any subject).

AWARDS: $1000, each category. Winners living in U.S. outside New York City receive travel, 1 night lodging expenses to attend awards luncheon.

JUDGING: By 4 newspaper professionals. May win 1 category only. Sponsor owns entries; no entries returned.

ENTRY FEE: None.

DEADLINES: Entry, April. Awards, October.

| 306 |

Penney-Missouri Newspaper Awards
School of Journalism
University of Missouri
Box 838
Columbia, Missouri 65205 U.S.A.
Tel: (314) 882-7771, 882-3731

March

National; **entry restricted to U.S. newspapers, journalists;** annual; established 1959. Purpose: to recognize, promote excellence in women's, people, lifestyle journalism. Sponsored by University of Missouri School of Journalism. Supported by J. C. Penney Company. Also sponsor annual Penney-Missouri Newspaper Awards Workshop; Magazine Awards.

NEWSPAPER CONTEST: Women's, People, Lifestyle Journalism, published October previous to September current year; 4 sets-copies each, tearsheets of complete page(s) or photostats. Categories (1 per person): General Reporting (Single Story on people, family lifestyle, philosophy, problems, activities, 2 bylines maximum; Series with 2 bylines maximum, published in full during awards year; 5 entries maximum per newspaper); Consumer Affairs, Fashion-Clothing (both Single or Series, 2 bylines maximum, 2 entries maximum per newspaper); Pages-Sections (Daily Newspaper Circulation Under 25,000, 25-100,000, 100-250,000, Over 250,000, Weekly-Semiweekly any Circulation) Dailies require 3 sections from 3 different days published in designated weeks. Weeklies-Semiweeklies require 3 sections from 3 different weeks published during designated weeks. No syndicated material in Fashion-Clothing.

AWARDS: General Reporting $1000, Single and Series. Consumer

Affairs and Fashion-Clothing, $1000 each. Best Pages-Sections $1000 First, $500 Second, $250 Third Place, each class. Transportation, hotel expenses for winners to Awards Workshop and Banquet. Honorable Mentions, Special Awards.

JUDGING: By 8 newspaper professionals. Based on thoroughness of research, coverage, organization, readability, style, news value, impact. Pages-Sections based on overall excellence of content, local coverage, reporting, editing, layout, and graphics. Illustration or layout not judged in Fashion-Clothing category. Director may rule on eligibility and category. First place 3-time winners not eligible for 2 years. No entries returned.

ENTRY FEE: None.

DEADLINES: Entry, October. Judging, December. Awards, March.

| 307 |

Vesta Awards Competition
American Meat Institute (AMI)
Jane Anderson, Director, Consumer Affairs
P.O. Box 3556
Washington, District of Columbia
20007 U.S.A. Tel: (703) 841-2400

September-October

International; **entry restricted to food editors, writers employed by daily newspapers;** annual; established 1950. Named after goddess of the hearth and family (Vesta). Purpose: to recognize food news reporting. Sponsored and supported by AMI. Recognized by Newspaper Food Editor's Association. Average statistics: 150 entrants, 18 awards. Held at Newspaper Food Editor's Conference.

NEWSPAPER CONTEST: Food News Journalism, published in daily newspaper August previous to July

current year; 3 original food pages, articles, columns, maximum per entry (continuing pages acceptable); series on one subject considered 1 article; 4 copies each (tearsheets, photostats); 2 entries maximum per newspaper. Require circulation verification. No weekly supplements or entire food sections. Categories: B&W and ROP Color; B&W and Rotogravure Color; ROP Color and Rotogravure Color. Circulation classes: Under 50,000; 50-200,000; over 200,000; Any Circulation.

AWARDS: Bronze Vesta Statuette, each category, class. Merit Certificate Plaques to Runners-up.

JUDGING: Panel of 6 judges rank top 5, each category. Based on reader service, nutrition information, journalistic style, illustrations-page makeup, originality, timeliness. No entries returned.

ENTRY FEE: None. Entrant pays first-class postage.

DEADLINES: Entry, April. Materials, July. Judging, August-September. Winners announced, September-October.

JOURNALISM (Regional-State)

About or from a Region-State.
Newspaper-Magazine Journalism, including CALIFORNIA, PACIFIC COAST, NEW YORK, CANADIAN, SPANISH.

| 308 |

Better Newspapers Contest
California Newspaper Publishers Association (CNPA)

Jackie Nava, Assistant General Manager
1127 11th Street, Suite 1040
Sacramento, California 95814 U.S.A.
Tel: (916) 443-5991

February

State; **entry restricted to California CNPA members;** annual. First, Second Prize Plaques to **California Newspaper Journalism,** including college and fraternity newspapers. Purpose: to encourage excellence in California newspapers. Sponsored by CNPA. Average statistics: 200-225 entries, 218 awards. Held at CNPA Annual Convention. Awards, February.

309

Deadline Club Journalism Awards Competition
Steven Osborne, President
P.O. Box 2503, Grand Central Station
New York, New York 10017 U.S.A.
Tel: (212) 644-2151

April

City; **entry restricted to New York City journalists;** annual. Sponsored by and held at Deadline Club, New York City Chapter of Sigma Delta Chi Society of Professional Journalists. Also sponsor $250 scholarships at New York City journalism schools.

NEWSPAPER-MAGAZINE CONTEST: **New York Journalism,** published in New York metropolitan area in previous year; unmounted tearsheets, unlimited entry. Story or series may be entered in multiple categories. Categories: Metropolitan Public Service (Newspaper, Wire Service), Business, Financial, Medical, Space, Biological or Physical Science (Newspaper, Wire Service, Magazine, Syndicate).

AWARDS: Deadliner Statuette, top winners each category. Special Achievement Plaques, 2 finalists, each category.

ENTRY FEE: $10 each. No entries returned.

DEADLINES: Entry, March. Awards, April.

310

Mike Berger Awards
Columbia University Graduate School of Journalism
Adelaide Katz, Director
Office of Special Programs, Room 706
Columbia University
New York, New York 10027 U.S.A.
Tel: (212) 280-3411

Spring

City; **entry restricted to New York reporters;** annual; established 1959. Purpose: to honor distinguished reporting in tradition of Mike Berger, Pulitzer Prize winning New York *Times* reporter (died 1959). Sponsored by and held at Columbia University Graduate School of Journalism. Supported by Lucille Lortel Schweitzer, widow of communications industrialist Louis Schweitzer. Also sponsor Paul Tobenkin Memorial Award (open to U.S. newspaper reporters for articles concerned with bigotry); Maria Moors Cabot Prizes for journalistic contributions to inter-American understanding and freedom of information (open to U.S., Canadian, Latin American journalists); National Magazine Awards.

NEWSPAPER CONTEST: **New York City Journalism,** work done during previous year, 3 copies of 5 clippings maximum; submitted by editors with letter, biographical resume. Preference to reporting providing insight into New York City life.

AWARDS: Mike Berger Awards *(Mike)*, Certificate and share of $1500 prize fund.

JUDGING: By committee.

ENTRY FEE: None.

DEADLINES: Entry,   January. Awards, Spring.

| 311 |

Pacific Coast Press Club (PCPC) Awards
Jay Beeler, First Vice President
P.O. Box 20261
Long Beach, California 90801 U.S.A.
Tel: (213) 594-6786

February-March

Regional;**entry restricted to Southern California PCPC members;** annual; established 1967. $25-$50 and Certificates for **Pacific Coast Journalism** (writing, photography, layout, publicity). Hunter-McCarthey Award for Overall Journalistic Excellence (periodic). Purpose: to recognize excellence in journalism. Sponsored and supported by Southern California businesses, associations. Average statistics: 150 entries, 50 entrants, 50 awards. Also sponsor student seminars, scholarships, community college newspaper contest. Awards, February-March.

| 312 |

Explore Canada Awards Competition for Best Canadian Publication
Tourism Industry Association of Canada (TIAC)
Suite 1016, 130 Albert Street
Ottawa, Ontario K1P 5G4 CANADA
Tel: (613) 238-3883

February

National; **entry open to Canada;** annual. Purpose: to arouse interest in Canadian heritage; promote Canadian travel. Sponsored by TIAC. Supported by Wine Council of Ontario. Held at TIAC Golden Jubilee National Conference in Toronto. Also sponsor awards for Area Promotion for travel, recreation, tourism promotion; Julian Crandall Trophy Conservation Award (founded 1952) to Canadian citizens.

NEWSPAPER-MAGAZINE CONTEST: **Canadian Culture, Heritage, History,** published during previous calendar year in Canadian newspapers, periodicals (news coverage, editorials, special features); clipping or tearsheets, mounted. Require supporting letter of purpose, results of material. Categories: National, Provincial-Regional Circulation.

AWARDS: Trophy each category.

ENTRY FEE: None. Entrant pays postage (include SASE).

DEADLINES: Entry,   January. Awards, February.

| 313 |

International Week Sea & Naval Film Festival Journalism Contest
Enrique Perez-Cuadrado de Guzman, Director
Plaza Castellini 5 & 7
Cartagena, SPAIN

January

National; **entry restricted to Spanish journalists.** Trophy, 15,000 pesetas to **Spanish Journalism, Articles published in Spanish national press** in preceding year. Awards, January.

JOURNALISM (Scientific, Technical,

Environmental)

Newspaper-Magazine Journalism, Book, including AGRICULTURE, AVIATION, CHEMISTRY, CONSERVATION, ENERGY, ENGINEERING, NUCLEAR ENERGY, SPACE, TREE, U.S. MARITIME. (Also see other JOURNALISM.)

314

AAAS-Westinghouse Science Writing Awards Competition
American Association for the Advancement of Science (AAAS)
Grayce A. Finger, Assistant Administrator
1515 Massachusetts Avenue N.W.
Washington, District of Columbia
20005 U.S.A. Tel: (202) 467-4350

January

National; **entry restricted to U.S. publications;** annual. Purpose: to encourage, recognize science writing and engineering-technological application; stimulate public interest and understanding. Sponsored by AAAS. Supported by Westinghouse Educational Foundation. Held at National Association of Science Writers Dinner during AAAS annual meeting.

NEWSPAPER-MAGAZINE CONTEST: **Popular Science Writing,** published in U.S. October of previous to September current year; single, series (over half published in current year), group of 3 unrelated stories, articles, editorials or columns (for newspaper); single or series (for magazine). 3 maximum per entrant per category, 6 copies each, tearsheets, clippings, reprints, or syndicate copy (8 1/2x11-inch maximum). Submit newspaper circulation statement. No medical, by AAAS or Westinghouse employees, or published in AAAS publications. Cat-

egories: Daily Newspapers (Circulation Over 100,000, Under 100,000), General Circulation Magazines.

AWARDS: $1000 Award, Honorable Mentions, each category. Travel, hotel expenses for winners to awards dinner.

JUDGING: By journalism, science, public affairs judges. Based on initiative, originality, scientific accuracy, interpretation clarity, promotional value. No entries returned.

ENTRY FEE: None. Entrant pays postage.

DEADLINES: Entry, October. Awards, January.

315

Arbor Day Awards
National Arbor Day Foundation
John Rosenow, Executive Director
411 South 13th Street, Suite 308
Lincoln, Nebraska 68508 U.S.A.
Tel: (402) 474-5655

April

National; **entry open to U.S.;** annual; established 1972. Purpose: to recognize outstanding tree-related activities in communications, education, planting projects. Sponsored by National Arbor Day Foundation (Arbor Lodge 100, Nebraska City, Nebraska 68410), nonprofit corporation of U.S. conservation, business leaders. Held at Steinhart Lodge (Nebraska City) for 1 weekend. Publish *Arbor Day News* (quarterly). Also sponsor awards for projects, advertising, public relations, education, communities, schools, organizations, media (motion picture, radio, television); J. Sterling Morton Award to individual who has best perpetuated Morton's tree-planting heritage; National Arbor Day Foundation Photo Contest.

NEWSPAPER-MAGAZINE CONTEST: Tree Journalism. Magazine, newspaper, or syndicated feature magazines (submit 6 copies) and daily, weekly newspapers eligible. Newspaper categories: Feature or Editorial Series, Special Section, Tie-In Premium Promotion.

AWARDS: Arbor Day Foundation Awards (plaques). Winner may use Arbor Day logo for 1 year.

JUDGING: By conservationists, communications authorities. May withhold awards, change categories.

ENTRY FEE: None. Entrant pays postage.

DEADLINES: Entry, November. Materials, December. Judging, January. Awards, April. Materials returned, May.

316

Aviation-Space Writers Association (AWA) Journalism Awards
William F. Kaiser, Executive Secretary
Cliffwood Road
Chester, New Jersey 07930 U.S.A.
Tel: (201) 879-5667

Spring

International; entry open to all; annual. Sponsored by Aviation-Space Writers Association (AWA). Also sponsor Earl D. Osborn Award for General Aviation Writing.

NEWSPAPER-MAGAZINE CONTEST: Aviation, Space Journalism, 3 copies in English, 10x14-inch maximum mailing package. Newspaper categories: Over 200,000 Circulation, Under 200,000. Magazine categories: Special Interest, Trade; General Interest.

BOOK   CONTEST: Aviation,

Space, 3 copies in English. Categories: Nonfiction, Technical-Training.

ELIGIBILITY: Published for public consumption during previous calendar year.

AWARDS: $100 Honorarium plus Scroll for Aviation and Space, each category, 1 award per person per year. Robert S. Ball Memorial Award, $500 and Trophy, for Space writing, reporting, any medium. James J. Strebig Memorial Award, $500 and Trophy, Aviation writing, reporting, any medium. Recognition Certificates.

JUDGING: May withhold, omit awards.

ENTRY FEE: None.

DEADLINES: Entry,   January. Awards, Spring.

317

Captain Donald T. Wright Maritime Journalism Awards
Southern Illinois University at Edwardsville
John A. Regnell, Chairman
Department of Mass Communications, Box 73
Edwardsville, Illinois 62026 U.S.A.
Tel: (618) 692-2230

Winter

International; entry open to all; annual; established 1970. Named after Captain Donald T. Wright, riverboat pilot, publisher of *Waterways Journal.* Purpose: to recognize outstanding achievement in maritime journalism contributing to better understanding of U.S. inland and intracoastal waterways. Sponsored by Southern Illinois University at Edwardsville (SIUE) Foundation, SIUE Department of Mass Communications. Supported by Mrs. Donald T. Wright. Average statistics: 20 entries, 2 awards. Held at various River Association meetings.

NEWSPAPER-MAGAZINE CONTEST: U.S. Maritime Journalism, about inland or intracoastal waterways; published; submit tearsheets.

BOOK CONTEST: U.S. Maritime Journalism, about inland or intracoastal waterways; published.

AWARDS: 2 or more Bronze Plaques (showing river transportation).

JUDGING: By SIUE Department of Mass Communication faculty. Not responsible for loss or damage.

ENTRY FEE: None.

DEADLINES: Entry, September. Awards, February-March.

| 318 |

Crops and Soils Magazine Award for Excellence in Agricultural Journalism
American Society of Agronomy (ASA)
William R. Luellen, Editor
677 South Segoe Road
Madison, Wisconsin 53711 U.S.A.
Tel: (608) 274-1212

Annual

National; entry restricted to articles published in Crops and Soils Magazine; annual; established 1978. Pen Set, Certificate Best Agriculture Journalism Articles. Honorable Mentions. Sponsored by ASA.

| 319 |

Earl D. Osborn Award for General Aviation Writing
Aviation-Space Writers Association (AWA)
William F. Kaiser, Executive Secretary
Cliffwood Road
Chester, New Jersey 07930 U.S.A.
Tel: (201) 879-5667

Spring

International; entry open to all; annual; established 1970. Named after Earl D. Osborn, aviation pioneer and founder (1925) of EDO Corporation. Purpose: to encourage, honor good writing, reporting, production on general aviation (private as opposed to military or commercial). Sponsored by AWA, EDO Corporation. Average statistics: 300 entrants. Presented at annual AWA meeting, held in various cities. Also sponsor AWA Journalism Awards. Second contact: Robert F. Kane, 12 East 41st Street, New York, New York 10017; tel: (212) MU5-6320

NEWSPAPER-MAGAZINE CONTEST: General Aviation Journalism, on private flying as opposed to military, commercial aviation. Other requirements not specified.

WRITING CONTEST: General Aviation, Any Medium, on private flying. Other requirements not specified.

AWARDS: $500 Earl D. Osborn Award and Trophy, Best Entry.

JUDGING: By AWA Committee. All entries read. Entrant retains all rights. Not responsible for loss or damage.

ENTRY FEE: None.

DEADLINES: Entry, not specified. Judging, January-April. Award, Spring.

| 320 |

Engineering Journalism Awards
National Society of Professional Engineers
Leslie Collins
2029 K Street N.W.
Washington, District of Columbia
20006 U.S.A. Tel: (202)463-2300

April

National; **entry restricted to U.S. newspaper journalists;** annual; established 1966. Purpose: to recognize journalists for contribution to public understanding of role engineering, technology play in contemporary American life. Sponsored and supported by National Society of Professional Engineers. Average statistics: 100 entries, 3 awards.

NEWSPAPER CONTEST: Engineering Journalism, original stories or series dealing with engineering subject matter as distinguished from science. Published in daily, weekly newspaper in previous year; mounted on 8 1/2x11-inch paper; unlimited entries.

AWARDS: $500 First, $300 Second, $200 Third Prize.

JUDGING: By 3 reporters and editors. Based on extent, manner in which journalist relates engineers to subject matter.

ENTRY FEE: None.

DEADLINES: Entry, January. Awards, April.

| 321 |

Forum Award
Atomic Industrial Forum (AIF)
MaryEllen Warren, Coordinator
7101 Wisconsin Avenue
Washington, District of Columbia
20014 U.S.A. Tel: (301) 654-9260

November

International; **entry restricted to professionals in electronic or print media;** annual; established 1967. Purpose: to encourage factual news coverage, public understanding of peaceful nuclear application. Sponsored by AIF, international, nonprofit, 600-member association concerned with peaceful application of nuclear en-

ergy. Recognized by Committee on Public Affairs and Information. Average statistics: 50 entries. Held at AIF Annual Conference, Washington, D.C., for 1 day.

NEWSPAPER-MAGAZINE CONTEST: Nuclear Energy Journalism, in English; 4 copies, 11 1/2x18-inch maximum size.

BOOK CONTEST: Nuclear Energy in English; 4 copies, 11 1/2x18-inch maximum size.

ELIGIBILITY: Professional nuclear-related projects for general public, appearing August previous to September current year.

AWARDS: $1000 and Framed Certificates Best Print Media. Money divided equally if tie.

JUDGING: By independent judges representing print, electronic media, trade press, industry, academic community. Based on accuracy, balance, perspective, timeliness, creativity, ingenuity of approach, contribution to public understanding of peaceful nuclear energy. Entries returned on written request.

ENTRY FEE: None.

DEADLINES: Entry, September. Judging, October. Event, November.

| 322 |

Heath Cooper Rigdon Conservation Writer Awards
Soil Conservation Society of America (SCSA)
Larry D. Davis
7515 N.E. Ankeny Road
Ankeny, Iowa 50021 U.S.A.
Tel: (515) 289-2331

Spring

International; **entry restricted to journalists;** annual; established 1975.

Purpose: to recognize outstanding efforts in communicating natural resource conservation, public understanding, appreciation of science and art of good land use. Sponsored by SCSA. Held at annual SCSA Council meeting. Also sponsor membership-only Commendation Awards for Service to own chapters, council of chapters, professional achievement.

NEWSPAPER-MAGAZINE CONTEST: Conservation Journalist. By persons actively engaged in writing for newspapers, magazines. Require nomination describing writing activities of individual. Include clipping examples.

AWARDS: Conservation Writer Award Plaques, Honorarium.

JUDGING: Recommendation by special committee. Final by SCSA Council.

ENTRY FEE: None.

DEADLINES: Entry, December. Award, Spring.

323

James T. Grady Award for Interpreting Chemistry for the Public
American Chemical Society
Dr. Justin W. Collat, Head, Grants & Awards
1155 Sixteenth Street N.W.
Washington, District of Columbia
20036 U.S.A. Tel: (202) 872-4481

March

International; entry open to all; annual; established 1955. Named after managing editor of American Chemical Society News Service (1922-1947). Purpose: to recognize, encourage, stimulate outstanding reporting directly to American public; materially increase public knowledge and understanding of chemistry, chemical engineering, related fields. Sponsored by 120,000-member, nonprofit American Chemical Society, largest association devoted to single scientific descipline.

NEWSPAPER-MAGAZINE AWARD: Chemistry Journalism. For noteworthy presentation by nominee through press. Require biographical sketch of nominee; identification of work on which nomination is based; samples (on 8 1/2x11-inch pages) of published work; evaluation, appraisal of nominee's accomplishments. Seconding letters not necessary unless contain additional factual information about nominee (maximum 2). Furnish 6 copies complete nominating document, letter-size and unbound.

BOOK-PAMPHLET   AWARD: Chemistry. For noteworthy presentation by nominee in book or pamphlet. Nomination requirements same as for Newspaper-Magazine.

AWARDS: $2000 James T. Grady Award and Gold Medal, Bronze Replica. $300 travel allowance.

JUDGING: By 5 judges.

ENTRY FEE: None.

DEADLINES: Nomination, March.

324

Oscars in Agriculture
DEKALB AgResearch
Ron Scherer, Public Relations Director
Sycamore Road
DeKalb, Illinois 60115 U.S.A.
Tel: (815) 758-3461

September

National; **entry restricted to U.S. professional editors;** annual; established 1961. Purpose: to encourage excellence in reporting of agriculture news. Sponsored by DEKALB

AgResearch. Held during DEKALB Communications Days at corporate headquarters in DeKalb, Illinois.

NEWSPAPER-MAGAZINE CONTEST: Agriculture Journalism, clippings of story-series in binder, 11x15 inches maximum; 1 maximum per individual, each limited to 1 theme-topic. Published June previous to June current year, by 1 professional editor on staff of commercial U.S. magazine-newspaper or through team effort. Require purpose, publication dates. Categories: Newspaper, Magazine, Team Effort.

AWARDS: Silver Agriculture Oscars to First Place, each category, for superior contributions furthering advancement of American agriculture. Plaques to employers.

JUDGING: By 7 judges, based on timeliness, depth of reporting, organization-clarity, production techniques-quality. May withhold awards.

ENTRY FEE: None.

DEADLINES: Entry, June. Winners announced, September.

| 325 |

Science in Society Journalism Awards Competition
National Association of Science Writers (NASW)
Diane McGurgan, Administrative Secretary
P.O. Box 294
Greenlawn, New York 11740 U.S.A.
Tel: (516) 757-5664

Fall

International; entry open to North America; annual; established 1972. Purpose: to recognize investigative, interpretive reporting about science, its impact for good and bad; encourage critical, probing articles. Sponsored and supported by NASW founded 1934 as society of professional writers of science for laypersons. Average statistics: 129 entries.

NEWSPAPER-MAGAZINE CONTEST: Science Journalism, single article or series; in English; for layperson; published June previous to May current year; 10 copies each entry; 3 entries maximum. News service stories acceptable. No book, book digests, straight science stories. Categories: Physical Science, Life Science.

AWARDS: $1000, Engraved Medallions, REcognition Certificates, each category. Certificate to publisher.

JUDGING: By professional science writers.

ENTRY FEE: Not specified.

DEADLINES: Entry, June. Awards, Fall.

| 326 |

Thomas L. Stokes Award
Washington Journalism Center
Julius Duscha, Director
2401 Virginia Avenue N.W.
Washington, District of Columbia
20037 U.S.A. Tel: (202) 331-7977

Spring

International; entry open to U.S. and Canada; annual; established 1959. Named after Thomas L. Stokes, syndicated columnist on natural resource issues. Sponsored by Washington Journalism Center.

NEWSPAPER CONTEST: Energy, Environment, Conservation Journalism, published in U.S.-Canadian daily newspaper during previous calendar year; about development, use, conservation of energy resources, environmental protection, conservation-natural resource issues. Require 10 work samples, summary letter.

AWARDS: Stokes Award, $1000 and Citation.

JUDGING: By journalist panel. Based on reporting, analysis, comment. No entries returned.

ENTRY FEE: None.

DEADLINES: Entry, February. Award, Spring.

327

Glaxo Fellowships for British Science Writers
Glaxo Holdings Limited
Geoffrey Potter, Group Public Relations Manager
6-12 Clarges Street
London W1Y 8DH, ENGLAND
Tel: 01-493-4060

Fall

National; **entry restricted to U.K. science journalists;** annual; established 1966. 1000 pounds Traveling Fellowship to **United Kingdom Science Writers** (National, Regional Newspaper, Science Magazine, Radio-Television). Purpose: to encourage communication of science knowledge to public. Sponsored by Glaxo Holdings Limited. Recognized by Association of British Science Writers. Event, Fall.

JOURNALISM (Sport, Hobby, Travel)
Newspaper-Magazine Journalism, Article, Script, including BOWLING, CANADIAN, HARNESS RACING, SKIWRITING, STAMP-COIN. (Also see other JOURNALISM.)

328

Bertha Weisz Memorial Awards for Stamp and Coin Columnists
Weiss Philatelic-Numismatic Features
Julius Weiss, Editor
16000 Terrace Road, #208
Cleveland, Ohio 44112 U.S.A.
Tel: (216) 451-3331

Spring

International; entry open to all; biennial (even years); established 1974. Named after Bertha Weisz, Cleveland stamp and coin enthusiast. Purpose: to give recognition to newspaper stamp and coin columnists. Sponsored and supported by Weiss Philatelic-Numismatic Features.

NEWSPAPER CONTEST: **Stamp-Coin Columns,** original, published (daily newspaper, 50,000 minimum circulation) from January to December in even numbered years. Original clippings, tearsheets showing by-line, date. Limit 2 entries. Categories: Stamp Column; Coin Column. No trade, hobby, hobby club paper columns. No columns based on government, agency press releases.

AWARDS: $50 U.S. Bond, plaque, each category.

JUDGING: By Weiss Features, based on originality, research, news. No entries returned.

ENTRY FEE: None.

DEADLINES: Entry, December. Awards, Spring.

329

Best Sports Stories Contest
Edward Ehre, Coeditor
1315 Westport Lane
Sarasota, Florida 33580 U.S.A.

Spring

International; entry open to all; annual; established 1944. Sponsored by *Best Sports Stories* (annual), published by E. P. Dutton, New York. Also have Sports-Photography Division.

NEWSPAPER-MAGAZINE CONTEST: Sports, published during current year, mounted with name of publication, photocopies accepted, maximum 3 articles per person. Require 50-word biography, permission to reprint. Categories: News-Coverage Story, News Feature Story-Column, Magazine Story.

AWARDS: $250 First Prize, each category. 40-50 best stories published in *Best Sports Stories,* copies to all included.

JUDGING: By 3 judges. No entries returned.

ENTRY FEE: None.

DEADLINES: Entry, December. Judging, February. Publication, Spring.

| 330 |

Bowling Magazine Writing Competition
American Bowling Congress (ABC)
Steve James, Public Relations Manager
5301 South 76th Street
Greendale, Wisconsin 53129 U.S.A.
Tel: (414) 421-6400

March

National; **entry open to U.S.;** annual; established 1953. Purpose: to reward outstanding bowling journalism. Sponsored by *Bowling,* monthly publication of ABC. Held at ABC Bowling Convention.

NEWSPAPER-MAGAZINE CONTEST: **Bowling,** published during

previous year, unmounted, 3 entries maximum per category. Categories: News, Editorial, Feature.

SCRIPT CONTEST: Bowling Radio-Television Broadcast. Requirements, restrictions same as for Newspaper-Magazine.

AWARDS: $200 First, $150 Second, $125 Third, $100 Fourth, $75 Fifth, $50 Sixth, $25 Seventh Prize, 5 Honorable Mentions, each category and division.

JUDGING: By 3 bowling journalists and 1 university professor. Sponsor may publish winners in *Bowling* magazine. Not responsible for loss or damage. No entries returned.

ENTRY FEE: None.

DEADLINES: Entry,   January. Awards, March.

| 331 |

Harold S. Hirsch Outstanding Skiwriter Award
United States Ski Writers Association (USSWA)
Don A. Metivier
7 Kensington Road
Glenn Falls, New York 12801 U.S.A.
Tel: (518) 793-1201

Spring

National; **entry restricted to professional ski writers;** annual; established 1965. Purpose: to improve overall quality of ski writing in U.S. Sponsored and supported by USSWA and Ski Industries America. Average statistics: 25-40 entries. Held at United States Ski Association annual convention. Second contact: United States Ski Association, Park City, Utah.

NEWSPAPER   CONTEST: Ski Writing, Submit 4-8 stories, columns.

AWARDS: Silver typewriter, plus

small keepsake, First Place. Honorable Mentions.

JUDGING: By journalism professors, ski industry executives.

ENTRY FEE: None.

DEADLINES: Entry, not specified. Awards, Spring.

| 332 |

John Hervey Awards for Excellence in the Reporting of Harness Racing
United States Trotting Association (USTA)
Philip Pikelny, Publicity Director
750 Michigan Avenue
Colombus, Ohio 43215 U.S.A.
Tel: (614) 224-2291

March

National; **entry restricted to U.S. freelance writers;** annual; established 1977. Named after John Hervey, author, sports journalist. Purpose: to encourage writing harness racing articles in U.S. newspapers, magazines. Sponsored by USTA, United States Harness Writers Association (USHWA). Supported by USTA. Average statistics: 40 entries, 14 semifinalists, 6 awards.

NEWSPAPER-MAGAZINE CONTEST: **Harness Racing,** published December previous to November current year; photostats acceptable; 1 entry per division. No USTA, race track publicity department employees. Divisions: Newspaper, Magazine. Categories: Essay, General Writing.

AWARDS: $500 First, $250 Second, $100 Third Place each division.

JUDGING: Entries from members, at-large members, nonmembers judged separately by local USHWA chapters, independent panel, university journalism educators. Grand Prize winner selected from 15 excellence

winners. Not responsible for loss or damage.

ENTRY FEE: None.

DEADLINES: Entry, November-December. Winners announced, January. Awards, Spring.

| 333 |

New Jersey Harness Writers Award
Edward C. Mueller, President
101 Marian Street
Toms River, New Jersey 08753
U.S.A. Tel: (201) 341-2081

March

State; **entry open to New Jersey residents or employees;** annual. Sponsored by Horse & Racetrack Bureau of New Jersey. Held at New Jersey Harness Writers annual dinner. Second contact: P.O. Box 372, Toms River, New Jersey 08753.

ARTICLE CONTEST: **Harness Racing,** any literary form; published in circulated media during previous calendar year (NJHW members), written or published during previous year (nonmembers). Submit published in original-duplicate; unpublished as typewritten, double-spaced. Categories: Members, Nonmembers. Sponsor may publish unpublished entries.

AWARDS: $100 to Best Entry.

ENTRY FEE: None.

DEADLINES: Entry, January. Winner announced, March.

| 334 |

Philatelic Press Club (PPC) Award
Ernest A. Kehr, Executive Chair
P.O. Box 114
Richmond Hill, New York 11419
U.S.A. Tel: (212) 843-4242

November

International; **entry restricted (nomination by PPC members);** annual. Award to Postal Administration for **Philatelic Journalism Information** (about stamps, postal services). Sponsored by PPC.

| 335 |

Explore Canada Awards Competition Best U.S. Publication

Tourism Industry Association of Canada (TIAC)
Suite 1016, 130 Albert Street
Ottawa, Ontario K1P 5G4 CANADA
Tel: (613) 238-3883

February

National; **entry open to U.S.;** annual. Purpose: to honor U.S. news, information media for best material publicizing Canada's tourist attractions, travel facilities; encourage wider spectrum of Canadian people, places, heritage. Sponsored and supported by TIAC. Held at TIAC National Conference in Toronto.

NEWSPAPER-MAGAZINE CONTEST: **Canada Tourism-Travel,** published in U.S. during previous calendar year, clipping or tearsheet, mounted in binder or scrapbook. Require supporting letter outlining purpose, results of material. No winners of 3 consecutive awards. Categories: Magazine, Newspaper (General Interest; Special Interest on particular attraction, events, activities).

AWARDS: TIAC Explore Canada Award, each category.

ENTRY FEE: None. Entrant pays postage (include SASE).

DEADLINES: Entry, January. Awards, February.

JOURNALISM (Other)

Newspaper-Magazine Journalism, Script, including HIGHER EDUCATION, HOUSE JOURNAL, READING. (Also see other JOURNALISM.)

| 336 |

American Association of University Professors (AAUP) Higher Education Writers Awards

Ellen A. Morgenstern, Public Information Officer
One Dupont Circle, Suite 500
Washington, District of Columbia
20036 U.S.A. Tel: (202) 466-8050

June

National; **entry open to U.S.;** annual; established 1969. Purpose: to recognize interpretive reporting on postsecondary education subjects and issues. Sponsored by AAUP, largest U.S. professional association of college-university teachers. Held at AAUP annual meeting.

NEWSPAPER-MAGAZINE CONTEST: **Higher Education Writing,** appearing March previous to March of contest year; 4 copies. Submit biographical statement.

SCRIPT CONTEST: **Higher Education Film, Television, Radio,** 4 transcripts. Other requirements, restrictions same as for Newspaper-Magazine.

AWARDS: Higher Education Writers Award (plaque).

JUDGING: By 3 English or journalism instructors chosen by AAUP president. 1 copy returned on request.

ENTRY FEE: None.

DEADLINES: Entry, April. Judging, May. Awards, June.

| 337 |

Council for Advancement and Support of Education (CASE) Recognition Program

Charles M. Helmken, Vice President
Eleven Dupont Circle, Suite 400
Washington, District of Columbia
20036 U.S.A. Tel: (202) 328-5917

June

International; **entry restricted to CASE members;** annual. Awards (monetary) and Certificates to **Institutional Periodicals-Publications** (Magazines, Tabloids, Newsletters, Brochures, Flyers, Reports) and **Newspaper Journalism.** Winning entries become property of sponsor. Sponsored by CASE. Average statistics: 3200 entries. Held in various U.S. cities. Have workshops, conferences. Awards, June.

| 338 |

International Reading Association (IRA) Print Media Awards Contest

Drew Cassidy, Public Information Officer
800 Barksdale Road
P.O. Box 8139
Newark, Delaware 19711 U.S.A.
Tel: (302) 731-1600

Spring

International; **entry restricted to professional journalists;** annual; established 1965. Formerly called ANNUAL NEWS AWARDS to 1971. Purpose: to honor outstanding reporting in newspapers, magazines, wire services on reading, related fields. Sponsored by IRA, 65,000-member, nonprofit, educational association with members in over 85 countries, dedicated to reading instruction im-

provement, reading habit development. Supported by Institute for Reading Research. Held at annual IRA Convention awards banquet. Also sponsor IRA Children's Book Award (to author showing unusual promise in children's literature); Albert J. Harris Award (diagnosis, remediation of reading, learning disabilities); Outstanding Dissertation of the Year Award (reading, related fields). Second contact: Dr. Donald Kenneth Maas, Education Department, California Polytechnic State University, San Luis Obispo, California 93407.

NEWSPAPER-MAGAZINE CONTEST: **Reading-Reading Education Journalism,** including in-depth studies of reading instruction, discussion of research, ongoing coverage of reading programs in community; published in previous calendar year; original article mounted on matboard, 8 1/2x14-inch (21 1/2x36 1/2 cm) maximum, plus 7 copies; unlimited entry. Require signed certificate of originality and noncollaboration. Translations accepted with original and verified English translation. Categories: Single Article or Single Connected Series in Metropolitan (100,000 or more daily circulation); Nonmetropolitan (under 100,000 daily circulation); Weekly Newspaper; Magazine (weekly, monthly, quarterly); Wire Service (newspaper syndicate).

AWARDS: $500, Medal (Overall Print Media). Certificates of Merit, each category. Second Place Awards.

JUDGING: By IRA special committee. Based on journalistic qualtiy, clear and imaginative writing, novelty, creativity in style, content. No entries returned. Not responsible for loss or damage.

ENTRY FEE: None.

DEADLINES: Entry, January. Awards, Spring.

| 339 |

British Association of Industrial Editors (BAIE) House Journal Competition
K. B. Barlett, Secretary General
3 Locks Yard, High Street
Sevenoaks, Kent TN13 1LT,
ENGLAND Tel: (0732) 59331

Spring

International; entry open to all; annual; established 1958. Sponsored by BAIE. Also have assessment and consultancy service to analyze content, writing, appearance of journals for improving effectiveness.

NEWSPAPER-MAGAZINE CONTEST: **House Journal,** published, 3 consecutive issues (2 consecutive for quarterly or less). Classes: Internal Newspapers, Magazines, External Newspapers, Magazines (circulation up to 10,000, 10-20,000, over 20,000). Special Categories: Newcomers (new editor of less than 5 years with First-Time journals, New Journal launched during previous year), Correspondents (News, Feature Article), International Design (outside U.K. for Best-Designed Newspaper, Magazine), Annual Report-Accounts for Employees (Newspaper, Magazine), Headlines (3 consecutive issues), Printing (by U.K. printers for House Newspaper, Magazine).

ELIGIBILITY: Published during previous calendar year, in English (except International Design), with editor verification.

AWARDS: Certificates, Awards, Trophies, Cups, each class, special category. Excellence and Merit Certificates at judges' discretion. Trophies held for one year.

JUDGING: By experts. Based on effectiveness as communications media in relation to objectives, design, presentation. Judges appraisal forms returned.

ENTRY FEE: Members, 12-19 pounds, nonmembers, 14-22 pounds, per class, special category.

DEADLINES: Entry, January. Judging, April. Awards, Spring.

JOURNALISM INTERN TRAINING PROGRAMS

Print Journalism, including CONGRESSIONAL-LEGISLATIVE, FOOD, MINORITY, NEWSPAPER and MAGAZINE EDITING. (Also see JOURNALISM SCHOLARSHIPS, FELLOWSHIPS, RESIDENCE GRANTS.)

| 340 |

AAAS Mass Media Intern Program
American Association for the Advancement of Science (AAAS)
Gail Breslow, Program Administrator
1776 Massachusetts Avenue N.W.
Washington, District of Columbia
20036 U.S.A. Tel: (202) 467-4310

Summer

National; **entry restricted to U.S. social-natural science college students;** annual; established 1974. Purpose: to provide opportunity to observe, participate in the news process, improve communication skills, increase understanding of editorial decision-making. Sponsored and supported by National Science Foundation; cosponsored by AAAS (112,000 members, founded 1848), world's leading general scientific organization dedicated to increasing public understanding, appreciation of science in human progress. Average statistics: 400 entrants, 20 finalists. Orientation in Washington, D.C.

JOURNALISM INTERNSHIP: Newspaper, Magazine Journalism, paid 10-12 week internship and travel expenses for 20 advanced undergraduate, graduate, postdoctoral students in social or natural sciences as mass media reporters, researchers, production assistants at newspapers, magazines. Require resume, writing examples, 2 faculty member recommendations; interim and final reports on internship.

JUDGING: Preliminary by experts in natural-social sciences, mass media. Final by AAAS staff. Based on study area understanding, commitment to promoting human understanding, appreciation of science, scientific methods.

DEADLINES: Entry, February. Announcements, April. Internship begins, June.

341

American Society of Magazine Editors (ASME) Magazine Internship Program
Robert E. Kenyon, Executive Director
Magazine Center
575 Lexington Avenue
New York, New York 10022 U.S.A.
Tel: (212) 752-0055

February

International; **entry restricted to college juniors (by nomination of academic dean or department head);** annual. Purpose: to integrate interests of journalism departments, magazine editors-staffs, magazine journalism students. Sponsored by ASME. Supported by Magazine Publishers Association. Average statistics: 54 interns working at 54 different magazines. Held in New York, New Jersey, Pennsylvania, Connecticut magazines.

MAGAZINE INTERNSHIP: Magazine Editing, Writing, stipend of $150 per week to college journalism majors completing junior year in May-June of internship year or humanities majors with journalism-creative writing courses or college newspaper-magazine staff members (nominated by academic dean or department head), for 10-week internship on editorial staff of national magazine (observing operations, handling reader mail, evaluating unsolicited manuscripts, researching, writing, interviewing) with weekly discussions on magazine publishing. For national judging, require dean, department head letter; writing samples; written reports from accepted interns; photo. No travel, board, personal expenses.

JUDGING: By dean, department head (1 candidate per college; 2 for schools with accredited magazine sequence). National judging of college candidates. Entrant pays postage (include SASE).

DEADLINES: Application, December. Notification, February.

342

Association for Education in Journalism (AEJ) Summer Journalism Internship for Minorities
Howard University
Dr. Lionel C. Barrow, Jr., Dean
School of Communications
Fourth & College Streets N.W.
Washington, District of Columbia
20059 U.S.A. Tel: (202) 636-7690

June

International; **entry restricted to minority college juniors;** annual; established 1968. Purpose: to encourage minority student education in mass communications; provide working condition information, job opportunities, graduate training, experience. Sponsored by AEJ, organization of 1000 mass communication college teachers; Minorities and Communications Division, Association for Education in Journalism; Institute of Afro-American Affairs, New York University Department of Journalism and Mass Communications; Howard University School of Communications. Average statistics: 10-14 finalists.

JOURNALISM INTERNSHIP: Minority Journalism, full-time internship to minority, junior-year students with 3 college journalism courses minimum, for 10-week summer journalism internship program in New York City area, and $175 per week minimum salary, plus tuition for 2-credit "Journalism and Minorities" course and arrangements for room-board on campus (intern pays room-board from weekly salary). Require 500-word autobiography of goals, journalistic interests, typed double-spaced; clips of previously published work; 2 faculty recommendation letters; college transcript; report of academic progress. No funds for travel, personal expenses. Job categories: Newspaper, Magazine, Public Relations.

JUDGING: By Internship Selection Committee.

DEADLINES: Application, February. Notification, June.

| 343 |

Congressional Fellowship Program
American Political Science Association (APSA)
1527 New Hampshire Avenue N.W.

Washington, District of Columbia 20036 U.S.A. Tel: (202) 483-2512

November-August

National; **entry restricted to U.S. professional journalists;** annual; established 1953. Purpose: to afford young journalists, political or social scientists, federal agency executives, or medical faculty opportunity for understanding of national legislative process. Sponsored by APSA. Supported by Edgar Stern Family Fund of New Orleans, Ford Foundation, IBM, Exxon, Andreas Foundation, Johnson Wax Fund, Merck. Average statistics: 15 per year.

JOURNALISM TRAINING PROGRAM: Congressional Journalism, $12,000 and travel expenses to journalists with BA degree, 2-10 years professional newspaper-magazine reporting experience, for training as congressional staff members with duties of legislative assistant or press secretary (no cost to Congress). Have 1 month orientation; congressional conferences; seminars with legislators, administrators, lobbyists, reporters, scholars; and 9 months as full-time aide to House, Senate members or congressional committee (including legislative drafting, lobbying coordination, briefing, strategy, speech-writing, arranging congressional hearings, campaign problems, international conferences abroad, travel to congressional district-state, research opportunities). Require detailed curriculum vita, resume; statement of goals; 3 professional reference letters; sample of best professional writing. Preference to candidates without extensive Washington experience.

JUDGING: By journalist, political scientist advisory committee. Based on quality training, professional competence, maturity, responsibility, relevance to career goals, advancement potential.

DEADLINES: Application, December. Winners announced, March. Fellowship, November-August.

344

National Newspaper Food Editor's Internship Program

Tupperware Home Parties
Mrs. Tina Engleman, Director of
Educational Services
P.O. Box 2353
Orlando, Florida 32802 U.S.A.
Tel: (305) 847-1958

May

National; **entry restricted to U.S. college juniors, seniors;** annual; established 1972. Purpose: to encourage newspaper food editing careers. Sponsored by Tupperware Home Parties and held in cooperation with participating major daily newspapers.

JOURNALISM INTERNSHIP: **Newspaper Food Journalism,** $2000 grant maximum to accredited college junior, senior majoring in journalism or home economics (planning career in newspaper journalism) for 10-week summer internship with major daily newspaper food editor. 2 $500 grants to runners-up for allied study-research, attendance at professional conventions. Require application; proposal letter; article (newspaper food story, real-life interview, or consumer interest) typed double-spaced, 3 pages maximum. No living expenses or transportation.

DEADLINES: Application, March. Notification, May.

345

Newspaper Fund Internships and Scholarships for College Students

The Newspaper Fund, Inc.
Janice M. Maressa, Administrative
Assistant
P.O. Box 300
Princeton, New Jersey 08540 U.S.A.
Tel: (609) 799-5600

May-August

International; **entry restricted to college juniors (Editing), minority college graduate students (Minority);** annual; established 1968 (Editing), 1979 (Minority). Purpose: to encourage newspaper editing; attract minority graduate students to newspapers as summer reporters, editors. Sponsored by Newspaper Fund, Inc., nonprofit foundation founded 1958 to encourage journalism careers for young people. Supported by Dow Jones & Company, Dow Jones News Services. Have workshops, teacher programs, Editor-in-Residence programs. Also sponsor Journalism Teacher Fellowship Program. Second contact: 55-57 Princeton-Hightstown Road, Princeton Junction, New Jersey 08550.

NEWSPAPER INTERNSHIP: **Newspaper Editing** *(Editing Internship Program),* maximum 40 internships at regular wages (paid by host newspapers) for summer work on daily newspaper, wire service copydesk (including copyediting pretraining, on-job copyediting, headline writing), to college juniors who will be seniors in fall. Require interest in newspaper career, 500-word personal essay, 2 recommendation letters, editing-writing exercise test, college course-grade list, reporting samples, final reports by interns-supervisors. No previous full-time professional newspaper journalism experience. Additional $700 scholarship to each intern completing full summer work.

Newspaper Minority Journalism *(Minority Internship Program)*, maximum 15 internships at regular wages (paid by host newspapers), for summer daily newspaper work with emphasis on editing (including news editing pretraining, postinternship workshop), to minority (Black, Hispanic, Asian, Pacific Islander, American Indian, Alaskan Native) graduate students, pending graduate students in Fall. Requirements same as for Editing Internship. No previous full-time professional newspaper, wire service journalism experience (3-month internships excepted). Additional $1000 scholarship to each intern completing full summer work.

JUDGING: Preliminary by sponsor, based on potential; final by host newspaper. Editing based on writing, editing, language communication, talent, interest. Commitments to host newspapers are binding.

DEADLINES: Entry, November. Winners announced, December (Editing), January (Minority). Pretraining, May-June. Internship, June-August.

| 346 |

Pulliam Journalism Fellowships
Indianapolis Newspapers, Inc. (INI)
Harvey Jacobs, Editor, The
Indianapolis News
307 North Pennsylvania Street
P.O. Box 145
Indianapolis, Indiana 46206 U.S.A.
Tel: (317) 633-9224

April

National; **entry restricted to U.S. college graduates;** annual; established 1974. Named after and founded by late Eugene C. Pulliam, publisher of 7 major newspapers. Purpose: to provide practical work-and-learn experience at major newspaper for top college graduates seeking newspaper careers. Sponsored and supported by Central Newspapers, Inc. (owner of *The Indianapolis Star, The Indianapolis News*). Have newsroom facilities, management-staff conferences, guest lecturers, job-related discussions. Also sponsor Photojournalism Fellowships.

JOURNALISM INTERNSHIP: **Newspaper Journalism,** 10 grants of $1665 paid in three installments to journalists committed to newspaper career, showing understanding of social-economic roles of free press, with proven potential in reporting, writing, editing, for 9 weeks' summer work at *Indianapolis Star* or *News*. Submit 3000-word maximum samples of writing, editing; 400-600-word editorial (any subject) written for this competition; 3 recommendation letters; college transcript; photo. No paid transportation, room-board.

ELIGIBILITY: College graduates within 1 year of graduation who were newspaper journalism majors, or liberal arts majors with some newspaper experience, and high scholastic achievement.

JUDGING: By INI staff. All entries read in entirety. Sponsor owns winning entries. Clippings of unsuccessful applicants returned. Not responsible for loss or damage.

DEADLINES: Application, February. Notification, April.

| 347 |

Summer Program for Minority Journalists
University of California, Berkeley
Nancy S. Kikuchi, Program
Coordinator
School of Journalism
607 Evans Hall
Berkeley, California 94720 U.S.A.
Tel: (415) 642-5962

Summer

National; **entry restricted to U.S. citizen, resident minorities;** annual; established 1969 and held at Columbia University Graduate Journalism School (to 1974); at University of California, Berkeley, since 1976. Formerly called MICHELE CLARK FELLOWSHIP PROGRAM to 1974. Purpose: to train beginning nonwhite reporters for daily newspapers; increase minorities in newsrooms. Sponsored by Institute for Journalism Education (Nancy Hicks, President). Supported by various foundations, newspaper organizations. Average statistics: 250 entrants, 50 semifinalists, 15-20 finalists. Held at U.C. Berkeley for 11-week summer program. Have visiting journalist seminars.

JOURNALISM TRAINING PROGRAM: Minority Print Journalism, 15-20 fellowships available to U.S. citizen, resident minorities (prefer age 21-35) with no or 1-year maximum newspaper experience (nomination by newspaper if latter) for 11 summer weeks' tuition, room-board, transportation to Berkeley and to interviews, incidentals, plus modest weekly stipend. For intensive journalism training, reporting, writing, editing 2000-circulation *Deadline* (weekly San Francisco newspaper). Graduates receive guaranteed full-time U.S. newspaper, wire service reporter job, including transportation to job, plus 15 undergraduate course credit units. Require 1000-word typed autobiography and newspaper analysis; reference letters; 35-word per minute typing speed; photo. Must agree to relocate to job city and be available for work. No college degree required. No funds for books, local or family transportation, or relocation.

JUDGING: Based on journalist reporting-writing potential, print journalism commitment, syntax, grammar, writing. Semifinalists interviewed and tested. Final acceptance by prospective newspapers.

DEADLINES: Application, January. Notification, April.

JOURNALISM RESIDENCE FELLOWSHIPS

Primarily for RESIDENCE STUDY and RESEARCH. Newspaper, Magazine, Wire Service Journalism, including BUSINESS, DANCE, FINANCIAL, FOREIGN AFFAIRS, EUROPEAN. (Also see JOURNALISM SCHOLARSHIPS, FELLOWSHIPS, INTERN PROGRAMS.)

348

American Dance Festival Dance Critics' Conference Fellowships
Lisa Booth, Administrative Director
P.O. Box 6097, College Station
Durham, North Carolina 27708
U.S.A. Tel: (919) 684-6402

June-July

National; **entry restricted to U.S. professional working journalists;** annual; established 1970. Purpose: to stimulate interest, expand knowledge, develop skills in dance criticism. Sponsored by American Dance Festival. Supported by NEA. Average statistics: 10 awards. Held in Durham, North Carolina for 3 weeks. Have workshops, discussions, scholarships. Also sponsor Video Apprenticeships; school for 250 dance students providing intensive dance training. Second contact: Judith Tolkow, ADF, 1860 Broadway, Room 1112, New York,

New York 10023; tel: (212) 586-1925.

JOURNALISM RESIDENCE FELLOWSHIPS: Dance Journalism. 10 fellowships for 3-week workshop to working professional journalists. Includes transportation, room and board, attending performances of dance companies on ADF program. Require explanatory letter, 2 samples published criticism (preferably on dance), 2 references.

JUDGING: Review and selection by workshop director.

ENTRY FEE: None. Entrant pays postage.

DEADLINES: Entry, April-May. Notification, May-June. Event, June-July.

349

Edward R. Murrow Fellowship for American Foreign Correspondents
Council on Foreign Relations (CFR)
Margaret Osmer, Secretary
58 East 68th Street
New York, New York 10021 U.S.A.
Tel: (212) 734-0400

September-June

National; **entry open to U.S. foreign correspondents;** annual; established 1949. Named after Edward R. Murrow, foreign correspondent. Purpose: to promote quality foreign events journalism that characterizes career of Edward R. Murrow. Sponsored by CFR, nonprofit 1800-member organization for international relations study, research, meetings, publishing. Supported by CBS Foundation. Publish *Foreign Affairs* (quarterly).

JOURNALISM RESIDENCE FELLOWSHIP: Foreign Affairs Journalism Newspaper, Magazine. Stipend equal to salary for office space and 9-month study-analysis-writing-research of international relations at CFR Harold Pratt House headquarters in New York City, and at a university, by U.S. citizen, newspaper or magazine correspondents-editors-producers serving abroad, or recently serving and planning to return. Prefer under age 40. Require 2500-word maximum statement of need, study-writing plans, career experience; leave-of-absence grant from employer; 5 journalism examples; 8x10 glossy photo; 5 references.

JUDGING: Based on performance, experience, education, program proposal, achievement prospects.

DEADLINES: Entry, March. Notification, June. Fellowship, September for academic year.

350

Fellowships in the Humanities for Journalists
University of Michigan
Graham Hovey, Director
3564 LSA Building
Ann Arbor, Michigan 48109 U.S.A.
Tel: (313) 763-2400

June

National; **entry restricted to U.S. professional journalists;** annual; established 1972. Purpose: to offer journalists academic year study in the humanities, and historical, social, cultural, philosophical dimensions of journalism; improve quality of journalism leadership. Sponsored by University of Michigan and Stanford University. Supported by NEH. Held at the University of Michigan (Ann Arbor) and Stanford University. Second contact: Director, C-14 Cypress Hall, Stanford University, Stanford, California 94305; tel: (415) 497-4937.

JOURNALISM RESIDENCE FEL-LOWSHIPS: **Journalist Humanities Study,** 12 at Michigan, 12 at Stanford of $18,000 each, plus tuition, $550 stipend for books and travel costs, to professional journalists for 9-month study in humanities-related areas (including course auditing, tutorials, library research, special seminars). Require 5 years minimum experience, leadership promise, journalism career commitment, leave of absence, interview of finalists. Submit 1000-word study statement and intellectual autobiography, biographical data, supervisor recommendation, 3 references, 10 work samples. No degree candidates, course credit, book-professional writing.

ELIGIBILITY: U.S. citizens or minimum 3-year residents who are fulltime employees of newspapers, wire services, TV-radio news departments, or magazine news, commentary, or public affairs departments; including film-TV documentarists, photojournalists, critics, reviewers. Need not be college graduate. No freelancers, employees in public information-relations jobs.

JUDGING: Based on professional performance, growth-achievement potential, motivation, aptitude, study ability, study plans.

DEADLINES:Application, February. Notification, June.

| 351 |

Jefferson Fellowship Program
East-West Communication Institute (EWCI)
1777 East-West Road
Honolulu, Hawaii 96822 U.S.A.
Tel: (808) 944-7333

January-May

Regional; **entry restricted to Asian, Pacific, U.S. journalists;** annual; established 1967. Coordinated by EWCI since 1971. Named after U.S. President Thomas Jefferson. Purpose: to encourage exchange of professional experience, promote learning of international news operations, expand knowledge related to current year's theme (varies). Sponsored by EWCI, national education institution founded 1960 to promote relations, understanding among U.S., Asian, Pacific nations through study, training, research. Supported by U.S. Congress, Asian and Pacific governments. Average statistics: 40 countries, 8-10 awards. Held in Honolulu for 3 1/2 months. Have on-campus housing, limited health insurance. Also sponsor graduate educational, research grants to Senior Fellows, scholarships, internships, other awards.

JOURNALISM RESIDENCE FEL-LOWSHIP: East-West Journalism. 8-10 $1500 stipends, round-trip fare to Honolulu.

ELIGIBILITY: Require vita-resume; statement (1000 words maximum) of reasons for interest, study areas, and intended projects proposal; letter from employer; 3 recommendation letters from senior journalists; 4 samples of professional work.

JUDGING: Final by East-West Center Selection Committee.

DEADLINES: Entry, May. Notification, June. Fellowships, January-May.

| 352 |

Joseph E. Hughes Fellowships
American Bankers Association (ABA)
Janell Bauer, Program Assistant
1120 Connecticut Avenue N.W.
Washington, District of Columbia
20036 U.S.A. Tel: (202) 467-4274

April

National; **entry restricted to U.S. professional journalists;** annual; established 1965. Purpose: to encourage media to keep up with changing environment of financial community. Sponsored by Stonier Graduate School of Banking, ABA. Average statistics: 15-20 entrants, 2 awards. Held at Rutgers University, New Brunswick, New Jersey, for 2 weeks. Have bank management simulation program, lectures by bankers, economists, academicians.

JOURNALISM RESIDENCE FELLOWSHIP: Financial Journalism, 2 tuition grants at Stonier Graduate School, room-board, plus $300 stipend and travel expenses; to U.S. journalists active in financial press (with 3 years minimum writing experience) for 2-week session providing financial education background. Submit recent articles from finance or business area.

JUDGING: By independent journalists.

DEADLINES: Application, March. Notification, April.

353

Newspaper Fund Teacher Fellowship Program
The Newspaper Fund, Inc.
Janice M. Maressa, Administrative Assistant
P.O. Box 300
Princeton, New Jersey 08540 U.S.A.
Tel: (609) 799-5600

Summer

National; **entry restricted to inexperienced high school journalism teachers, publications advisers;** annual; established 1960. Purpose: to provide journalism-publications teachers, advisers with basic skills, knowledge. Sponsored by The Newspaper Fund, Inc., nonprofit foundation funded 1958 to encourage journalism careers for young people. Supported by Dow Jones & Company, Dow Jones News Services. Average statistics: 1000 entrants, 250 finalists, 50 winners. Have workshops, teachers' programs, Editor-in-Residence programs. Also sponsor college student Newspaper Internships, Scholarships.

JOURNALISM RESIDENCE FELLOWSHIP: Journalism-Publications Teacher Training, up to $350 for workshop tuition, books, room-board, transportation. Winners choose workshop from list provided by sponsor. Teachers responsible for expenses over $350.

DEADLINES: Event, Summer.

354

Nieman Fellowships for Journalists
Nieman Foundation for Journalism
Daphne B. Noyes, Program Officer
Walter Lippmann House
One Francis Avenue
Cambridge, Massachusetts 02138
U.S.A. Tel: (617) 495-2237

September-June

National; **entry open to U.S.;** annual; established 1938 by Agnes Wahl Nieman, wife of Lucius W. Nieman, founder of *Milwaukee Journal* newspaper. Purpose: to promote, evaluate standards of journalism in U.S. by providing journalists mid-career opportunity to study, broaden intellectual horizons. Sponsored by Nieman Foundation for Journalism. Supported by Ford Foundation, U.S. and Canadian newspapers, magazines. Average statistics: 150 entries, 40 finalists, 12 fellows. Held at Harvard University. Have non-U.S. citizen fellowships. Publish *Nieman Reports* (quarterly journal). Also sponsor Louis Stark

Memorial Fund (established 1961) to support labor-reporting fellows; Robert Waldo Ruhl Fund (established 1973) to support associate fellows from abroad; occasional funding for other journalism fields.

JOURNALISM RESIDENCE FELLOWSHIP: Journalism Newspaper, Magazine, Press Service. Approximately 12 fellowships, including $300 weekly stipends (partially tax-exempt), tuition for classroom, library, Faculty Club costs, athletic and child care expenses, to full-time journalists with at least 3 years' professional experience in media, for 9-month nondegree academic study at Harvard University in any subject, including 1 complete required course, 2-4 audit courses per term, independent and supervised reading, independent research, seminars, consultations, travel in New England and abroad. Require 12 samples of current writing in quadruplicate (fit or folded to 8 1/2x11 inches), 2 1000-word essays (journalistic background, proposed study at Harvard), 4 recommendation letters, letter from immediate supervisor, agreement to return to former job, employer verification of leave of absence. Spouses may attend classes, libraries, seminars. No professional writing during fellowship or formal credit for studies.

JUDGING: By Nieman Curator, 3 Harvard faculty, 4 media professionals. Based on promise as contributor to craft. Finalists interviewed. Sponsor keeps writing samples.

DEADLINES: Application, February. Judging, February-May. Notification, June. Fellowships, September-June.

355

Walter Bagehot Fellowship Program in Economics and Business Journalism
Columbia University
Chris Welles, Director
Graduate School of Journalism
New York, New York 10027 U.S.A.
Tel: (212) 287-2711

September-May

National; open to U.S. professional journalists; annual; established 1974. Named for Walter Bagehot, 19th-century British economist. Purpose: to provide mid-career study in economics and business for professional journalists. Sponsored by Columbia University Graduate School of Journalism. Supported by various corporations. Average statistics: 50 entrants, 10 awards.

JOURNALISM RESIDENCE FELLOWSHIP: Economic-Business Newspaper, Magazine, Wire Service. $14,000 stipend and free tuition to full-time editorial employees with 4 years journalistic experience for 2 semesters (8 courses minimum) study in business, economics, international affairs, law at Columbia University. Have guest speakers, twice weekly seminars, dinners. Require leave-of-absence (employers expected to make up salary loss differential). Columbia University Certificate to fellows. Submit at least 6 samples of work, 3 references, 1000-word maximum (each) essays on professional career and business or economic trend.

JUDGING: By journalism faculty. Based on demonstrated journalistic excellence.

DEADLINES: Entry, April. Notification, May. Fellowship, September for academic year.

356

**Journalists in Europe
Scholarships**
Centre de Formation et de
Perfectionnement des Journalistes
(CFPJ)
Philippe Uiannay, Executive Manager
33 rue du Louvre
F-75002 Paris, FRANCE
Tel: 5088671

October-June

International; **entry restricted to
professional journalists;** annual; established 1946. Purpose: to provide
journalists with training, opportunity
to study European community institutions and discover political, economic, social, cultural realities of
EEC-member countries. Sponsored by
CFPJ, nonprofit organization founded
1974 (Hubert Beuve-Mery, founder).
Supported by European Economic
Community (EEC), UNESCO. Average statistics: 135 awards, 40 countries. Held at Journalists in Europe International Training Center, Paris.
Have study rooms, documentation
service. Publish yearbook. Also sponsor preliminary language courses;
summer retraining sessions (limited
entry) in specialized journalism media.

JOURNALISM   RESIDENCE
SCHOLARSHIP: European Journalism Newspaper, Magazine, News
Agency. 40,000 francs for living expenses (comparable to student lifestyle) to professional journalists to
conduct inquiries on European current
events, problems. Does not include
transportation to, from Paris. Require
letter in English, French, or German;
university, work references; press
clippings; evidence of language proficiency; statement of study intent. All
documents require signature of diplomatic or consular representative.

ELIGIBILITY: Professional journalists aged 25-35 with proficiency
(speak and understand) in French and
English; 4 years experience with
agency, newspaper, magazine.

JUDGING: By professional committee.

ENTRY FEE: Varies.

DEADLINES: Application, February. Notification, June. Scholarship,
October-June.

JOURNALISM SCHOLARSHIPS, FELLOWSHIPS, GRANTS

*For STUDY, RESEARCH, and
WRITING. Print Journalism, including
ELECTRICAL LIVING,
ENVIRONMENTAL CONSERVATION,
INVESTIGATIVE, LATIN AMERICAN,
RELIGIOUS, SCIENCE. (Also see
JOURNALISM INTERN-TRAINING
PROGRAMS and RESIDENCIES.)*

357

**Alicia Patterson Foundation (APF)
Fellowship Program for
Journalists**
Maria Casale, Program Coordinator
122 East 42nd Street
New York, New York 10168 U.S.A.
Tel: (212) 697-0868

December

National; **entry restricted to U.S.
professional journalists;** annual; established 1965. Named after Alicia
Patterson (1904-1963), 23-year editor
and publisher of *Newsday*. Purpose:
to enable journalists to travel, study,

write on significant areas-problems. Sponsored by APF Fellowship Program. Average statistics: 125 entrants, 8 finalists, 3-5 awards. Publish *APF Reporter* (bimonthly magazine). Have annual conferences on journalism issues.

JOURNALISM FELLOWSHIP: Journalistic Writing, 3-5 fellowships

up to $20,000 to U.S. citizen newspaper, magazine, wire service, broadcast journalists, editors, freelance writers with 5 years' professional journalism experience, for 1-year travel, study, writing of their choosing. Require application, project proposal, professional autobiography, 4 references. Require 1-year leave of absence from present job; report in periodic newsletter. Not for book preparation.

JUDGING: Finalists by staff and outside judges. Winners by panel of 7-9 nonstaff writers, editors, journalists. Work reprinted in *APF Reporter,* distributed to editors. Sponsor may reprint freely with proper credit for 1 year after publication date.

DEADLINES: Application, June-October. Notification, December.

358

Electrical Women's Round Table (EWRT) Julia Kiene Fellowship

Jean P. Keele, Chair
Central Power & Light Company
P.O. Box 2190
Alice, Texas 78332 U.S.A. Tel: (512) 664-0961

Spring

International; **entry restricted to women graduate students;** annual; established 1956. Named for Julia Kiene, former National President of EWRT and member of National Board of Directors. Purpose: to promote efficient use of electricity; encourage college graduates to further study toward advanced degree in electrical energy related field. Sponsored by 800-member EWRT, founded 1927 as independent national organization of women associated with electrical industry, allied fields.

JOURNALISM FELLOWSHIP: Electrical Living Journalism, Advertising.

$2000 (in 2 payments during 1 year) to woman graduate student working toward advanced college degree in field related to electrical living. Require background, goals, 4 references, college transcripts. No EWRT members.

JUDGING: By 5-member committee. Based on academic aptitude, vocational promise, character, financial need, willingness to continue career in field related to electrical energy.

DEADLINES: Entry, March. Award, Spring.

359

Environmental Conservation Fellowships

National Wildlife Federation (NWF)
Thomas L. Kimball, Executive Vice President
1412 16th Street N.W.
Washington, District of Columbia
20036 U.S.A. Tel: (202) 797-6800

April

International; **entry restricted to U.S., Canadian, Mexican graduate students;** annual; established 1957. Purpose: to encourage advanced study in wildlife, natural resource management, protection of environmental quality. Sponsored by NWF, founded 1938 to educate general public about resource, environmental problems; American Petroleum Institute (API). Also sponsor API matching-funds grants for oil-related research; conservation research grants.

JOURNALISM RESEARCH FEL-LOWSHIP: Environmental Conservation Journalism, Communications Research. Up to $4000 for 1 academic year to U.S., Canadian, Mexican citizens in college, university graduate program or law school (accepted for fall semester to conduct course work). Half given in September, half in January upon receipt of satisfactory progress report. Require transcripts, GRE scores, statement, references from major adviser, department head or chair. Research may be conducted outside U.S. Upon completion provide copy of publication, thesis, report resulting from study or supported by program; acknowledgment of NWF support and 1-page abstract.

JUDGING: By NWF Board of Directors. Based on completeness, clarity of application; relevance of proposed project to NWF interests, programs; value of study to natural resource conservation; scholastic standing; satisfactory credentials.

DEADLINES: Application, December. Acceptance, April. Grant in fall for academic year.

| 360 |

Fund for Investigative Journalism Grants
Howard Bray, Executive Director
1346 Connecticut Avenue N.W.
Room 1021
Washington, District of Columbia
20036 U.S.A. Tel: (202) 462-1844

Continuous

International; entry open to all; continuous; established 1969. Purpose: to aid, encourage investigative reporting through grants; increase public knowledge about concealed, obscure, complex aspects of public matters.

Sponsored by Fund for Investigative Journalism (Nick Kotz, Chairman). Supported by foundations, individuals.

JOURNALISM GRANT: Investigative Journalism Articles, Books, Broadcast Scripts, to probe abuses of authority, malfunctioning of institutions-systems that harm public, including environmental hazards, political corruption, invasion of privacy, organized crime, threats to civil rights, defense-foreign policy, abuses of corporate and union authority. Require letter describing proposed investigation (subject, significance, proof in hand, further evidence needed, approach), itemized budget, resume, published work samples, publisher statement of intent. Book grants require chapter outline, publisher contract, grant repayment if book makes money beyond advance.

DEADLINES: Open.

| 361 |

Inter American Press Association (IAPA) Scholarship Program
2911 N.W. 39th Street
Miami, Florida 33142 U.S.A.
Tel: (305) 634-2465

October

International; **entry restricted to U.S., Canadian young journalists, students;** annual; established 1954. Purpose: to exchange young journalists between countries of Western hemisphere. Sponsored by IAPA to foster knowledge, interchange among American people in support of free society, individual liberty. Held at IAPA annual meeting in Toronto, Canada. Statistics (all awards): 285 scholarships to date. Also sponsor 5 scholarships per year to Latin American journalists for study in U.S., Canada; IAPA-Tom Wallace Awards (named for late editor of *Louisville Times)* to U.S., Canadian newspaper (plaque) or journalist ($500, scroll) for inter-American friendship, understanding (nomination by IAPA members); IAPA-Pedro Joaquin Chamorro Awards (established 1952), to Latin American newspaper, magazine (plaque), 5 Latin American journalists, photographers, cartoonists ($500, certificate) for freedom of the press.

JOURNALISM SCHOLARSHIP: Latin American Journalism, 7 $3500 scholarships for 6-9-month study, reporting in Latin American country at university of entrant's choice, to U.S., Canadian journalists, journalism students, age 21-35, fluent in Spanish or Portuguese. Require 3 years professional journalism experience or journalism degree, language speaking, writing, and comprehension ability; 2 courses at university, research project article, report; 1 story per month to IAPA minimum for recipients.

DEADLINES: Application, September. Notification, October.

| 362 |

Journalism Foundation of Metropolitan St. Louis Journalism Scholarships
Marilee Martin, Scholarship Coordinator
CASA, Saint Louis Conservatory & School for the Arts
560 Trinity Avenue
St. Louis, Missouri 63130 U.S.A.

May

Regional; **entry restricted to St. Louis Metropolitan area resident college students;** annual; established 1969. Sponsored by Journalism Foundation of Metropolitan St. Louis. Supported by Society of Professional Journalists (Sigma Delta Chi), Women In Communications, International As-

sociation of Business Communicators, Association of Black Journalists, Newspaper Guild. Average statistics: 90 entries, 12 awards, 440 attendance. Held at annual banquet in St. Louis. Tickets: $15. Second contact: Barbara Abbett, Fleishman-Hillard, Inc., Memorial Drive, St. Louis, Missouri 63102.

JOURNALISM SCHOLARSHIP: College Journalism, 12 $600-$750 scholarships available for journalism degree study at accredited department-school of journalism. Require 3 recommendation letters, 2 writing samples, 300-500-word statement, biographical information, photo.

ELIGIBILITY: Junior, senior, graduate college student residents of Metropolitan St. Louis (St. Louis City; Franklin, Jefferson, St. Charles, St. Louis Counties in Missouri; Madison, Monroe, St. Clair Counties in Illinois) enrolled in accredited journalism school.

JUDGING: By 6 members of participating organizations. Based on aptitude for, interest in journalism, communications career, academic standing, financial need. Not responsible for loss or damage.

ENTRY FEE: None. Entrant pays postage (include SASE).

DEADLINES: Application, March. Notification, May.

| 363 |

Nate Haseltine Fellowships in Science Writing
Council for the Advancement of Science Writing (CASW)
William J. Cromie, Executive Director
618 North Elmwood
Oak Park, Illinois 60302 U.S.A.
Tel: (312) 383-0820

Continuous

National; **entry restricted to U.S. journalists, journalism graduate students;** established 1977. Replaces AMERICAN MEDICAL ASSOCIATION SCIENCE JOURNALISM AWARDS (established 1964). Named for Nate Haseltine, late medical writer for *Washington Post.* Purpose: to teach science-medicine writing, reporting. Sponsored by AMA; CASW, organization of science journalists, scientists seeking to increase public understanding of science by upgrading writing quality. Also sponsor Dr. Morris Fishbein Fellowships in Medical Journalism.

JOURNALISM FELLOWSHIPS: Science Writing Newspaper, Magazine, Wire Service Journalism, up to $1500 per year to working journalists, journalism graduate students for career in mass media general-public science writing. Working journalists may use funds for part-time schooling-directed study, reference-science books, magazine subscriptions, science meeting travel, on-job training with science writer. Require resume, 3 employer-faculty recommendations, 3 writing samples, 500-word career-study goals; from students, undergraduate journalism-science degree, transcripts, science writing-study resources available at school.

ELIGIBILITY: Employed by daily newspapers, wire services, news magazines (those with 2 years' experience given priority). Students with undergraduate degrees in science or journalism, proven ability and motivation to pursue career in science writing. No fellowships for careers in public relations, public information work.

JUDGING: By selection committee.

DEADLINES: Open.

364

Quill and Scroll Foundation Journalism Research Grants
Quill and Scroll Society
Richard P. Johns, Executive Secretary
University of Iowa
School of Journalism
Iowa City, Iowa 52242 U.S.A.
Tel: (319) 353-4475

Continuous

International; **entry restricted to graduate students;** continuous. Sponsored by Quill and Scroll Society (International Honorary Society for High School Journalists). Supported by Quill and Scroll Foundation. Publish *Quill and Scroll* (quarterly). Also sponsor National Writing Contest (for U.S. junior-senior high school students), 10 $500 Edward J. Nell Memorial Scholarships in Journalism (open to senior class Writing, Photography, Current Events Quiz contest winners), George H. Gallup Award Newsmedia Evaluations (for member high school news publications), Current Events Quiz and Photography Contest (both open to U.S. junior-senior high school students).

JOURNALISM GRANT: High School Journalism-Scholastic Publications Research, grants of reimbursement for actual costs (postage, supplies, printing, questionnaires, etc.; no payment for work), to graduate students for research in high school journalism-scholastic publications. Require proposal letter from student, endorsement letter from thesis-study supervisor.

DEADLINES: Open throughout year.

365

Ralph McGill Scholarship Fund
Jack Tarver, Chairman
Box 4689
Atlanta, Georgia 30302 U.S.A.

Fall

Regional; **entry restricted to U.S. Southern third-, fourth-year college students;** annual. Named for Ralph McGill, late publisher of *The Atlanta Constitution*. Purpose: to award scholarships to students who have demonstrated long-time interest in news and editorial newspapering. Sponsored by Ralph McGill Scholarship Fund. Supported by Cox Foundation.

JOURNALISM SCHOLARSHIP: Undergraduate Newspaper Journalism, up to $1500 for 1 academic year to entrants with at least 2 years of college, roots in South, interest in news and editorial newspapering, intentions for career in dailies, weeklies. Require 500-word application letter, photo, college-authority recommendation letter; "B" average to maintain scholarship.

DEADLINES: Application, April. Notification, Fall.

366

Scripps-Howard Foundation Scholarships and Grants
Edward Forte, Administrator
200 Park Avenue, Room 4310
New York, New York 10166 U.S.A.

Spring

National; **entry open to U.S.;** annual. Purpose: to encourage ambitious, talented young people to prepare for careers in journalism, allied arts. Sponsored by Scripps-Howard Foundation, founded 1962 as charitable nonprofit organization. Also spon-

sor Robert P. Scripps Graphic Arts Grants and various Scripps-Howard Foundation Journalism Awards.

JOURNALISM SCHOLARSHIPS: Student Newspaper Journalism *(Roy W. Howard-Margaret Rohe Howard Journalism Scholarships),* up to $2000 to students interested in editorial, business aspects of newspapers, willing to work to provide part of costs. Require application letter, school transcripts, faculty recommendations.

Professional Journalism *(Ellen Browning Scripps Journalism Scholarships),* 10 fellowships yearly to persons currently working in journalism who wish to increase their knowledge in any field through graduate work. Require application letter stating purpose, goals.

JOURNALISM GRANTS: Journalism Special Projects, to projects related to journalism and journalism education, including but not limited to seminars, minority student, internship programs.

DEADLINES: Application, April. Notification, Spring.

367

Stoody-West Fellowship for Graduate Study in Journalism
United Methodist Communications (UMC)
Gene W. Carter, Assistant General Secretary
307 Fenway Drive
Walnut Creek, California 94598
U.S.A. Tel: (415) 935-0247

February

International; entry open to all; annual; established 1964. Formerly called RALPH W. STOODY FELLOWSHIP to 1980. Purpose: to assist Christian person engaged in religious journalism in graduate study at accredited school or journalism department. Sponsored by UMC. Average statistics: 1 award.

JOURNALISM FELLOWSHIP: Graduate Religious Journalism, $6000 grant for full-time journalism graduate study. Require 500-word maximum statement of interest in religious journalism, 2 recommendation letters, religious writing examples, published articles list, undergraduate transcripts, report of academic progress throughout year, photo.

JUDGING: By 3 UMC Board members. Based on academic record, writing examples, statement of professional goals, promise of future usefulness, sincerity, and commitment. All entries reviewed in entirety; returned at sponsor's expense. Not responsible for loss or damage.

DEADLINES: Application, January. Notification, February.

RESIDENCE GRANTS

Primarily for RESIDENCE STUDY, RESEARCH, and WRITING. Includes Book, Dissertation, Publishing, Script. (Also see other SCHOLARSHIPS, FELLOWSHIPS.)

| 368 |

American Antiquarian Society (AAS) Research-Writing Fellowship Awards
Marcus A. McCorison,
Director-Librarian
185 Salisbury Street
Worcester, Massachusetts 01609
U.S.A. Tel: (617) 755-5221

March

International; **entry restricted to scholars;** annual. Purpose: to make available research resources in early American history and culture. Sponsored by AAS, founded 1812 as third oldest historical society in U.S. Supported by NEH, private endowments. Have library materials to year 1876; informal seminars, colloquia.

WRITING RESIDENCE FELLOWSHIPS: Early American History-Culture Scholarly Research-Writing, **Short-Term Visit** *(Fred Harris Daniels Fellowship),* up to $1800 for 1-3 months full-time residence at AAS, to scholars residing over 50 miles from Worcester, for research, doctoral dissertation writing.

Long-Term Visit *(National Endowment for the Humanities Fellowship),* up to $22,000 for 6-12 months full-time residence at AAS, to U.S. citizens or minimum 3-year residents. No outside teaching assignments or activities, advanced degree study, or concurrent major fellowships (except sabbaticals, grants from own institutions).

Doctoral Dissertation Research *(Frances Hiatt Fellowship),* $1000 for minimum 6 weeks study at AAS to graduate student researching doctoral dissertation.

Early American Bibliography or Printing-Publishing History *(Albert Boni Fellowship),* up to $1250 for 1-2 months work at AAS library.

ELIGIBILITY: Submit formal application, 3 reference letters. Recipients are to be in regular and continuing residence at AAS library during grant period.

JUDGING: Based on scholarly qualifications, project interest, appropriateness of inquiry to Society's holdings.

ENTRY FEE: None.

DEADLINES: Entry, January. Awards, March.

| 369 |

Appalachian Studies Fellowships
Berea College
Loyal Jones, Director
Appalachian Center
College P.O. Box 2336
Berea, Kentucky 40404 U.S.A.
Tel: (606) 986-9341, ext. 513
Continuous

Regional; **entry restricted to Appalachian residents;** continuous. Purpose: to provide financial assistance to scholars engaged in Appalachian research at Weatherford-Hammond Mountain Collection and Museum in Berea. Sponsored by Berea College Appalachian Center. Supported by Andrew W. Mellon Foundation. Have symposium on Appalachian Research. Also sponsor W. D. Weatherford Award Competition.

WRITING RESIDENCE FELLOW-SHIP: **Appalachian Studies Research,** costs of travel, lodging, meals, supplies to experienced scholars and those with plans to publish.

JUDGING: By selection committee.

DEADLINES: Open.

| 370 |

Fulbright-Hays Grants
Institute of International Education
(IIE)
Theresa Granza, Manager
809 United Nations Plaza
New York, New York 10017 U.S.A.
Tel: (212) 883-8265
Spring

National; **entry open to U.S.;** annual; established 1946 by legislation authorizing use of foreign currencies accruing to U.S. abroad for educational exchanges (1961 *Fulbright-Hays Mutual Educational and Cultural Exchange Act* authorizes congressional appropriations for these exchanges). Named after Senator J. William Fulbright. Purpose: to increase mutual understanding between U.S. and other nationals through foreign study. Sponsored by IIE, Founded to promote peace, understanding through educational, cultural exchanges in all academic fields; U.S. International Communication Agency (USICA). Supported by annual appropriations from U.S. Congress, other governments. Average statistics: 3000 entrants. Have grants to visiting scholars, American scholars-professionals, predoctoral fellowships, teacher exchanges, Hubert H. Humphrey North-South Fellowship Program (study-internships), Faculty Research Abroad Program, Doctoral Dissertation Research Abroad Program, Group Projects Abroad. Fulbright-Hays program booklets available from USICA, 1776 Pennsylvania Avenue N.W., Washington, D.C. 20547. Also sponsor Fulbright Awards for University Teaching and Advanced Research Abroad.

WRITING RESIDENCE GRANT: **Creative Arts Foreign Study,** round-trip transportation, language and orientation course, tuition, books, health-accident insurance, single-person maintenance for 6-12 months study in 1 foreign country (doctoral candidates may receive higher stipends).

ELIGIBILITY: U.S. citizens with majority of high school, college education in U.S., B.A. or equivalent (or 4 years professional experience-study in proposed creative art field). Require host-country language proficiency, certificate of good health, study plan, project proposal, reasons for choosing particular country, what contribution foreign experience will make to professional development, work samples, possible interview.

JUDGING: Professional juries and binational commissions in field of expertise prepare nominations to Fulbright agencies abroad, U.S. Board of Foreign Scholarship.

DEADLINES: Application, November. Judging, November-December. Preliminary notification, January. Awards, April-June.

371

Fulbright Awards for University Teaching and Advanced Research Abroad
Council for International Exchange of Scholars (CIES)
Suite 300
Eleven Dupont Circle
Washington, District of Columbia
20036 U.S.A. Tel: (202) 833-4950

Spring

National; **entry open to U.S.**; annual; established 1946 by legislation authorizing use of foreign currencies accruing to U.S. abroad for educational exchanges (1961 *Fulbright-Hays Mutual Educational and Cultural Exchange Act* authorizes congressional appropriations for these exchanges). Named after Senator J. William Fulbright. Purpose: to increase mutual understanding between U.S. and other nationals through foreign study. Sponsored by CIES, U.S. International Communications Agency (USICA). Supported by annual appropriations from U.S. Congress, other governments. Average statistics: 2500 entrants, 1000 semifinalists, 500 awards. Have other grants for teacher-scholar exchanges, research abroad. Also sponsor Fulbright-Hays Grants.

WRITING RESIDENCE GRANT: University Teaching, Advanced Research, stipend, round-trip transportation, other allowances for 1 academic year or less of university teaching and-or postdoctoral research abroad.

ELIGIBILITY: U.S. citizens, scholars, creative artists, professionals, institutions. Require host-country language proficiency if needed; university teaching experience; doctorate, if specified by host country (for teaching); doctorate or recognized professional standing (for research); project presentation, other documentation.

JUDGING: 50 discipline-area committees and binational commissions assist CIES in preparing nominations to Fulbright agencies abroad and U.S. Board of Foreign Scholarship. All entries reviewed.

DEADLINES: Application, June (American Republics, Australia, New Zealand), July (Africa, Asia, Europe). Judging, September-December. Notification, January-April. Awards given 12-18 months following notification.

372

Helene Wurlitzer Foundation of New Mexico Residencies
Henry A. Sauerwein, Jr., Executive Director
P.O. Box 545
Taos, New Mexico 87571 U.S.A.
Tel: (505) 758-2413

Continuous

International; entry open to all; continuous. Sponsored by Helene Wurlitzer Foundation of New Mexico. Have 12 studio apartments in Taos, New Mexico. Also accept painting, sculpture, choreography, allied fields.

WRITING RESIDENCE GRANT: Writing, furnished studio apartment (including linen, utilities) for 3-12 months. Residents purchase, cook, serve own meals; clean apartments. No families, transportation, living expenses, materials.

DEADLINES: Open.

373

Howard University Press Book Publishing Institute Scholarships
Janell E. Walden, Program Director
2900 Van Ness Street N.W.
Washington, District of Columbia
20008 U.S.A. Tel: (202) 686-6498
Spring

International; entry open to all; annual; established 1980. Purpose: to prepare individuals for entry-level positions in book publishing industry. Sponsored by Howard University Press. Supported by Time, Inc., other publishing companies. Recognized by AAP Education for Publishing Program. Held in Washington, D.C., for 5 1/2 weeks. Have lectures, workshops, tours, discussions. Tuition: $900.

PUBLISHING RESIDENCE SCHOLARSHIP: Book Publishing, scholarships to attend Institute to students demonstrating financial need, high motivation, appreciation for books; for tuition, housing, books, meals, transportation to classroom. Must be college senior or hold bachelors degree, wish to begin career in book publishing. Certificates awarded on successful completion of course. Categories: Editorial, Design-Production, Marketing, Business.

JUDGING: Applicants reviewed by admissions committee.

ENTRY FEE: $25.

DEADLINES: Entry, April. Acceptance, May.

374

Indiana University Writers' Conference Scholarships
Roger Mitchell, Director
464 Ballantine Hall
Indiana University
Bloomington, Indiana 47405 U.S.A.
Tel: (812) 337-1877
June

International; entry open to all; annual; established 1941. Purpose: to provide constructive, professional guidance-criticism for writers and their work. Sponsored by Indiana University. Average statistics: 150 entries. Held at Indiana University in June. Have workshops. Fees: $150 tuition plus 1 week room-board. Also sponsor Founder's Award, Indiana Women's Press Association Award, other cash awards to conference participants.

WRITING RESIDENCE SCHOLARSHIP: Nonfiction, fees and tuition for attending conference to entrants submitting best manuscript.

JUDGING: By Conference screening committee. Not responsible for loss or damage.

ENTRY FEE: $15 (refundable). Entrant pays postage (include SASE).

DEADLINES: Entry, April. Acceptance, May. Conference, June.

375

MacDowell Colony Residence Grants
680 Park Avenue
New York, New York 10021 U.S.A.
Continuous

International; entry open to all; continuous; established 1907 by American composer Edward MacDowell. Purpose: to help creative professional artists pursue work under optimal conditions. Sponsored by and held at MacDowell Colony (Peterborough, New Hampshire), nonprofit membership corporation providing working, living accommodations and solitude (no instruction) for writers, visual artists, filmmakers, composers of demonstrated talent. Supported by NEA, private donors. Average statistics: 190 residents (98 writers, 58 visual artists, 34 composers), 39-day average stay, nearly 2000 residents to date. Have 30 isolated studios, 3 residence cottages, graphics workshops, library, main hall, on 450 acres of fields, woods. Also sponsor Edward MacDowell Medal, presented to major artist annually in August. Second contact: MacDowell Colony, High Street, Peterborough, New Hampshire 03458.

WRITING RESIDENCE GRANT: Writing, tuition waiver, based on number of accepted applicants (selected from writers, filmmakers, composers, visual artists) and financial need, for room, board, private studio. Require sample manuscripts, publications list, recommendations.

JUDGING: By professionals in each discipline. Based on talent shown in submitted work samples, recommendations.

DEADLINES: Entry, January (for June-August), April (September-November), July (December-February), October (March-May). Request application from New York office.

376

Niagara Frontier Christian Writers' Workshop Scholarships
Don Booth, Director
6853 Webster Road
Orchard Park, New York 14127
U.S.A. Tel: (716) 662-5259
June

International; entry open to all; annual; established 1970. Purpose: to challenge, encourage writers to share faith in Christ through nonfiction, devotionals. Sponsored by Niagara Frontier Christian Writers' Workshop. Average statistics: 45 attendance. Held for 1 day at Houghton College (910 Union Road, West Seneca, New York 14224; 716-674-6363). Have manuscript criticisms, marketing suggestions. Tickets: $17 registration. Also sponsor Fiction Writing Residence Scholarships.

WRITING RESIDENCE SCHOLARSHIPS: Chirstian Nonfiction, to attend Christian Writers' Workshop. Submit up to 2000 words. Categories: Book, Article, Essay, Script, Journalism.

JUDGING: By workshop leaders. Entries reviewed in entirety.

DEADLINES: Application, May. Notification, June.

377

Northwood Institute Creativity Fellowships
Alden B. Dow Creativity Center
Judith O'Dell, Director
3225 Cook Road
P.O. Box 1406
Midland, Michigan 48640 U.S.A.
Tel: (517) 631-1600, ext. 208
Summer

International; **entry restricted to English-speaking persons;** annual; established 1979. Named after Alden B. Dow, AIA. Purpose: to encourage creative thought; provide time, work facilities for creative persons to concentrate on ideas without financial worries; establish internationally recognized center for creativity technology. Sponsored by Northwood Institute, Alden B. Dow. Average statistics: 6 awards. Held at Northwood Institute, Midland, Michigan.

WRITING RESIDENCE FELLOWSHIP: Creative Project, for study, creation, innovation, appreciation. 3-month study at Northwood Institute; includes room, board, professional counsel. Considered applicants flown to personal interview. Applicants welcomed from all disciplines, areas of interest covering spectrum of written communications (e.g., language development, publishing, distribution of literature). Require description of proposed project, resume, budget projection. College credit arranged upon request. Special certificates, recognition upon successful completion.

JUDGING: By Board of Directors, Advisory Panel, Northwood Institute Alden B. Dow Creativity Center. All entries viewed in entirety. Project ideas remain property of applicant. Not responsible for loss or damage.

ENTRY FEE: None. Entrant pays postage (include SASE).

DEADLINES: Entry, December. Judging, December-March. Winners announced, April. Award, June-August.

378
Science for Citizens Program Grants
National Science Foundation (NSF)
G. Triml, Program Director
Science Education Directorate
1800 G. Street N.W.
Washington, District of Columbia
20550 U.S.A.

Various

National; **entry restricted to U.S. Organizations;** various throughout year. Purpose: to encourage scientists to participate in public-policy-related activities; provide scientific, technical expertise to citizen groups. Sponsored by NSF Science Education Directorate, dedicated to understanding between scientific, technological communities and general society. Also sponsor Technological Innovation in Education Program Grants (to innovative educational television and communication technology in science education institutions), Public Understanding of Science Grants.

WRITING RESIDENCE GRANT: Science Public Service, $18,000-$35,000 to scientific, educational, service, charitable organizations (or to individuals through such organizations) not primarily for profit, for residencies allowing scientists-engineers up to 1 year with organizations in need of expertise, resulting in handbooks, articles, literature on scientific needs of citizens.

JUDGING: Reviewed by scientists, engineers; professional, institutional leaders.

DEADLINES: Vary throughout year.

379
Smithsonian Institution Research Fellowships
Smithsonian Institution
Room 3300, L'Enfant Plaza
Office of Fellowships and Grants
Washington, District of Columbia
20560 U.S.A.

Continuous

International; entry open to all; continuous. Purpose: to further research training of scholars, scientists in early stages of professional careers. Sponsored by Smithsonian Institution, founded 1846 to increase and diffuse knowledge. Considered largest historical-research museum in U.S. Also have Materials Analysis Fellowship (for study of application of scientific techniques to humanities, arts, social sciences), Short-Term Visits Grants, and various scholarships, fellowships, internships. Also sponsor Guggenheim Fellowship, Woodrow Wilson International Center for Scholars Residential Research Fellowships.

WRITING RESIDENCE FELLOW-SHIP: Academic Research and Writing *(Visiting Research Program),* minimum $8000 (predoctoral), $14,000 (postdoctoral) for 6-12-month scholarly research-writing; also provide allowance for research-related expenses, relocation. Require residence at Smithsonian facilities; detailed research proposal indicating why Smithsonian is best place to conduct proposed work. Categories: Predoctoral (for candidates researching dissertation), Postdoctoral (for candidates with recently completed doctoral degrees or equivalent in experience, education).

ELIGIBILITY: All qualified scholars evaluated on academic standing, scholarly competence, experience, suitability of project to Smithsonian's facilities-programs.

DEADLINES: Application, January. Notification, continuous.

| 380 |

United States and Japan Exchange Fellowship Program
Japan United States Friendship Commission
Francis B. Tenny, Executive Director
1875 Connecticut Avenue N.W.
Suite 709
Washington, District of Columbia
20009 U.S.A. Tel: (202) 673-5295

April, October

National; **entry restricted to mid-career U.S. and Japanese artists;** semiannual; established 1975. Purpose: to aid education and culture at highest level; enhance reciprocal people-to-people understanding; support close friendship and mutuality of interests between U.S. and Japan. Sponsored by Japan United States Friendship Commission, NEA (U.S.), Agency for Cultural Affairs (Japan). Have fellowships in dance, design, folk arts, music composition, theater, visual arts, crafts. Also sponsor Journalism Fellowships, Book Translation Awards, American Performing Arts Tours in Japan, Japanese Cultural Performances in U.S. Second contact: Nippon Press Center Building, 2-1 Uchisaiwai-cho, 2 chome, Chiyoda-ku, Tokyo; tel: 508-2380.

WRITING RESIDENCE FELLOW-SHIP: Literature Work-Study in Japan. 5 fellowships of $1600-monthly stipends plus round-trip transportation for 6-9 months to creative and practicing artists well established in field, to observe Japanese traditional and contemporary artistic developments. (Overseas travel fares for spouse, children to 18 also provided.) Require completed training; not recent resident or working in Japan at time of application. Funds also available for additional expenses. Written report required at conclusion. No historians, scholars, art critics, students. Proficiency in Japanese not required.

JUDGING: Reviewed by private citizens, experts, in respective fields. American selection committee chooses semifinalists. Final by Japanese awards committee.

DEADLINES: Entry, March, September. Fellowships, October, April.

381

U.S. Army Center for Military History (USACMH) Resident Fellowships
Maurice Matloff, Chief Historian
Washington, District of Columbia
20314 U.S.A.

September-May

National; **entry restricted to U.S. civilian graduate students;** annual. Purpose: to stimulate unofficial scholarly research and writing in military history. Sponsored by USACMH. Have desk space, staff assistance. Publish books, monographs, pamphlets on military history.

DISSERTATION RESIDENCE FELLOWSHIP: U.S. Military History, 2 $4000 stipends for dissertation writing during academic year at Center. Require undergraduate-graduate transcripts, academic recommendation letters; academic approval of dissertation topic, research proposal, 10-25-page writing sample.

ELIGIBILITY: U.S. civilian graduate students writing dissertation on American military history. Must have completed by September all Ph.D. requirements except dissertation. No previous recipients of Department of Defense agency equivalent fellowships.

JUDGING: Preliminary by civilian academic historians, Army officers. Final by Chief of Military History at Center. Based on academic achievement, faculty recommendation, demonstrated writing ability, nature-location of proposed research, utility to project of federal archival centers in Washington.

DEADLINES: Entry, January. Notification, April. Fellowship, September-May (academic year).

382

U.S. Department of Energy Visiting Scholar Program
Dr. Jack Holl, Chief Historian
Historian's Office
Room 7G-033, Forrestal Bldg.
Washington, District of Columbia
20585 U.S.A. Tel: (301) 353-5431

Continuous

National; **entry open to U.S.;** continuous. Purpose: to aid scholars in work requiring extended research in Washington, D.C., area. Sponsored by U.S. Department of Energy.

WRITING RESIDENCE SCHOLARSHIP: U.S. Energy History Curriculum Development, up to full salary, fringe benefits, travel money, secretarial assistance, use of office and computer facilities, for 1 year at Department of Energy Headquarters. On history of U.S. energy policy, production, use. Submit undergraduate-graduate curriculum proposals (7 typed pages maximum), syllabus and evaluation of course currently teaching, resume, budget, copies of major publications.

U.S. Energy History Research, benefits, services same as for Curriculum Development. Submit research proposal-design (7 typed pages maximum), resume, budget, copies of major publications.

ELIGIBILITY: Full-time employees of college, university, state or local agency. For research, preference to imaginative proposals leading to publication on topics relating to utilization-development of energy systems, policies, technologies in 20th century.

DEADLINES: Application, May. Awards, continuous (as vacancies occur).

383

Wesleyan Writers Conference Scholarships and Fellowships
John W. Paton, Executive Secretary
Wesleyan University
Middletown, Connecticut 06547
U.S.A. Tel: (203) 347-9411, ext. 602

June

International; entry open to all; annual; established 1956. Formerly called SUFFIELD WRITER-READER CONFERENCE. Purpose: to provide intensive workshop for writers. Sponsored by and held at Wesleyan University for 1 week. Supported by Connecticut Commission on Arts and Humanities, publishers, bookstores. Average statistics: 25-30 awards, limited to 100 attendance. Have writing classes (novel, short story, poetry, for young people, for performance, factual), speakers, writing appraisals. Tuition: $295 room-board; $250 day student; $90 1 seminar only; $25 registration. Also sponsor Fiction Writing Residence Scholarships and Fellowships.

WRITING RESIDENCE SCHOLARSHIP: Nonfiction, 20 full or partial scholarships to writers, college students, literature-writing teachers, working journalists, for 1 week tuition, room-board. Require experience, aspirations; welcome supporting letters. One $295 full scholarship to woman writer (Connecticut Federation of Women's Clubs); preference to Connecticut resident. One full scholarship (Xerox Corporation) to individual writing for young people. Several scholarships (Adelphi Literary Society); preference to college or recently graduated students. Submit 1-2 nonfiction chapters or articles.

JUDGING: By writing professionals on Advisory Board. All entries read in entirety. Not responsible for loss or damage.

DEADLINES: Application, May. Notification, June.

384

William Flanagan Center for Creative Persons Residencies
Edward F. Albee Foundation
14 Harrison Street
New York, New York 10013 U.S.A.

June-October

International; entry open to all; annual; established 1978. Sponsored by Edward F. Albee Foundation. Held at William Flanagan Memorial Creative Persons Center on Long Island (South Fairview Avenue, Montauk, New York 11954).

WRITING RESIDENCE GRANT: Writing, for room-board for at least 1 month to writers, painters, sculptors. Require intention letter, recommendation, sample manuscript.

DEADLINES: Application, January-April. Notification, June-October.

SCHOLARSHIPS, FELLOWSHIPS
Primarily for STUDY and RESEARCH. Includes Book, Essay, Dissertation. (Also see RESIDENCE GRANTS.)

385

Appalachian Writers' Workshop Tuition Scholarships
Mike Mullens, Coordinator
Hindman Settlement School

Hindman, Kentucky 41822 U.S.A.
Tel: (606) 785-5475

August

International; entry open to all; annual; established 1978. Sponsored by Hindman Settlement School, founded 1902 for promotion, preservation of culture and history of Appalachia. Held in Hindman, Kentucky. Have readings, workshops, conferences, field trips. Fees: $70 tuition, $70 room-board. Also sponsor Appalachian Family Folk Week, Appalachian Visual Arts Week.

WRITING SCHOLARSHIP: **Appalachia Essay,** covers tuition for needy individuals who submit manuscript for evaluation. Submit sample essay.

DEADLINES: Not specified. Conference, August.

| 386 |

Graduate Fellowship in Illinois History
Illinois State Historical Society (ISHS)
William K. Alderfer, Executive Director
Old State Capitol
Springfield, Illinois 62706 U.S.A.

May

International; **entry restricted to doctoral candidates;** annual; established 1967. Sponsored by ISHS.

DISSERTATION FELLOWSHIP: **Illinois History Graduate Dissertation,** $2500 (paid quarterly) for academic year to doctoral candidate in accredited institution. Require 3 recommendation letters, financial statement, application letter; completion of dissertation in 5 years.

JUDGING: 7-member ISHS Educational Affairs Committee. Sponsor

keeps 1 copy for Illinois State Historical Library.

ENTRY FEE: None.

DEADLINES: Entry, January. Judging, February. Notification, May.

| 387 |

Lucy Martin Donnelly Fellowship
Bryn Mawr College
Office of the President
Bryn Mawr, Pennsylvania 19010
U.S.A.

Periodic

International; **entry restricted (nomination by college);** periodic. **Fellowship to Women for Belles Lettres** (including Writing, Playwriting); U.S.-British Commonwealth citizens, without regard to financial circumstances. Request visits to college for workshops, readings, talks. Sponsored by Bryn Mawr College.

| 388 |

Rockefeller Foundation Humanities Fellowships
1133 Avenue of the Americas
New York, New York 10036 U.S.A.
Tel: (212) 869-8500, ext. 392

March

International; entry open to all; annual; established 1975. Purpose: to support humanistic scholarship intended to illuminate and assess contemporary social, cultural issues. Sponsored and supported by The Rockefeller Foundation. Average statistics: 1000 entrants, 140 semifinalists, 35 awards. Also sponsor Rockefeller Foundation Research Fellowship Program for Minority-Group Scholars; 5-6 Rockefeller Foundation Human Rights Research Fellowships.

WRITING FELLOWSHIP: Contemporary Humanities Issues Research and Writing, 35 1-year fellowships up to $20,000 (usually $10-$15,-000) to writers-scholars (or through tax-exempt institutions with which they are affiliated) in traditional humanistic disciplines and social sciences with clear humanistic implications, for salary, benefits, travel, secretarial-research support, materials for projects analyzing-evaluating contemporary issues. Require (in English) 3 copies each 500-1000-word project description typed double-spaced, applicant vita and publications bibliography, 3 references. Upon sponsor request, require 7 copies each of vita, developed proposal.

JUDGING: By panel of scholars.

DEADLINES: Application, September. Proposal request, December. Notification, March.

| 389 |

Rockefeller Foundation Research Fellowship Program for Minority-Group Scholars
1133 Avenue of the Americas
New York, New York 10036 U.S.A.
Tel: (212) 869-8500

April

National; **entry restricted to U.S. minorities;** annual; established 1979. Purpose: to influence understanding and resolution of U.S. minority-group issues. Sponsored and supported by The Rockefeller Foundation. Average statistics: 15 awards. Also sponsor Rockefeller-Foundation Minority Social Science Program; 5-6 Rockefeller Foundation Human Rights Research Fellowships, Humanities Fellowships.

WRITING FELLOWSHIP: Minority Humanities, 15 1-year fellowships up to $25,000 (usually $18-$21,000) to minority scholars (or through tax-exempt institutions with which they are affiliated) in traditional humanistic disciplines for maintenance, travel, other costs of projects providing humanistic perspective on minority-group issues. Require 5 copies each (typed double-spaced) 15-page proposal, 2-page abstract, budget, 3 references. Not for completion of graduate-professional studies; fiction, poetry writing-translation; holders of other major fellowships (those receiving small stipends, sabbatical salaries are eligible); or less than 1 year work.

JUDGING: By panel of humanistic scholars. Based on relevance to current issues, creativity of approach, conceptual clarity, presentation effectiveness, analytical methods, project feasibility.

DEADLINES: Application, January. Notification, April.

| 390 |

Santa Cruz Writers' Conference Scholarships
University of California, Santa Cruz (UCSC)
Santa Cruz, California 95064 U.S.A.

June

International; entry open to all; annual. Purpose: to focus on writing as craft, expression, exploration, art. Sponsored by and held at UCSC for 2 weeks. Have workshops; lecture series; option for housing. Tuition: $305 plus $20 nonrefundable application fee. Also sponsor Fiction Writing Residence Scholarship.

WRITING SCHOLARSHIP: Nonfiction, scholarships to Writers' Conference. Submit recent, unpublished manuscript; typed double-spaced; 5000-word minimum and outline. 1 entry per category. Require letter indicating experience, financial need.

ENTRY FEE: Entrant pays postage (include SASE).

DEADLINES: Application, May. Notification, June.

| 391 |

Stanford Writing Scholarship
University of Melbourne
P. G. Morgan, Assistant Registrar (Arts)
Faculty of Arts
Parkville, Victoria 3052, AUSTRALIA
Tel: 345-1844

Fall

National; **entry restricted to young Australians;** annual. $4000 **Writing Scholarship** for 1-year study at Stanford University Writing Center (Palo Alto, California, U.S.A.). Sponsored by University of Melbourne. Held during academic year.

SCRIPT (Film, Television, Radio)
Includes Script Production, Book, Book-Publication Design, and Article.

| 392 |

Alfred I. DuPont Awards in Broadcast Journalism
Columbia University
Graduate School of Journalism
New York, New York 10027 U.S.A.

Fall

International; entry open to all; annual; established 1942. Sponsored by Columbia University since 1969. Supported by Alfred I. DuPont Foundation. Average statistics: 800 entries. Televised by PBS. Also sponsor other media awards.

SCRIPT AWARD: Journalism Television, Radio Broadcast, news-public affairs aired July previous to June of current year by local or network station, and syndicated material. Require reasons for submission.

AWARDS: For Singular Achievement in Broadcast Journalism.

JUDGING: By jury based on outstanding achievement in news-public affairs through research done in annual DuPont-Columbia Survey of Broadcast Journalism. Sponsor keeps all entries.

ENTRY FEE: None.

DEADLINES: Entry, July. Awards, Fall.

| 393 |

Chicago
Communications Collaborative
410 South Michigan Avenue
Suite 433
Chicago, Illinois 60605 U.S.A.
Tel: (312) 633-9566

Summer

International; entry open to all; annual; established 1978. Purpose: to recognize finest communications nationally and internationally through Chicago shows. Sponsored by Communications Collaborative, organization of Chicago communication associations. Recognized by Art Directors Club of Chicago, Artists Guild of Chicago, American Society of Magazine Photographers, Graphic Arts Council. Have visual media categories. Publish *Chicago Annual* (yearbook of winners).

SCRIPT CONTEST: Film, Television, Slide, produced or unproduced; written after March previous year.

Require 5 copies, original printed or typed.

BOOK CONTEST: Any Type, published or unpublished. Requirements same as for Script.

BOOK-PUBLICATION DESIGN CONTEST: Design, Typography, published. Book categories: Hardcover, Jacket, Paperback, Typography, Entire Book. Publication categories: Consumer, Trade (Black & White, Two-Color, Four-Color Cover; same for Body); Company (Black & White, Two-Color Cover; same for Body); Newspaper-Magazine (Black & White, Two-Color); House Organ.

NEWSPAPER-MAGAZINE CONTEST: Article, published or unpublished. Requirements same as for Script. Categories: Consumer, Trade, Company Magazine, Company Newsletter; Newspaper.

WRITING-PUBLICATIONS CONTEST: Various, published or unpublished. Requirements same as for Script. Categories: Catalog, Booklet, Folder, Brochure, Instructions or Teaching Guides, Other.

AWARDS: Best of Category, Best of Show at judges' discretion. Winners exhibited for 1 month.

JUDGING: By media experts, based on 5-point scale.

ENTRY FEE: Single $15, Campaign $35. Not-for-Profit Public Service Single $7, Campaign $17. Acceptance: Single $50, Campaign $150. Not-for-Profit Public Service Single $25, Campaign $75. Entrant pays postage. No entries returned.

DEADLINES: Entry, August. Event, Summer.

394

Houston International Film Festival (Festival of the Americas) Script Contest

Cinema America Inc.
J. Hunter Todd, President-Founder
P.O. Box 56566
Houston, Texas 77027 U.S.A.
Tel: (712) 757-0028

April

International; entry open to all; annual; established 1968. Formerly called ATLANTA INTERNATIONAL FILM FESTIVAL to 1974, VIRGIN ISLANDS INTERNATIONAL FILM FESTIVAL to 1977, GREATER MIAMI INTERNATIONAL FILM FESTIVAL to 1978. Purpose: to honor excellence in film and TV. Sponsored and supported by Cinema America, Houston Film Society. Recognized by IFFPA, IAIFD, Paris. Average statistics (overall festival): 2100 entries, 900 entrants, 30 countries, 600 semifinalists, 150 winners, 50 exhibitions, 15,000 attendance. Held at Stouffers Hotel, Greenway Plaza, Houston, Texas, for 6 days. Tickets: $4 each premiere, $50 series. Second contact: Rikki Kipple, Assistant Director, 2100 Travis, Central Square, Suite 626, Houston, Texas 77002.

SCRIPT CONTEST: Documentary Feature, Short Screenplay, any type, produced or unproduced; completed in previous 2 years, in shooting script form. Categories: Feature, Short or Experimental.

AWARDS: Grand Prize, each category, includes assistance in option and production. Short Award includes raw stock and cameras.

JUDGING: International Blue Ribbon Committee of 100 selects top 3, each category. Final by International

Grand Awards Jury of 7. May change categories.

ENTRY FEE: $75. Sponsor pays return postage.

DEADLINES: Entry, March. Event, April.

395

Humanitas Prize
Human Family Institute
Judy Conway Greening, Executive Director
P.O. Box 861
Pacific Palisades, California 90272 U.S.A. Tel: (213) 454-8769

July

National; **entry open to U.S.;** annual; established 1977. Considered largest money prize for entertainment industry writers. Purpose: to encourage, recognize, sustain U.S. writers of teleplays communicating human values; bring insights of Judeo-Christian vision of human condition to bear on contemporary life. Theme: Values That Most Enrich the Human Person. Sponsored by Human Family Institute, which seeks to promote greater appreciation of human dignity.

SCRIPT CONTEST: **Humanitarian Television Broadcast.** Written, produced, aired (on ABC, CBS, NBC) 7p.m.-11p.m., first televised May previous to May current year. Require 2 copies, 1-page typed storyline summary. Categories: 90 Minutes, 60 Minutes, 30 Minutes.

AWARDS: $25,000 (90 Minutes), $15,000 Prize (60 Minutes), $10,000 Prize (30 Minutes). Also give nonmonetary prizes to producers, directors, story editors, production companies, networks of these entries, and to news-documentary program.

JUDGING: All entries read by Exec-

utive Committee, Trustees. No entries returned.

ENTRY FEE: None.

DEADLINES: Entry, April. Awards, July.

396

Irvine Writers' Conference Awards
University of California Extension, Irvine
Laura Ferejohn
P.O. Box AZ
Irvine, California 92716 U.S.A.
Tel: (714) 833-5192

August

International; **entry restricted to Conference participants;** annual; established 1981. $100, $50, and Honorable Mention Certificates to **Film-Television Scripts** (unpublished; entrant enrolled in workshop). Purpose: to give writers recognition, opportunity to share experiences. Sponsored by U.C. Irvine Extension and Stephen Cannell. Average statistics (including Fiction): 50-75 entries, 6 awards, 100 attendance. Held at U.C. Irvine for 4 consecutive Saturdays. Entry, June. Awards, August.

397

AWGIE Awards
Australian Writers Guild (AWG)
Angela Wales, General Secretary
83 York Street, Suite 505
Sydney 2000 NSW, AUSTRALIA
Tel: (02) 29-1402

June-August

National; **entry restricted to Australian AWG members;** annual; established 1968. AWGIE Awards to **Australian Film, Television, Documentary Scripts.** Purpose: to encourage, award excellence in scriptwriting.

Supported by AMPOL Petroleum Ltd. Average statistics (including Fiction): 80 entries, 65 entrants. Publish *Viewpoint* (monthly newsletter). Awards, June-August.

398

Canadian Motion Picture Distributors Association (CMPDA) Script Development Program
Joan London
22 St. Clair Avenue, Suite 1703
Toronto, Ontario M4T 2S4 CANADA

Continuous

National; **entry open to Canada;** continuous; established 1978. Purpose: to provide writers access to Canadian motion picture industry; allow member companies review of commercial script properties. Sponsored by CMPDA.

SCRIPT PRODUCTION: Documentary Feature Film, typewritten. Require waiver of claims against similar-identical idea, plot, situation, story, treatment, theme, scheme.

AWARDS: Accepted scripts forwarded to production heads of U.S., Canadian CMPDA-member companies for possible purchase, development.

JUDGING: Preliminary by sponsor; final by member companies. Based on commercial potential. No scripts returned.

ENTRY FEE: None. Entrant pays postage.

DEADLINES: Open.

ALPHABETICAL
EVENT/SPONSOR/AWARD INDEX

Alphabetical index to each EVENT, SPONSOR, and AWARD (followed by identifying CODE NUMBER of the event).

A

AAAS Mass Media Intern Program: 340

AAAS Socio-Psychological Prize Competition: 25

AAAS-Westinghouse Science Writing Awards Competition: 314

AAUP Higher Education Writers Awards: 336

AAUW Award: 166

"Ability Counts" Research Writing Contest: 26

Adolph Bentinck Prize: 70

AEJ Summer Journalism Internship for Minorities: 342

African Studies Association: 105

Agriculture Oscars: 324

AHAM Awards: 302

AIAA Literature Awards: 189

AIP-U.S. Steel Foundation Science Writing Award: 190

AJL Book Awards: 103

ALA Awards and Citations Program (Children's): 71

ALA Awards and Citations Program (Librarianship): 112

ALA Awards and Citations Program (Reference): 143

Alan Marshall Award: 152

Alba Prize: 141

Albert Boni Fellowship: 368

Albert J. Harris Award: 29

Alberta Culture, Film and Literary Arts: 173

Alberta Culture Literary Awards: 173

Alberta Nonfiction Award: 173

Alberta Regional History Award: 173

Alberta Writing for Young People Award: 173

Alden B. Dow Creativity Center: 377

Alexander Prize Essay: 24

Alfred I. DuPont Awards in Broadcast Journalism: 392

Alice Davis Hitchcock Book Award: 52

Alice Leigh Gift: 1

Alicia Patterson Foundation (APF) Fellowship Program for Journalists: 357

Allan Nevins Prize: 19

Alliance Francaise National French Contest: 42

ALMA Awards Program: 302

Alvine-Belisle Prize: 90

Amaury Talbot Prize: 111

American Antiquarian Society (AAS) Research-Writing Fellowship Awards: 368

American Association for the Advancement of Science (AAAS): 25, 314, 340

American Association of Law Libraries (AALB): 67

American Association of Nurserymen (AAN): 205

D

H

H. W. Wilson Library Periodical Award: 112

Hannen Swaffer National Press Awards: 255

Hans Christian Andersen Awards for Books for Children: 79

Harold S. Hirsch Outstanding Skiwriter Award: 331

Harriet Monroe Poetry Award: 104

Harry S. Truman Book Award: 120

Harry S. Truman Library Institute: 120

Harshe-Rotman & Druck: 206

Harvard University Press: 200

Haseltine Fellowships in Science Writing: 363

Headliner Achievement Awards in Journalism: 249

Headliner Awards: 289

Health Education Writers Awards: 275

Health Journalism Awards: 276

Hearst Foundation Journalism Awards: 271

Heath Cooper Rigdon Conservation Writer Awards: 322

Helene Wurlitzer Foundation of New Mexico Residencies: 372

Henry E. Dorfman, Director: 15

Herbert J. Davenport Fellowships in Economics Reporting: 267

Herbert W. Putnam Honor Award: 112

Hermann-Hesse Prize: 139

Hermon Dunlap Smith Center for the History of Cartography: 198

Herskovits Award: 105

Hervey Award: 332

Heywood Broun Journalism Award: 283

Highway Safety Editorial Awards Contest: 259

Hindman Settlement School: 385

Hinkhouse-Derose Awards: 284

History of Science Society (HSS) Writing Awards: 195

Hitchcock Book Award: 52

Horn Book Awards: 72

Horse & Racetrack Bureau of New Jersey: 333

Hospitalized Veterans Writing Project (HVWP): 2

Houghton Mifflin Company: 149

Houghton Mifflin Literary Fellowship: 149

Houston Film Society: 394

Houston International Film Festival (Festival of the Americas) Script Contest: 394

Howard R. Marraro Prize: 133, 177

Howard University: 342

Howard University Press Book Publishing Institute Scholarships: 373

Howard W. Blakeslee Awards: 277

Hudson's Bay Company Prize: 207

Hughes Fellowships: 352

Hugo Science Fiction Achievement Awards: 196

Human Family Institute: 395

Humanitas Prize: 395

Hunter-McCarthey Award: 311

I

IAFF International Awards Program: 260

IAPA Scholarship Program: 361

IAPA-Pedro Joaquin Chamorro Awards: 361

ILAB Bibliographical Prize: 115

Illinois State Historical Society (ISHS): 386

Illinois Wesleyan University (IWU) Writers' Conference Awards: 3

Indiana University Writers' Conference Scholarships: 374

Indiana Women's Press Association Award: 374

Indianapolis Newspapers, Inc. (INI): 346

Institute Manuscript Award: 121

Institute of Early American History and Culture: 121

Institute of International Education (IIE): 370

T

U

V

W

Y

SUBJECT/CATEGORY INDEX

Index to AREAS OF SPECIAL INTEREST (followed by identifying CODE NUMBER of each event).

HAVE WE MISSED A CONTEST/EVENT?

Please let us know so that we may
correct our future editions. Thank you.

FESTIVAL PUBLICATIONS
P.O. Box 10180
Glendale, California 91209 U.S.A.

LEARNING RESOURCES
CENTER

ILLINOIS CENTRAL COLLEGE
MCMLXVI

East Peoria, Illinois